The Devil's Music
Giles Oakley

THE DEVIL'S MUSIC

A HISTORY OF THE BLUES

GILES OAKLEY

SECOND EDITION, UPDATED

DA CAPO PRESS • NEW YORK

Library of Congress Cataloging-in-Publication Data

Oakley, Giles.
  The Devil's music: a history of the blues / Giles Oakley—1st Da Capo
Press ed.
     p. cm.
  "An unabridged republication of the second edition published in Lon-
don in 1983, which was a revision of the first edition published in London
in 1976, here supplemented with a new afterword by the author"—T.p.
verso.
  Discography:
  Includes bibliographical references (p.   ) and index.
  ISBN 0-306-80743-2 (alk. paper)
  1. Blues (Music)—History and criticism. I. Title.
ML3521.O18   1997
781.643' 0973—dc21   96-52633
                                                                    CIP
                                                                     MN

Edited by Maddalena Fagandini to accompany a series of
programmes prepared in consultation with the BBC Further
Education Advisory Council and broadcast in 1976

First Da Capo Press edition 1997

This Da Capo Press paperback edition of *The Devil's Music* is an
unabridged republication of the second edition published in London
in 1983, which was a revision of the first edition published in London
in 1976. It is here supplemented with a new afterword by the author,
and is reprinted by arrangement with Taplinger Publishing Company and
BBC Worldwide Publishing.

Published by Da Capo Press, Inc.
A Subsidiary of Plenum Publishing Corporation
233 Spring Street, New York, N.Y. 10013

Contents

CONTENTS

Preface to the second edition

This book was originally published in connection with a five-part documentary film series made for BBC Television in 1976 called *The Devil's Music*, and it draws extensively from the interviews with blues singers filmed for that project in Chicago, New York, St Louis, Memphis and different parts of Mississippi.

The intention of both the book and the films was to explore the blues in relation to the way of life that spawned them, looking at the rise and spread of the music from a succession of different perspectives. Some chapters concentrate on close-up biographical accounts of specific singers while others widen the focus to examine blues in particular states and cities as a whole, or deal with the recording and entertainment business. There are also passages surveying the historical background, including slavery, segregation, migration, the Depression, racism, and the rise of Soul.

Throughout the book the personal experiences of people close to the music have been used to shape the overall historical structure. By taking singers from different backgrounds and performing in different styles, it was hoped to demonstrate that there is not *one* blues but many.

As the role and status of black people has been modified over the course of this century so the music has changed, and in order to chart that process the book refers to economics and sociology as well as history. Too frequently creative or artistic activities are presented as being the province of inspired individuals safely removed from other social and political concerns. This has been especially true of much writing about popular music which often amounts to little more than biographies of successive stars.

American black music is self-evidently deeply political in the important sense of having clear and perceived connections with the oppressed position of black people in American society. This is particularly true of the blues, called the Devil's Music by (usually black) opponents who have feared its power as a *social* force, whether for 'disruption', 'irresponsibility', 'irreligion' or for sexual freedom. To some extent the blues negotiate the tensions between opposition to the status quo, accommodation to it, and transcendence of it through the joy of sensual release.

This book is intended to be an accessible introduction to the blues and a heart-felt celebration of the lives and music of those numberless blues singers who have created some of the most enduringly expressive and emotionally charged music in western popular culture.

Regrettably, since the publication of *The Devil's Music* several of the artists we filmed have died. Accordingly this edition has been revised to take account of these sad developments and also to include further new material from the 1976 film trip and from other sources. Blues research and publishing is continually expanding so changes have been made in the light of new information where appropriate. However no major structural alteration has been attempted, except for the addition of a lengthy afterword, bringing the story of the blues up to date.

Giles Oakley, 1983, 1996

Introduction

'Then one night in Tutwiler, as I nodded in the railroad station while waiting for a train that had been delayed nine hours, life suddenly took me by the shoulder and wakened me with a start.'

This was how W. C. Handy described the occasion in 1903 which led him to see what we now call the blues 'with the eye of a budding composer'. A lean, ragged and loose-jointed black with toes poking out of his shoes started playing the guitar as Handy slept on the tiny Mississippi station. As the sad-faced guitarist played he pressed a knife on the strings.

'The effect was unforgettable. His song, too, struck me instantly.

> Goin' where the Southern cross the Dog
> Goin' where the Southern cross the Dog
> Goin' where the Southern cross the Dog.'[1]

It was the weirdest music Handy had ever heard, and the tune stayed in his mind. As a band-leader and music publisher, Handy was later to formalize and publicize this 'earth-born music', and to become known as 'Father of the Blues'.

But this accolade is wrong. There was no one person who gave birth to the blues, and if there was, it was certainly not W. C. Handy as he himself was the first to admit. The blues were emerging all over the Southern States of America simultaneously, in Mississippi, in Alabama, Georgia, Louisiana and in Texas and elsewhere. Hundreds of nameless and forgotten singers and musicians, cotton-pickers, levee camp, saw-mill and turpentine camp workers, roustabouts and farm hands, were singing and playing the blues, alone or in groups, at work or at their ease.

Some say the blues began in 1903, some say in 1890, or in 1902 or almost any time around those years. In 1960 James Butch Cage told Paul Oliver:

'They comes from back in slavery time. When we was on the slavery – colored time was on the slavery – we was eatin' the bones and the skin and the hog jaws. That's what they eat back there, and the white folks eat all the good meat. They was hard times and they made a song about it. My mama learned it to me; she wasn't a slave but my grandmaw was, and they used to sing it:

> Black nigger baby, black feet and shiny eyes.
> Black all over to the bone and india rubber thighs,
> Turn that nigger round and knock 'im in the haid,
> 'Cause white folks say, "We're gonna kill that nigger dead!"
> The white folks eat the hog in the skillet,
> Niggers was no-good, so very little in it,
> Old Uncle Dicker-Dagger eat up the grease – say,
> "Get up in the mawnin', I'll be free!"
> Black nigger baby gonna take care of myself,
> Always carry a great big razor and a pistol in my vest,
> Turn that nigger round and knock 'im on the haid,
> 'Cause white folks say, "We're gonna kill that nigger dead".[2]

Another blues singer, Booker White, makes the same claim.

'You wanted to know where did the blues come from. The blues came from behind the mule. Well now, you can have the blues sitting at the table eating. But the foundation of the blues is walking behind a mule way back in slavery time.'[3]

But as a form of music or a type of song, the blues did not come 'from back in slavery time'. No slaves sang what are now called blues, and the term was not in use to refer to music. What Butch Cage told Oliver simply expresses a mythological or poetic truth about the music's origins. The lives of all black people in America have been fundamentally shaped by the racial experience of slavery; the memory of enforced servitude in the past has moulded attitudes and feelings in the present and has conditioned the black American's stance in the world. Since the end of slavery the black communities have been searching for their identity – in relation to white culture, in relation to them-selves and in relation to their past. And much of that search is dominated by the memory of what slavery meant. In 1963 LeRoi Jones described what slavery does to a person:

'The weight of his bondage makes impossible for the slave a great many alternatives into which the shabbiest of free men can project himself. There is not even a separate identity the ego can claim. "What are you going to be when you grow up?" "A slave."'[4]

Though the memory of slavery, or the idea of slavery may tell us that the slave could have no separate identity, could have no free ego, that is not the whole story. Even the raucous little song from 'slavery' days which Butch Cage and his friend Willie Thomas performed for Paul Oliver in 1960 shows a toughness of spirit and a will to survive.

Black nigger baby gonna take care of myself.

To understand the part played by the blues in American society, we need to consider what psychological impulses the black inherited from the days of slavery, and also what cultural and artistic forms existed in those times – the spirituals, the plantation songs, work songs, banjo music, fiddle tunes and dances. All these elements were there, and to see how and why the blues emerged at the end of the nineteenth century, we must first look at slavery society.

Part One

Slavery

When in 1863 President Lincoln's Emancipation Proclamation was read out loud in Boston's Tremont Temple, the audience sang:

> Sound the loud timbrel,
> O'er Egypt's dark sea;
> Jehovah hath triumphed,
> His people are free.[1]

The joyful cry of freedom for the slaves ended a period of history which had begun three centuries earlier, when the first of the several millions of Africans who were eventually to be taken into slavery were shipped to the New World. The first slaves taken to the North American colonies were mainly indentured servants who could gain their freedom after working a fixed period of years. But by the late 17th century complete slavery was widespread.

The New England colonies, with their small farming communities already prosperously developing, had no use for a large, cheap work force. It was in the sparsely settled, almost tropically fertile South that labour was in short supply. White labourers were insufficient and in any case not keen to apply themselves on the scale required to develop these territories to their full potential. In 1661 the Virginia colony legalised slavery and the other colonies soon followed.

Tobacco was the first major crop to draw on slave labour, quickly to be followed by rice, sugar and cotton. In ever increasing numbers, Africans were tricked, trapped, captured and cajoled into the slaving ships and in the most horrific conditions transported across the Atlantic. Many had been bartered for with molasses and rum extracted from sugar-cane grown by slaves who had preceded them. Chained and overcrowded below deck, countless died in passage of disease, dehydration or asphyxia, their corpses tossed into the sea. Of the 35 to 40 million involved in the trade to the Americas over a period of nearly three centuries, an estimated 15 million survived the journey.

At the time of the American War of Independence (1775–1783), the Northern States declared slavery illegal, but the South did not. The wealth of the Southern planters depended on it, as did the prosperity of the slave traders of Bristol and Liverpool.

Eli Whitney's invention in 1793 of the cotton gin – a machine which successfully separated the cotton from seed and other impurities – led to a boom in the commodity and, among other consequences, helped the growth of the Lancashire textile industry. Output increased in Georgia and South Carolina, and the cotton belt spread West to Alabama, Mississippi, Louisiana and eventually to Texas.

When the slave trade was officially abolished in 1807, the Southern States virtually ignored it and illicit trade continued. The ban had the effect of increasing the value of slaves and breeding was intensified to the extent, in some cases, of establishing stud farms where the most able-bodied men and women were used to produce saleable offspring.

Slaves not only created the wealth of the South, but also the landscape. Their labour was used to build houses, docks, bridges, roads and later the railroads. Based on the plantations, gangs of them were leased by their owners to the construction companies, causing considerable resentment among the poor whites who were competing for the same jobs. Throughout the Southern States these gangs of slaves were an ever present and – to some – a threatening sight.

It was the American Civil War of 1861–1865 which finally dealt the death blow to slavery in the South.

Torn from their own environment, terrified and bewildered, the survivors of the Atlantic crossing brought with them what little they could of their own way of life. In a book published in London in 1816, George Pinckard described a newly arrived shipful:

'They have great amusement in collecting together in groups and singing their favorite African songs; the energy of their action is more remarkable than the harmony of their music.'[2]

He later watched a group on a ship from Guinea in the harbour of Savannah, Georgia.

'We saw them dance, and heard them sing. In dancing they scarcely moved their feet, but threw about their arms, and twisted and writhed their bodies into a multitude of disgusting and indecent attitudes. Their song was a wild yell devoid of all softness and harmony, and loudly chanted in harsh harmony.'[3]

But for the majority of Africans, their culture was rapidly suppressed. Tribes were deliberately split up, their religions banned and in some instances even their music stopped. The Black Codes of Mississippi for example put an end to the beating of drums out of fear that the slaves could communicate and concert a revolt. It was only those elements of African life which suited the interests of the Master which were allowed to remain, like the rhythmic group work chants which had been a traditional part of farming in Africa.

Work song was not the only form of music licensed by the white owners. It was an amusing diversion to observe the slaves performing their strange hybrid music. In his *Journal* of 1774, Nicholas Cresswell described slaves in Maryland dancing to a banjo made out of a gourd 'something in the imitation of a Guitar, with only four strings'. They would sing in a 'very satirical manner' about the way they were treated. 'Their poetry is like the Music – Rude and uncultivated.'[4]

Musical skills could even add to the market value of a slave. There are frequent references to musical talents in the slave advertisement columns of early American newspapers. These adverts were either offering slaves for sale or for hire (by the day, week, month or even year), or frequently they were offering rewards for the capture of runaways. Such and such a runaway 'makes fiddles' or 'can play upon the fiddle' or the flute; another might be 'artful and can both read and write and is a good fiddler'.[5]

Punishment for escape was swift and summary, but not necessarily a deterrent. The mundane brutality of plantation life is witnessed in the following notes in the diary of Spooner Forbes, a Mississippi slave-owner.

July 11, 1859	Jake and Harrison ran away. Harrison came to Town and took his whipping and went back. Jake not heard from.
July 20, 1859	Jake come home again and got a good whipping.
June 28, 1860	Jake ran away at dinner time.
July 15, 1860	Jake came in this morning.
July 16, 1860	Whipped Jake today for going in Town.
Mar. 18, 1862	Jake ran away, sent to Jo Willis and got his dogs but did not catch him.
Mar. 20, 1862	Jake came in at half past four o'clock and took his whipping and acknowledged his stealing.[6]

The cycle of forced labour and servitude, running away, tracker dogs, beatings and whippings, the capricious world where the Master's word was law and where the slave was at the mercy of his every whim and mood, was hard indeed. There is no doubt the memories of former slaves were true enough.

'I's hear tell of them good slave days, but I ain't never seen no good times then.'

'Lord, Lord, honey! Them was awful days.'[7]

Slave memories have been handed on from generation to generation, like the stories blues singer Sam Chatmon heard from his ex-slave father:

'Yeah, he told me, he told me plenty about slaves. He said when he was a child big enough to remember it, they'd go to these barns and get this corn, was mixed with this rat stuff, rat waste I'll call it, I won't say the other part ... The old ladies would take that on to the children right out there in the pen and mix that stuff up in a big wooden trough, and they'd get down and eat it, just like hogs ... And papa say he'd never seen a piece of meat, they'd grease all the children's mouths on a Sunday, and he'd linger behind and he'd get to eat the meat skin.'[8]

Booker White heard similar stories from relations and older people, like the 110 year-old former slave he met in Memphis:

'I always had it on my mind what was happening back there in them days. She said, "Well Book, I'll tell you. Back there in them days they sold my mother. I never did see her, I was five years old and they sold my mother away from me. I didn't see my mother no more, I was 5 years old when they taken me away from her and they sold my mother."'[9]

William Howard Russell of the London *Times* travelled through Louisiana in the early months of the Civil War:

'It struck me more and more ... as I examined the expression on the faces of the slaves, that deep dejection is the prevailing, if not universal, characteristic of the race.'[10]

Most plantation owners were resident Masters, personally responsible for all they ruled. Part of their responsibility was a network of obligations towards their slaves, providing protection and care in the form of food and shelter. In a sense, the entire society of the Southern States was shaped by slavery and not least because of this pattern of paternalism.

At its best, paternalism could protect both Masters and slaves from the worst excesses of the system – the tendency of the Master to cruelty and tyranny in the execution of his considerable power, and the tendency of the slave to be crushed and oppressed by his servitude. Masters saw themselves as fathers who presided over an extended and subservient family which included both white and black. Of course this could all too easily grow into an imperious domination over disobedient 'children'. It helped foster the image of the slave as, at best, an irresponsible, childlike simpleton. And it exacted obedience from women – the 'Pure White Womanhood' of Southern mythology – and from children.

The whole ideology of paternalism, seen as a justification for involuntary and forced labour, often led to a self-blinding, myth-building arrogance in the owner, the belief in the superiority of Southern 'Good Manners', 'Graciousness', 'Courtesy' and 'Liberality of Spirit'. These self-images grew out of the planters' view of their role and their commitment to the notions of Family, Fortune and Honour. The system was believed to be as ordered and as stable as the façades of their stately mansions, the 'Big Houses', and the tiers of class and authority within the world of the plantation were felt to be immutable. Master and Mistress and Sons and Daughters, Cousins, overseers and yeomen, slave-drivers, house-slaves, mammies and field slaves – all had their place and all were in some way locked into the structure. The rigidity of this world, maintained even in the face of the growing clamour of abolitionist sentiment, left the South ill-prepared for the shocks it was to receive in the Civil War and Emancipation.

Just as the world of the planter was an edifice built around The Family, so too was that of the slave. Despite the widespread practice of splitting families, of separately selling off a husband, a wife, or any surplus children with a callous disregard for the pain and suffering it would cause, the family was still the basic unit of the slave quarters. Within the comparative stability and regularity of plantation life, relationships of gentility and tenderness developed, and the extended ties of family and friends provided a communal strength of great significance.

The slaves had developed a way of accommodating to the dominance of the Masters.

> Got one mind for the boss to see,
> Got another mind for what I know is me.[11]

The old woman who told Booker White about slavery time told him the men and women would be in the fields ploughing and chopping and they would 'sing them songs so pitiful, and so long' till they would be crying; but 'when they see the boss coming they would make like a gnat got in their eye. 'Cos you know, the boss didn't want them to feel that-a-way, you know, they had to be cool, play it cool, you know.'[12]

As their African heritage was stripped from them, or had withered away, whatever was imposed upon them or they embraced of their own volition was transformed into a culture of their own.

Their African religions were suppressed and replaced by Christianity, especially when their owners began to feel that 'the deeper the piety of the slave, the more valuable he is in every respect'.[13] Religious instruction was initially used as a form of social control, as this early catechism shows.

Q 'What did God make you for?'
A 'To make a crop.'
Q 'What is the meaning of "Thou shalt not commit adultery"?'
A 'To serve our heavenly Father, and our earthly master, obey our overseer, and not steal anything.'[14]

But the Masters' intentions were easily bypassed, as an ex-slave explained:

'When I starts preaching I couldn't read or write and had to preach what Master told me, and he say tell them niggers iffen they obeys the Master they goes to Heaven; but I knowed there's something better for them, but daren't tell them 'cept on the sly. That I done lots. I tells 'em iffen they keeps praying, the Lord will set 'em free.'[15]

Religion as adapted by slave society undoubtedly provided a source of communal strength and reassurance; it was a refuge and a symbol of hope. It could convey the message that freedom was in 'heben' and that God would set His people free.

> Yes, we all shall be free,
> Yes, we all shall be free,
> Yes, we all shall be free,
> When the Lord shall appear.

But this same hymn might be sung with different lines when out of the Masters' hearing, as happened during the Civil War:

> Yes, we all shall be free,
> When the *Yankee* shall appear.[16]

We don't have to see the spirituals only as covert political anthems in order to appreciate their importance. The great flood of travel narratives and slave autobiographies published in the 19th century and later reveal many views of the part the spiritual played in the lives of the slaves. Not everyone approved:

'In the *blacks'* quarter, the coloured people get together and sing for hours together short scraps of disjointed affirmations, pledges, or prayers, lengthened out with long repetition *choruses.* These are all sung in the merry chorus-manner of the Southern harvest field, or husking-frolic method, of the slave blacks; and also very greatly like the Indian dances. With every word so sung, they have a sinking of one or other leg of the body alternately; producing an audible sound of the feet at every step, and as manifest as the steps of actual negro dancing in Virginia, etc. If some in the meantime sit, they strike the sounds alternately on each thigh. What in the name of religion, can countenance or tolerate such gross perversions of true religion! but the evil is only occasionally condemned.'[17]

For some, the more exuberant spirituals were evidence of the 'unalloyed contentment and happiness.'[18] of the slaves. For others such apparent joyfulness reflected the slaves' uncrushable spirit and will to survive. But it was the long and mournfully slow chants, with their swooping cadences, which seemed to many to reflect the infinite sadness and despair of an oppressed people.

> When Israel was in Egypt's land,
> Let my people go.
> Oppressed so hard they could not stand,
> Let my people go.
> Go down, Moses, way down in Egypt's land,
> Tell old Pharaoh,
> Let my people go.[19]

Frederick Douglas, a slave who escaped at the age of twenty-one and who dedicated his life to the cause of Abolition in lectures, speeches and writings, described how the slaves on his old plantation would 'make the dense old woods, for miles around, reverberate with their wild notes. These were not always merry because they were wild. On the contrary, they were mostly of a plaintive cast, and told a tale of grief and sorrow. In the most boisterous outbursts of rapturous sentiment, there was ever a tinge of deep melancholy.'[20]

Many spirituals were sung in the call-and-response form of some traditional African music, and the same style was used in the slaves' secular music, especially in the work song. In a typical plantation narrative, *The Old Plantation and What I Gathered*

There in an Autumn Month, written in 1859, James Hungerford described the scene when the slaves rowed a party of white folks along a local creek. One slave, 'Charley', led the singing and the other oarsmen answered in chorus, all timing the strokes of their oars to the measure:

> Farewell, ole plantation!
>   Oho! Oho!
> Farewell, de ole quarter,
>   Oho! Oho!
> Un daddy, un mammy,
>   Oho! Oho!
> Un marster, un missus,
>   Oho! Oho!

'The tone of voice in which this boat-song was sung was inexpressibly plaintive, and, bearing such a melancholy tune, and such affecting words, produced a very pathetic effect. I saw tears in the eyes of the young ladies, and could scarcely restrain my own.'

Hungerford was clearly interested in music, and describes much of what he saw of the slaves, chiefly looking for the picturesque and the quaint, and all with a sentimental and faintly patronising eye. But his book contains much valuable evidence of pre-blues forms of slave music, in particular in his description of a singer named Clotilda and of old Uncle Porringer, a fiddle player, at a dance.

He says Clotilda was a 'queer being' with a wild, unsettled glance and a 'weird, or, rather elfish expression'. Hungerford's cousin Lucy tells him that Clotilda 'can make you rhymes all day long, and is a great help to the corn-bank singers, furnishing them with any number of jingling lines for the corn-husking season, and with tunes for them too; for she can make melodies as well as rhymes.'

Later that evening the cousins go down to the slave quarters at the edge of the wood near 'the house', and there they are greatly amused by the 'merriment' in the moonlight.

'Upon benches placed against the outside wall of the hut upon each side of the door sat several of the older negroes of both sexes from the neighbouring quarters. Ike was singing the *words* of a jig in a monotonous tone of voice, beating time meanwhile with his hands alternately against each other and against his body. To this music about a dozen or so negro boys and girls were dancing on the hard beaten ground ... As soon as she joined the throng, Clotilda, without a moment's pause, whirled herself among and through the crowd of dancers, till, having gained the opposite side to that at which she had entered, she turned and faced them, and began to recite the following verses in a shrill sing-song voice, keeping time to the measure, as Ike had done, by beating her hands sometimes against her sides, and patting the ground with her feet . . .

JUBER DANCE

Laudy! How it make me laugh
T'er see de niggers all so saf';
See um dance de foolish jig,
Un neber min' de juber rig.

Juber!

Juber lef' un Juber right;
Juber dance wid all yo' might;
Juber here un Juber dere,
Juber, Juber ebery where.

Juber!'

And so the performance went on, with increasing uproar and confusion, until the Juber dancers ended up in a 'struggling heap' amid 'unrestrained laughter by everyone'. With the help of a bucket of 'hard' cider sent over from 'the house', Uncle Porringer was persuaded to take up his fiddle and play for the dancers. As Hungerford and the others left, the slaves were dancing into the night to a 'lively and rattling jig tune.'[21]

Nigger Minstrels and coon songs

By the last years of slavery, white people had begun to take an interest in some aspects of black culture. But ironically the vogue for slave music was created not by the real 'Niggers', but by *white* performers, the 'Nigger Minstrels', who in the 1840's took the entertainment world by storm.

This was just the first of successive waves of absorption of black music, and others soon followed. In the brief wake of pro-Negro sentiment after the Civil War, the spirituals became for many the symbol of a noble people just freed. In the 1870's the famous Fisk Jubilee Singers, with finely honed and smoothly presented performances in concert halls around the world, helped create an image of black music which lingers on to this day. They prepared the way for anyone with a trained voice to sing 'spirituals'. But these concert hall spirituals are far removed from the originals 'whose wailing cadences, borne on the night air, are indescribably melancholy'. Writing in *Befo' de War Spirituals*. E. A. McIlhenny describes what the authentic material was like.

'It is almost impossible to get exact wording of spirituals for even the same singer never sings one twice exactly the same. The singer will vary the words, lines and melody every time . . . begins with a simple sweet melody, but as the singer becomes more . . . uplifted and enthused by oft repeated lines, all sorts of quavering notes and melodious expression will be improvised.'[1]

Back in the 1840's, well before the popularity of the spirituals there had already been a growing white taste for minstrel songs like *Old Zip Coon* and *Jump Jim Crow*, performed by Dan Emmett and the Virginia Minstrels, and later by other groups. Though their music ultimately derived from the plantations, these were 'black-face' performers. There were many such troupes over the years – The Ethiopian Serenaders, the Moore and Burgess Minstrels – and they generally performed highly entertaining parodies of black music and musicians, playing banjos, tambourines, bones and fiddles.

Probably the most famous of the black-face groups were the Christy Minstrels, who became so popular (especially in England where the style soon took root after they performed in London) that Edwin P. Christy's name became virtually synonymous with minstrelsy. In 1849 they published their *Ethiopian Glee Book* by Elias Howe who gave himself the name 'Gumbo Chaff', banjo-player to some imaginary African Chieftain. This songbook contained a good selection of fairly authentic folk material, music genuinely derived from plantation life, and which in its way was a testament to the charm and power of black music of the time. In his preface, Gumbo dedicated the collection to 'Antislabery 'Cieties trout de World', adding that 'De 'Scriber am pressed wid de vast 'sponsibility ob presentin' to de whole . . . Popalashun ob dis world de genus ob de colored professors ob de 'vine art.'[2]

Probably the most famous of the early minstrel songs, *Jump Jim Crow* (written by the actor Tom Rice in about 1828), took its inspiration from the strange walk of a deformed black stable-hand in Louisville, Kentucky.

> First on de heel tap, den on de toe,
> Ebery time I wheel about I jump Jim Crow,
> Wheel about and turn about an do jis so,
> And ebery time I wheel about I jump Jim Crow.[3]

It was only later that the phrase 'Jim Crow' would take on its sinister connotation of segregation and racism, but that connection is probably not entirely coincidental; while in the early years of nigger minstrelsy the parodies were almost certainly performed with good-natured affection, later they were to turn into cruel ridicule. While the burnt cork entertainers may have prepared the way for blacks to appear in their own right, they also defined the terms in which they could do so: portrayed as 'coons', blacks were expected to behave like it. And there were at least two well-established images they had to live up to:

'One was the good-hearted simpleton, loose-jointed, shuffling, and awkward, who could paradoxically break into an intricate buck and wing, or make the banjo talk. The other was the Negro dandy, who wore the habiliments and the customs of his white "superiors" so absurdly, and whose dignity, though preposterous, was highly diverting.'[4]

Examples of minstrel show images abound in the literature of the years after the Civil War. Novels and magazine stories, anecdotes and cartoons of the time all used the same kind of derisive terms as were current in songs: 'nigger', 'niggah', 'darkey', 'coon', 'pickaninny', 'Mammy', 'aunt', 'uncle', 'buck', 'light-complected-yaller', 'yaller hussy' and so on. Blacks were thick-lipped, they had flat noses, big ears and feet, kinky or woolly hair, and most were given ludicrous names like 'Solomon Crow', 'Abraham Lincum', 'Piddlelcins', 'Had-a-Plenty' and 'Wanna-Mo'. And just about every derogatory stereotype was applied to them – they were improvident, emotional, gossipy, high-tempered, vain, dishonest, idle, liars, cheats, superstitious, dull, stupid, ignorant, happy-go-lucky, immoral, criminal, thieves and drunkards. They liked high-flown languages they couldn't understand, they liked gaudy clothes and trinkets, all had a love for stolen chickens, 'water millions', 'split weet-'taters' (perhaps with 'brown gravy leakin' down es sides',), 'possum' and of course liquor.[5]

But there were stereotypes of black life other than those of the weak-minded, child-like, unreliable buffoons of the coon songs and novelettes. The minstrel shows also featured the absurdly sentimental and romanticised view of plantation life of Stephen Foster. The Christy Minstrels especially made a feature of Foster's hugely popular *Plantation Melodies* and similar material by other popular song writers both black and white. Tony Russell has described the image they presented:

'Coon songs were not always comic, there were the sentimental "darkey" effusions, the great line that stretched each side of *Old Black Joe*. Judging black life by these – as European audiences very probably did in watching the "nigger minstrel" shows, having nothing else to go on – one summons up a peaceful picture of woolly-headed slaves strumming their banjos, fishing in the sun and courting little octoroons with improbable names . . . of chain gangs and beatings and slave-drivers we hear not a whisper; nor of Massa's hot intentions towards the estate's little octoroons, though that particular abuse was sometimes romanticised into such songs as *My Pretty Quadroon*:

> Massa had gardens and bowers,
> And flowers that were always in bloom,
> He begrudged me my pretty wild flower,
> Cora, my pretty quadroon.[6]

Again these images permeated much contemporary writing in magazines like *Harper's*, or *Atlantic Monthly*. If black men and women were not seen as laughable idiots, they were presented in a way which left them safely remote from serious concern with any real issues of racism, bigotry, or of poverty and violence. It was all too easy for people fed on a diet of unreality, in which a black person was never seen as being human in the same way as themselves, but always as a caricature, to accept more overt kinds of prejudice. An anonymous traveller in the 'great black' regions of the South talked of 'the uncouth strangely-shaped animal-looking Negro or mulatto, who seems mentally, even more than by his physical characteristics, to belong to a race entirely distinct from that of the white race around them.' The writer went on to explain what he took to be white women's fear of Negroes, which he understood because they were 'a race alien, animal, half savage, easily made sullen or aroused to fury'.[7] It was in this climate of opinion that black people found themselves in their struggle to create a new way of life after the end of slavery.

From emancipation to segregation

In 1865, free from legal bondage and no longer tied to the white man's absolute control, the shattered slave society began the struggle to find a new way of life. But with that freedom came an uncertainty and instability, and a kind of isolation.

Slaves had been born into a rigid, fragile society, where decisions were made for them and where the planters' paternalism denied them any ultimate form of independence. It is true, of course, that many slaves had held positions of authority and status within their own stratified society. At least two-thirds of the slaves had worked under black foremen, or overseers, and it would not have been uncommon for these supervisors to run the whole plantation in the Master's absence. Then there was the 'Mammy', that almost legendary figure of many a sentimental novel and film, a woman who had to be extremely tough and resourceful in the face of wide duties within the 'Big House', and was required at all times to be obedient, obliging and cheerful. The driver, the Mammy, and of course the preacher, these were people of position within slave society. Outside the plantations there were also the freedmen – successful runaways, or those who had been freed either out of their owner's respect and affection, or because they were their owner's own illegitimate children. At the time of Emancipation there were about half a million free blacks, compared with a slave population of around 4 million.

This élite, including the freedom who had concentrated in Northern cities and in the border States, were to provide black leadership after the War.

But the paternalism of the Old South had left its mark, and for many respect was still sought from the white man on the white man's terms. Slavery had generated a kind of alliance between the white upper classes and the slave élite which many blacks found hard to abandon when that system was abolished. When the Southern economy was shattered by the Civil War, it took with it the planters' leadership. The War had destroyed much agricultural land and property, and had drained the South of its finances while industry in the North boomed. With little capital to revive its economy, the plantation system gone, the inheritance left to slaves, and whites, was meagre indeed.

Freed from slavery, large numbers of blacks fled the South with its poverty and chaos and moved North and West to where communities had already been established by the freedmen. But the vast majority remained, to face a legacy of bitterness and a backlog of presumed racial inferiority.

There was a brief period of 'Reconstruction', when blacks played an active part in the political regeneration of the South and some State governments even managed considerable reforms (in North Carolina the provision of public schooling was increased by 500 per cent). But it seems clear that whatever opportunities there were for establishing a stable and sharing community, they were eventually to be abandoned. The economic collapse was general, and the bitterness of the large numbers of poor whites – who had always existed and whose plight had been largely forgotten in the myth of the Old South – was growing.

The black community, now broken up along with the old plantations, had no structure of its own on which to build. It had never been expected or allowed to work together for economic or political ends. The periodic slave revolts and the organising of the 'Underground Railway' (to 'conduct' runaways to freedom), though demanding enormous courage and resourcefulness on the part of many individuals, were not enough to teach the freed slaves the art of widely based, group action.

As early as 1877, when the victorious Federal troops who had occupied the defeated South after the war were withdrawn, it was clear that Reconstruction was a failure and that the black had been abandoned as a ward of the nation. The North quietly acquiesced in the South's demand that the whole problem be left to the disposition of the dominant Southern whites. Gone was the attempt to guarantee the freedman his civil and political equality, and gone was the support for his attempts to create a secure and equable status. It was a long, gradual and uncertain course which decided exactly what that status might be, for there were divisions among the whites themselves – differences of class and political persuasion, differences of economic strength and social attitudes; but it became increasingly apparent that these divisions were to be healed at the expense of the black. By the turn of the century it was clear that the blacks would be effectively disenfranchised throughout the South, and would be firmly relegated to the lowest rungs of the economic ladder. And it was clear too that they were to be afforded neither true equality (enshrined in the token legal formula for Segregation 'Separate but Equal') nor even the chance to aspire towards equality.

Blacks had the constant reminder of their inferior position in the series of Segregation Statutes, or 'Jim Crow' laws, passed in the late 1890's and early 1900's. They were the public symbols, the most elaborate and formal expression of the South's determination to maintain white supremacy. In bulk and in detail, in intent and in execution, the Segregation codes gave the sanction of law to an almost total racial ostracism. And where the law was not enough, violence and lynching could be made to reinforce it.

Whether by law or by custom, that ostracism extended to housing and jobs, education, schools, churches, eating and drinking, virtually all forms of public transportation, to sports and recreations, to hospitals, prisons, orphanages, asylums, morgues (even in death) and to cemeteries.

Socially, educationally and politically, the blacks were pushed out and disadvantaged, so much so that the status conferred upon them by the white world was almost as low as it had been under slavery. The vast majority of blacks were left uneducated and unskilled, their lives circumscribed by conditions beyond their control or understanding. Most were still living in the Southern States – 75 per cent of them in 1880 – and most were still involved in the same kind of agricultural work as they had been as slaves.

There were manual jobs outside farming, like constructing or rebuilding roads and railroads, repairing and grading the river levees to control flooding, or working in the saw-mills and turpentine camps of the expanding timber industry, but although such work was carried out almost entirely by blacks, these jobs were far outnumbered by those in agriculture. For most blacks, life was limited to the semi-feudal system of farm tenancy and sharecropping which replaced the old slave plantations.

A cropper would work for a planter in return for a share of the crop at harvest time. He and his family would be allocated a certain number of acres on a plantation which he could regard as 'his', and the planter would provide the 'furnishings' – housing, food, clothes, seed, and the tools needed to work the land. At first this seemed a reasonable and equable arrangement, giving the tenant a measure of independence and the planter a stable work force. But in practice the system was tense and insecure, open to all kinds of abuses, and it locked the cropper into a cycle of dependence, debt and despair. The tenant was totally at the mercy of the boss who provided the furnishings on credit, and who did all the financial calculations – 'the figgurin'' – at settlement time. At the end of the year the cropper usually found himself in debt to the landowner, left with only fading dreams of one day making enough from his share to buy his own land. Sam Chatmon, who was born on a plantation and was himself a cropper for many years, explained what it meant:

'The white man is supposed to furnish everything and you supposed to furnish the labor, but now he don't furnish nothing but the land and the cotton seeds. You pay for everything else that he put out there on that. Then he get half of your crop. All right, if you make 10 bales of cotton, that's 5 for you and 5 for him. Well now, you can get 30 dollars a month, you don't get furnished but 6 months, and then when that's turned round, that

30 dollars a month, how can you owe 5 or 600 dollars, if that's all you owe? So I told him one day, I said, "You know one thing?" I said, "Farming's all right but there's too many *its* in share-cropping." He say, "*It?*" I told him, "Yeah!". "What sort of *its?*" I said, "You got to work *it*, plough *it*, hoe *it*, pick *it*, then there's nothing in *it!*".[1]

Most cropper families lived in poorly constructed, unpainted, weatherbeaten and leaking wood-frame cabins. They were prone to chronic diseases which their poverty, ignorance and fatalism did little to forestall. They would loosely talk of 'weakness', or of having 'spells' which they might try to cure with patent medicines from travelling 'Doctors' who touted their wares with groups of itinerant entertainers.

Sharecroppers would raise as large a family as they could, because every new child meant an extra pair of hands to dig, plough, chop weeds, or pick cotton. This meant that as many relations as possible would be part of the household and women were valued for their fertility in much the same way as they had been by the slave-owners. Sam, who was born in 1899, was one of the youngest in the large Chatmon family, who lived on a Mississippi plantation:

'Well there was 9 whole brothers, I can't tell you how many halves I had. My daddy had three wives, and my mother had less children than the others, she had 13 children.'[2]

Women provided such stability as there was in the system, rearing as many children as survived (twenty was not un-common). They could also bring in additional money as domestic servants or by working in the white folks' kitchens. The emotional and physical demands on these women were enormous, and those who accepted these responsibilities were frequently repaid by the desertion of their men-folk when settle-ment time came and increased debts were the only result. Some women moved from the farms to the cities where their ability to get domestic jobs gave them an advantage, but for the men vir-tually the only freedom was to move from one share to another. So blacks moved into a phase which lasted into our own times, an era characterised by constant movement and migrations over short distances and long, from one plantation to another, end-lessly seeking freedom or better opportunities.

In this instability, this constant movement and rambling, the one thing which could not be suppressed, and may even have helped give them a sense of unity was their music. Out of slavery they had brought their ability to make music with any instrument, improvised or otherwise, to express their feelings and tell their stories in song, to recognise and entertain one another whether at home on the plantation, in the back street dives, or on the minstrel stage.

From minstrels to ragtime

'It goes without saying that minstrels were a disreputable lot in the eyes of a large section of the upper-crust Negroes . . . but it is also true that all the best talent of that generation came down the same drain. The composers, the singers, the musicians, the speakers, the stage performers – the minstrel shows got them all . . . Mahara's outfit, like the Georgia Minstrels, the McCabe and Young Colored Minstrels, was the genuine article, a real *Negro* minstrel show!!'[1]

W. C. Handy came from a fairly prosperous and well-established black family in Alabama (his father was a Methodist preacher) and given the appalling image of the race the 'black face' minstrel shows had helped perpetuate and reinforce, it is not surprising to find a defensive note creep into his discussion of the 'genuine article'. There were increasing numbers of black entertainers on stage after the Civil War, and the kind of thing they performed was broadly similar to the burnt cork brigade. If a spiritual was sung at all it was likely to end up a lively burlesque or a reel:

> Get on boa'd, little chillun',
> Get on boa'd, *big* chillun',
> Get on boa'd, *all* de chillun',
> Daddy and Mammy, too![2]

Most of these troupes, like Handy's own outfit the Mahara Minstrels, had trained bandsmen who would perform a wide variety of 'classical' pieces, such as the *William Tell* overture, selections from *The Mikado*, or the latest Broadway hits. But if these minstrels were perhaps more conventional and European in their choice of music than others, most of them retained many elements in common with ordinary black folk music.

Slaves on the old plantations had absorbed many kinds of European music – Wesleyan hymns, Scottish and Irish fiddle music, and ballads of all kinds. Transformed and shaped by their own African traditions, this music became the basis of the nigger minstrel shows. And this same music was not then simply lost to the 'folk' world; more frequently it became reabsorbed itself. As minstrel music became more and more popular in the late 19th century, the music of the plantation shack returned to the shack, via the concert stage, the printed music and of course the travelling minstrel show itself. One example of the way this could happen is the case of *Old Zip Coon*, a very early minstrel song. Several composers claimed to have written it, but it seems to have originated as a folk song and to have made its first stage appearance in a Baltimore theatre in 1834.

> O there once was a man with a double chin,
> Who performed with skill on the violin.
> Well, he played in time and he played in tune,
> But he wouldn't play anything but *Old Zip Coon*.
>
> *Chorus*
> Old Zip Coon he played all night,
> Till the owls and the bats took flight,
> He fiddled and he sawed by the light of the moon,
> But he wouldn't play anything but *Old Zip Coon*.[3]

And so on for any number of verses.

This song, with many verbal variations, passed back into oral culture as *Turkey in the Straw* and has been performed by black and white musicians, including some blues singers, virtually ever since.

Minstrel show bands not only played coon songs and classics, but also dance music and plantation melodies, much of which was not far removed from the kind of thing many blacks performed for their own entertainment. This description of a barn dance on a rainy night in Ashtabula, Ohio, comes from the *Illustrated London News* of February 1897, written by an English woman traveller.

'Very seldom have I enjoyed an entertainment more, either before or since. The quaintest dances imaginable, accompanied by fiddlers and plantation songs, with one man always told off to shout out the different figures, and how they were to be danced . . . One dance by the younger members especially enchanted us. This is the *Plantation Quadrille*, the principal figure like this: a long grand chain, with the couples stationed some distance apart, and before the hand of the next person could be reached, each one, but particularly the women, did a *pas seul* composed of different swaying movements of the body, which were most graceful and pretty. The older people seated round the room kept rhythmic time to the music and dance by clapping their hands together, then on one knee, then on the other, stamping the foot the while, and singing the following verse with great gusto –

Hoe de corn, hoe de corn, Moses,
Hoe de corn, Moses, hoe de corn;
Come away from dat winder,
My lub and my dub,
Come away from dat winder
Don't you hear me? Oh, my!
Come some odder night,
For there's going to be a fight!
There's be razors a-flying in de air.

'. . . The origin of that elegant expression, "taking the cake", had previously been an enigma to me, if I had ever thought about it before, but it was suddenly in an unexpected and most practical way (revealed to me). Just before the ball was declared finished a long procession of couples was formed, who walked in their very best manner round the room three times before the criticising eyes of a jury of a dozen old people, who selected the best turned-out pair, and gravely presented them with a large plum cake.'[4]

By the late 1890's the world of entertainment was beginning to absorb a new music to emerge from black culture. This was ragtime, and the dance craze which went with it, the 'cakewalk'. And that same period also saw the early glimmerings of jazz and blues, both of which had much to do with ragtime, and all of which had something to do with black folk culture – the world of the unknown, untrained musician in 'honky-tonks', 'barrel-houses', 'bawdy houses' and levee camps.

Ragtime was a new syncopated music which seems to have foot-tapped its way out of banjo rhythms. Writing in 1899, Rupert Hughes explained its origins.

'Negroes call their clog dancing "ragging" and the dance a "rag", a dance largely shuffling. The dance is a sort of frenzy with frequent yelps of delight from the dancer and spectators and accompanied by the latter with hand clapping and stomping of feet. Banjo figuration is very noticeable in ragtime music and division of one of the beats into two short notes is traceable to the hand clapping.'[5]

All over the Mid-West and South, along the Missouri, Mississippi and Ohio Rivers, bands performed at functions or toured with minstrel shows, with carnivals, like the De Kreko Bros. Carnival Show, and with tent shows and circuses. One musician remembers a street fair in Sedalia, Missouri (where the King of Ragtime, Scott Joplin was based), in 1898:

'They would play for the trapeze act and then to each event in turn. For the circus they played "quick time" which were marches played in double time."[6]

These shows, and the ten-, twenty- and thirty-cent dramatic shows in theatres and on river steamboats, all saw the rise of ragtime. Rag was also played in 'honky-tonk' saloons, pool halls, cabarets, restaurants, confectionery stores, by groups or with just a pianist. As a form it is best remembered as piano music, and written music at that. It was transcribed for other instruments and published in orchestral form, but it was originally written for the piano, and it has the grace and delicacy of a Victorian drawing-room. Its almost prim simplicity is enlivened by march and dance rhythms which give the music its 'body', while the shifting syncopations generate an infectious and happy lightness. But the recurring themes, especially those in the bass figures of the left hand, give ragtime its faint hint of underlying melancholy. This elusive, slightly wistful sadness which permeates the best ragtime compositions, suggests connections with blues piano, but though related, the styles are really separate.

As with ragtime, we can never really know who the early blues experimenters were. Roy Carew, a music-lover working in New Orleans at the turn of the century, commented on the connection between ragtime and a powerfully rhythmic form of piano blues which was later to be called boogie-woogie.

'I would say that Boogie-Woogie was the bad little boy of the rag family who wouldn't study. I heard crude beginnings of it in the back streets of New Orleans, in those early years following 1904, but they were really back streets, . . . such music never got played in the "gilded palaces".'[7]

The ragtime pianist and composer Eubie Blake remembers a William Turk who played a similar kind of ragtime and boogie in Baltimore. He was six feet tall and weighed more than three hundred pounds. According to Eubie:

'He had a left hand like God. He didn't know what key he was playing in, but he played them all. He could play the ragtime stride bass, but it bothered him because his stomach got in the way of his arm, so he used a walking bass instead. I can remember when I was thirteen – this was 1896 – how Turk would play one note with his right hand and at the same time four with his left. We called it "sixteen" – they call it boogie-woogie now.'[8]

Early New Orleans jazz and blues

'The one blues I never can forget out of those early days happened to be played by a woman that lived next door to my godmother's in the Garden District. The name of this musician was Mamie Desdoumes. Two middle fingers of her right hand had been cut off, so she played the blues with only three fingers on her right hand. She only knew this one tune and she played it all day long after she would first get up in the morning.

> I stood on the corner, my feet was dripping wet,
> I asked every man I met . . .
> Can't give me a dollar, give me a lousy dime,
> Just to feed that hungry man of mine . . .'[1]

That is how the ragtime, blues and jazz pianist Jelly Roll Morton remembered a blues singer he heard in New Orleans in 1902.

At the turn of the century a process of cross-pollination of many kinds of music was taking place in New Orleans. Marches, French quadrilles, Spanish rhythms, black dance music and of course ragtime were all being played by white, creole and black bands. At some point, no-one can say precisely when, jazz emerged out of the amalgam. What made this music distinctively different was the fusion of its two main ingredients: the light airy music of ragtime and the heavier, more emotional strains of the blues.

The legendary Buddy Bolden was one of the earliest trumpet 'Kings' of New Orleans and he was much in demand in the city at least by 1900 with his kind of early ragtime band. They had four horns and three rhythm instruments and played a very low-down kind of blues – singing charming little ditties like *If You Don't Like My Potatoes Why Do You Dig So Deep?*; *All the Whores Like the Way I Ride*; *Make Me a Pallet On Your Floor*, or *Funky Butt*. His band members would arrive for work 'playing the dozens' – hurling scatological insults at each other which had gained for them what Martin Williams in his *Jazz Masters of New Orleans* calls 'the reputation of the nastiest talking men in the History of New Orleans'.[2]

Bunk Johnson claimed to have joined Bolden at this time because he was 'crazy to play blues. Bolden was playing blues of all kinds, so when I got with Bolden, we helped to make more blues . . .'[3] 'Old King Bolden played the music the *Negro* public liked.'[4]

Jelly Roll Morton remembered Bolden too:

'The tune everybody knew him by was one of the earliest variations from the real barrelhouse blues. Some of the old honky-tonk people named it after him and sang a little theme to it that went like this . . .

> I thought I heard Buddy Bolden say,
> "Dirty, nasty stinky butt, take it away,
> Dirty, nasty stinky butt, take it away,
> And let Mister Bolden play . . ."

'This tune was wrote about 1902, but, later on, was, I guess I'll have to say it, stolen by some author and published under the title of the *St Louis Tickle*. Plenty old musicians, though, know it belonged to Buddy Bolden, the great ragtime trumpet man.'[5]

The second chorus of this old song, which Jelly Roll recorded himself, begins:

> I thought I heard Judge Fogarty say . . .[6]

and there is no better illustration of the interrelation of ragtime, jazz, blues and the ordinary, rather crude forms of black folk culture. Newman Ivey White in his *American Negro Folk Songs* quotes a work song sung by labourers in Augusta, Georgia and in it Judge Fogarty appears as Judge Pequette.

> Thought I heard – huh!
> Judge Pequette say – huh!
> Forty-five dollars – huh!
> Take him away – huh![7]

White recalls also hearing the song in Statesville, North Carolina, in the year 1903.

Jelly Roll Morton went on to become one of the finest ragtime and jazz composers and pianists, but he never forgot his early grounding in the blues in New Orleans.

'Music was pouring into the streets from every house. Women were standing in the doorways, singing or chanting some kind of blues – some very happy, and some very sad.'[8]

And it seems that the audience for the blues, at least in New Orleans, were the 'cotton-picking Negroes'. Danny Barker, a guitar- and banjo-player and jazz band vocalist from New Orleans, describes the people who also liked the 'slow, low-down gut-struts' of the blues trumpeter Chris Kelly, who was dark of colour and 'talked a real broken patois, African almost'.

'Now there was a caste system in New Orleans that's died out now. Each one of those caste systems had its own trumpet player, and Chris Kelly played for those blues, cotton-picking Negroes, what they called in the old days "yard and field" Negroes. They were real primitive people who worked in the fields, worked hard. They wore those box-backed suits and hats with two-coloured bands on them, shoes with diamonds in the toe, or a two-dollar gold piece in the toe . . . Chris Kelly played for those people. They would give a ball at the New Hall, which was the young men's charity hall, and every time they gave something there, the undertaker would be glad because there were three or four bodies, and sometimes women's titties would be chopped off . . . Chris Kelly played for people like that.'[9]

Work and song

At the same time that blues, or what were later remembered as blues, were being played and sung in turn-of-the-century New Orleans, all over the Southern States the ordinary black workers could be heard singing the blues in its earliest form.

> I got de blues,
> But I'm too damn mean to cry.[1]

Typically the blues originated as an expression of individual feeling, a personal statement of utter simplicity, perhaps consisting of a single line repeated and repeated again.

> Gwine take morphine an' die
> Gwine take morphine an' die
> Gwine take morphine an' die.[2]

Many singers themselves used the term 'one-verse songs' which meant the entire song was based on the repetition of a single line. For field hands and cotton-pickers, such songs could be found in their most rudimentary form as a 'holler', a lonely, rambling shout which would echo round the cotton fields. The holler had its roots in slavery time, as Frederick Olmsted described in 1853 when he saw a gang of South Carolina slaves who had been hired out to a railroad company.

'One raised such a sound as I had never heard before, a long, loud, musical shout, rising, and falling, and breaking into falsetto, his voice ringing through the woods in the clear, frosty night air, like a bugle call. As he finished, the melody was caught up by another, and then another, then by several in chorus.'[3]

These cries could be made by slaves in gangs, or they could be made by the voice of one lonely worker to a companion hundreds of yards away in another field. Such calls were common all over the South well into this century, sometimes known as 'corn field hollers', 'cotton field hollers', 'whooping', or just 'loud-mouthing'. At their most rudimentary they were little more than a strident lament, in which every phrase was exploited purely for its sound qualities in the empty air.

Woh hoo-oo, woh hoo!
Woh hoo-oo, woh hoo![4]

They might be short and sharp, or long wavering swoops which thinned out and quietly disappeared. Others might be functional calls, like the shouts to a water-carrier. Under the burning sun in a corn field or cotton-row, the water boy or girl was in constant demand. The singer Huddie Ledbetter, who had been a farmer in Texas, had in his repertoire a water call which he sang to the accompaniment of his twelve-string guitar.

Bring me a little water, Silvie,
Bring me a little water now.
Bring me a little water, Silvie,
Every little once in a while.[5]

But the call or holler of the field hand had not entirely replaced the old group work songs of slavery days. While gang-work was far less widespread after Emancipation, and people more often worked in isolation, there were still many kinds of group song.

Well, she ask me – whuk – in de parler – whuk
An' she cooled me – whuk – wid her fan – whuk
An' she whispered – whuk – to her mother – whuk
Mama, I love that – whuk – dark-eyed man – whuk.[6]

This was a song collected by the folklorists Howard Odum and Guy Johnson who say it was sung to any kind of work demanding long and rhythmic movement of the body; work such as pulling, striking or digging to the sound 'whuk'. They remark 'Happily works the dusky figure while he and his companion sing'.[7]

The work songs were more than simply a means to ease hard physical labour, they were also the vehicles for comments of the kind Odum and Johnson found in this grading song from a levee camp.

Well, captain, captain, you mus' be blin',
Look at yo' watch! See ain't it quittin' time?
Well, captain, captain, how can it be?
Whistles keep a-blowin', you keep a-workin' me.[8]

Another work song they collected revealed 'something of the attitude of the Negro toward the white man, but which the white man rarely has the privilege of hearing'.

Ain't it hard, ain't it hard,
Ain't it hard, to be a nigger, nigger, nigger?
Ain't it hard, ain't it hard?
For you can't get yo' money when it's due.

Well, it make no difference,
How you make out yo' time,
White man sho' bring a
Nigger out behin'.

Nigger an' white man,
Playin' seven-up;
Nigger win de money –
Skeered to pick 'em up.[9]

Illustrating both the tenacity of certain verses and sayings in black folk culture and the close connections between work song and the blues is the stanza about the 'Nigger an' white man, playin' seven-up'. A version of that same stanza was collected by Lafcadio Hearn as far back as the 1870's. He quoted it in a newspaper, the *Commercial* of Cincinatti, Ohio, when writing about the songs of the roustabouts working on the city's levee waterfront.

Nigger an' a white man playing seven-up,
White man played an ace, an' nigger feared to take it up,
White man played an ace an' nigger played a nine,
White man died, an' nigger went blind.[10]

In 1926 a blues singer named Julius Daniels recorded a similar stanza in Atlanta, Georgia, while in 1939 the Mississippi singer Tommy McClennan used the same theme in his popular *Bottle Up and Go*.

The hollers and work songs were not just primitive forms of blues, they were and continued to be a separate but parallel form of music. They were part of the musical environment from which blues singers could draw ideas. Chester Burnett, who as 'Howling Wolf' was one of the most commercially successful blues singers of the 1950's, grew up in Mississippi where he was born in 1910.

'There was a lot of music around there. Work songs. Some of the fellows was making songs like "I worked old Maude, and I worked old Belle" – things like that. They'd just get out there and sing as they worked. Plowing songs, songs to call mules by. They'd get out there mornings and get to plowing and get to hollering and singing. They'd make these songs up as they go along.

'They make their sound and their music just like they feel . . . They made up the work songs as they felt. If they felt . . . somebody had taken something from them, that's what they sang about ... But you take myself: I never did have no ups and downs. I came from a good family, and I came up on a good plantation, and I was treated like a man.'[11]

Booker White grew up in Mississippi at the same time, and he has similar memories:

'Now, way back there in them days when they milking them cow, I've heard old folk out there milkin', singin':

> But I'm glad to see the evenin' sun go down,
> So I can go back home and lay back down.

I had to stop for many days propped up on the railing fence, no wire fence, railing fence, and hell, I did a lot of singing. I'd ease on up and get that song and put it down, you know. Oh, I bin around. I knowed exactly who's gonna sing 'em when they come out in the field. I know exactly who's gonna sing 'em.'[12]

The early blues were simple expressions of personal feelings and it was a natural development for the one-verse songs to demand rhymes and additional verses to amplify and underline the emotion.

> Some folks say de fo' day blues ain't bad,
> But de fo' day blues am de wust I eber had.[13]

One of the classic work song themes which went straight into the blues is the famous *John Henry*. The story has been traced to an incident in the 1870's, when a 'steel drivin' man' John Henry competed with a steam drill during the construction of the Big Bend Tunnel on the C. and O. Railroad. Some versions claim he died in the attempt through physical exhaustion, but it is at least as likely that he was crushed in a cave-in of the kind which killed dozens of workers. It probably started as a simple work song.

> This old hammer – WHAM!
> Killed John Henry – WHAM!
> Can't kill me   – WHAM!
> Can't kill me   – WHAM!

But the enormous variety of versions gave the story a mythical life of its own, and it must have been known in nearly every railroad gang or prison camp in the South. So widespread did the song become that it was also part of the repertoire of many white musicians, in a common stock of folk material shared by blacks and whites alike. It gradually took on the form of a ballad, even drawing in elements of an old Scottish ballad, but nearly every performance would be personalised and different. It was a theme which could express a number of quite different attitudes, or it could be sung just as a good old song.

Some versions of *John Henry* appear to take a kind of racial pride in the steel driver's fight against impossible odds.

> John Henry said to the captain,
> That a man is not but a man.
> Said before the steam drill beat me down,
> I'll hammer my fool self to death,
> I'll hammer my fool self to death.[15]

There is a piquant irony in the adoption of John Henry as a hero of this kind; for many whites the black man was only good for mindless hard labour. This belief in his brutish physicality easily extended into images of the black's animal lust and sexual prowess. Such symbolism was doubtless not lost on singers themselves.

> John Henry had a little girl,
> Her name was Polly Ann.
> John was on his bed so low,
> (She) drove with his hammer like a man,
> Drove with his hammer like a man.[16]

If for some *John Henry* was a ballad of self-destruction or physicality, for others it could be a vehicle for a more placid view of life. The version Mississippi John Hurt recorded in 1928 as *Spike Driver Blues* gently suggests that he at least has no intention of competing.

> Take this hammer and carr' it to the captain, tell him I'm gone,
> Tell him I'm gone, you can tell him I'm gone,
> Take this hammer an' carr' it to the captain, an' tell him I'm
>   gone,
> Jes' tell him I'm gone, I sure is goin'.
> This is the hammer that killed John Henry, but it won't kill me,
> But it won't kill me, but it won't kill me . . .[17]

John Henry is just one of a number of ballad-type songs which passed into wide currency among folk musicians. They were more or less narrative songs about external events, often dealing with heroic figures, or epic 'bad-men', or with almost legendary incidents like the fights celebrated in *Frankie and Albert* (or *Frankie and Johnny*, with its famous catch line: 'He was her man, but he done her wrong'). Countryman Mississippi John Hurt included not only *Frankie* in his repertoire but also another popular ballad character, known variously as *Stagger Lee* and

Stack-O-Lee. Accompanied by his fluently picked ragtime guitar *Stack O'Lee Blues* (1928) shows how happily the early blues 'songsters' drew on a wide range of source material and performed it in their own personal way.

> Standin' on the gallows, head way up high,
> At twelve o'clock they killed him,
> We was all glad to see him die,
> That bad man,
> Oh, cruel Stack O'Lee.[18]

W. C. Handy

W. C. Handy was one of the first to see the commercial possibilities of the blues. In 1903 he accepted an offer to direct the Knights of Pythias band of Clarksdale, Mississippi, and with them he travelled around the small towns and local communities in the area, playing for dances and socials, in night-spots and in the stately plantation mansions. His was the music of 'respectable and conventional bands' and as a trained musician he had a good knowledge of European music. Throughout his childhood and youth he had heard the music of illiterate and poor blacks, and had absorbed many melodies and snatches of song but without giving them much thought. It was his experience in the Mississippi of 1903 which changed that.

Apart from the occasion on Tutwiler railway station when he was so impressed by the ragged musician who sang:

> Goin' where the Southern cross the Dog,

while sliding a knife on the strings of his guitar, Handy's real enlightenment came at a dance in the town of Cleveland. He was leading his orchestra in a dance programme when a note was passed up with the request that they play some of 'our native music'. The old time Southern melody they tried only led to a second note. Would they object if the local coloured band played? Handy's group graciously retired from the stand as the locals took over.

'They were led by a long-legged chocolate boy and their band consisted of just three pieces, a battered guitar, a mandolin and a worn-out bass. The music they made was pretty well in keeping with their looks. They struck up one of these over-and-over strains that seem to have no very clear beginning and certainly no ending at all. The strumming maintained a disturbing monotony, but on and on it went, a kind of stuff that has long been associated with cane rows and levee camps. Thump-thump-thump went their feet on the floor. Their eyes rolled. Their shoulders swayed. And through it all that little agonizing strain persisted. It was not really annoying or unpleasant. Perhaps "haunting" is a better word, but I commenced to wonder if anybody besides small town rounders and their running mates would go for it.'

Handy's answer was not long in coming. A rain of dollars, quarters and halves poured on to the floor at the feet of the little string band, and soon the three of them had collected more silver dollars than the nine men in Handy's orchestra were being paid for the whole night.

'Then I saw the beauty of primitive music. They had the stuff the people wanted. It touched the spot.'[1]

From that time on Handy started orchestrating local tunes, and went on to make a name for himself as a composer and publisher of blues tunes based on authentic folk strains.

His place in blues history is as a popularizer and publisher rather than as a blues performer. The style of his orchestra was always too formal to be considered the genuine article. But in formalizing the music which was springing up all over the South in a disparate and incoherent way, he helped give it an identity. In 1912 he became the third person within a few months to publish a piece of music under the name 'blues', the famous *Memphis Blues*. Up to that point the word blues was probably only loosely applied to a wide spectrum of songs – work songs, love songs, devil songs, 'ditties', 'ballits' (ballads), the over-and-overs, the slow drags, pats, stomps and all kinds of barrelhouse music. By about 1910 the form had probably achieved enough of a separate status to be known specifically as 'the blues', but most were still merely independent verses, with no particular title beyond their first line to distinguish one from another. The Rev. Ledell Johnson, who was born in Mississippi in 1892, remembers the music of his uncles who had a band, 'an old hobby-horse outfit'. His uncle George 'didn't know nothing about these blues. He played these little old love songs . . . see, they had these little jump up songs . . . The little old blues they had to my idea wasn't worth fifteen cents. One thing I can remember was some kind of little old song they had:

> Buck up to me, buck up to you,
> That's the way my honey do.'[2]

Sam Chatmon was four in 1903, and he claimed that he was then singing:

> Run down to the river thought I'd jump in an' drown,
> I thought about the woman I lovin' and I turn around.

At that time Sam didn't hear the word 'blues' used for music:

'No, in *them* days I didn't know nothin' but square-dancing and foxtrot and waltz, two-step and then they got up with another dance – come out a little later they called it "The Dip". And you'd play this fast music, this ragtime, and then the white folks would be doin' the Dip in that dance, Dip! That's the way I learnt how to play all that kind of fast music.'[3]

Another singer, Henry Townsend, who was born in Mississippi in 1909, recalls what the blues used to be called when he was young:

'Well they used to have several names for them songs, used to call them, let's see, a corn song, they used to call them reels – and I consider them, yes, they *are* real, 'cos they're telling the truth!'[4]

To some extent the publication of Handy's *Memphis Blues* and the others of 1912 crystallised the music into a coherent form, using the twelve-bar structure by which it is still best known. What is probably his most famous composition, *St Louis Blues*, has the classic form of the opening line repeated and then followed by a third, rhyming line:

> I hate to see de ev'nin' sun go down,
> Hate to see de ev'nin' sun go down,
> 'Cause ma baby, he done lef dis town.[5]

Countless blues follow that structure: three lines of verse, twelve bars of music. Ask almost any jazz or pop musician to play a blues and that's what you'll get – a 'twelve-bar blues.'

But while many authentic blues performers stick to this pattern, just as many others play an irregular and erratic number of bars – eight bars, eleven bars, twelve and a half – whatever suits the mood of the piece. It is the personalised combination of vocal, rhythmic and formal elements which gives the music its individual expressiveness, because, according to Little Brother Montgomery, 'Blues comes from within, the music come from within a person, it don't come out of a conservatory.'[6]

Few of Handy's compositions are within the repertoire of modern blues musicians. As the singer T-Bone Walker remarked:

'Now, you take a piece like *St Louis Blues*. That's a pretty tune and it has a kind of bluesy tone, but that's not the blues. You can't dress up the blues . . . I'm not saying that *St Louis Blues* isn't fine music you understand. But it just isn't blues.[7]

To many blues historians it is not at all surprising that W. C. Handy's 'enlightenment' should have occurred in Mississippi. Many are convinced that the blues actually originated there at some uncertain date in the 1890's. One of these writers is Samuel Charters who concludes that, despite the conflicting evidence, 'it was in the Mississippi delta counties that the first blues were sung'.[8] True or not, it is something of a moot point; what is more important has been the enormous richness of Mississippi music, providing a diversity of styles which have had a continuing and shaping influence on American popular culture. There have been an almost astonishing number of first-rate blues singers who came from Mississippi, many of whom moved on to other parts of the country and to the cities of the North, taking with them the powerfully emotional sound of the Mississippi blues.

By the 1890's there was a greater concentration of black people in Mississippi than in any other part of the country. In some areas blacks outnumbered whites by as many as two or three to one. This was especially true of the so-called Mississippi Delta. The term does not refer to where the river fans out into the gulf of Mexico, like the Nile Delta does into the Mediterranean; it is the local term loosely applied to that part of the State flanked on the West by the Mississippi River, roughly from Memphis to Vicksburg, and on the East by the Yazoo River. It is a flat plain, for centuries washed over by uncontrolled river floods accumulating some of the richest earth in the South. The land had been levelled and planted by slaves, who constituted a majority of the population as early as the 1840's. Levees were banked up to control the river flow and the area became more and more densely populated after the Civil War. As railroads and roads were developed, larger and larger numbers of poor and illiterate blacks were attracted to the area, drawn by promises of higher pay made by labour agents working for the white planters. Virtually limited to sharecropping and working on the new plantations owned by the whites, raising cotton to the exclusion of everything else, life in the Mississippi Delta was the essence of the black's segregated social isolation. Gus Cannon, who was born in Red Banks, Mississippi in 1883 remembered what conditions were like in the Delta when he was a boy. 'Did I work? Sure I worked! That cotton tall, taller than me – with my brother. Got a whipping too! But no schooling. Mmm . . . I done

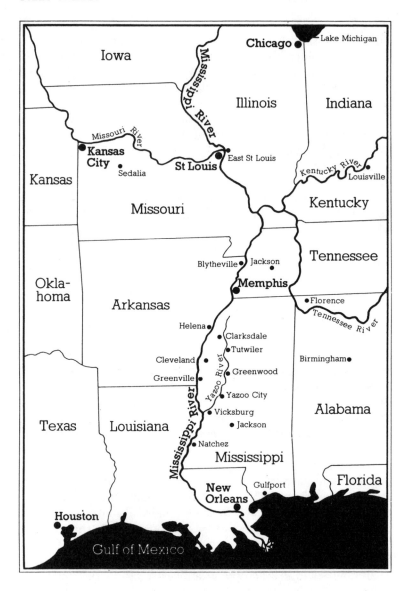

killed, I've killed two bears in my life, and one deer. Deer, wolf, wild cat and everything else down there. Oh when I was down in the Delta, just below, I mean south of Clarksdale, Clarksdale wasn't a big city there, at that time. Wasn't nothin', some plank walks and all the roads were mud roads . . . I don't know but one bridge across the Sunflower River. That was the railroad. There's a gang of 'em through there now.'[9]

The dominance of the white minority was absolute, economically, educationally, politically and socially. Mississippi had a reputation for racism and bigotry from the earliest days of Emancipation; its record of lynching, reaching a bloody peak in the early days of the Jim Crow laws, was appalling. The *Vicksburg Evening Post* described the lynching of a man and his wife in 1904 by a mob of over a thousand people in Doddsville, Mississippi:

'Luther Holbert and his wife, negroes . . . were tied to trees and while the funeral pyres were being prepared, they were forced to hold out their hands while one finger at a time was chopped off. The fingers were distributed as souvenirs. The ears of the murderers were cut off. Holbert was beaten severely, his skull was fractured and one of his eyes, knocked out with a stick, hung by a shred from the socket.

'Some of the mob used a large corkscrew to bore into the flesh of the man and woman. It was applied to their arms, legs and body, then pulled out, the spirals tearing out big pieces of raw, quivering flesh every time it was withdrawn.'[10]

It was also reported that two blacks had already been killed by a posse in mistake for Holbert, who was alleged to have killed his white planter boss.

During the Civil Rights Campaigns of the 1960's, the State was still a by-word for repression and racism, with several bombings and slayings designed to keep down the 'uppity niggers'. In 1963, when squads of gun-wielding and club-swinging police beat and shoved 600 black children into patrol wagons and garbage trucks during a demonstration in the city of Jackson, a Civil Rights worker said it was 'just like Nazi Germany'.[11]

Blacks were socially and racially ostracised, economically exploited and politically crippled in Mississippi, as in other parts of the South. Segregation and humiliation, sometimes massive, sometimes petty, was the lot of every black, whether poor or not. But within the black community, within the confines of deprivation, they set about creating a way of life.

A major part of that life was centred on the Church, that stronghold of communal strength under slavery. In his book *The Negro Revolt*, Louis E. Lomax says that:

'By listening and fervently responding to the pure poetry of the Negro preacher, the Negro masses got a sense of history and moral philosophy. There is something incredibly informative about sitting Sunday after Sunday and year in, year out, listening to a minister trace out the history of the Jews from the day God spit out the seven seas to the time John the Revelator closed the Bible and said all truth has been revealed. Even those of us who couldn't read came to think of history as a moving, changing thing; we were never allowed to doubt that man as a created thing had purpose and that we, to be sure, were a part of that purpose.'[12]

The Church as a social institution and as a system of belief did perhaps give the black community an overall universal context in which it could place itself, a structure which for some was a buffer against the grimmer aspects of reality, and a refuge and a source of strength for others. It could confer status upon its elders and leaders, and the emotionality and exuberance of its services and its music provided an outlet for repressed feelings, or for shared joys. There was however a parallel world to that of the Church, the world of secular amusement which lay alongside it, uneasily and with much tension; this was where the blues were sung. The music considered 'sinful', or 'the devil's music', blues singers were constantly being called to repentance, and children were always being warned away from the blues by their parents. For the blues singer the counter-accusation might be that the preacher was a hypocrite, an immoral philanderer and exploiter of other peoples' superstitions. Despite the conflicts between them, the two worlds frequently overlapped, with many a singer 'getting religion', or a preacher turning to the blues. The blues singer was able to articulate feelings and attitudes less frequently touched on by the Church. The global view provided by religion was complemented by the interior world of personal feeling, of emotions experienced by individuals but shared by the group. When asked to define the blues, most blues singers reply that 'the blues is a feeling'.

Booker White: 'Well sure, blues is a feeling! But you can write the truth with the blues . . . You see, I tell you, you gotta feed your mind with something all the time, you think about something all the time. Sometimes you can have a good feelin', sometimes you have a bad feelin'. But now, in the blues line it's always being up on somebody you love or somebody that quits you.'[13]

Henry Townsend: 'It really is this to me: it's a relief, for pressure.'[14]

Houston Stackhouse: 'Hard working people, been half-mistreated and done around – I believe that's what the blues come from you know . . . Well, the blues come from black people . . . The blues come out of colored people. That's where I say it come from.'[15]

These singers were all born in Mississippi in 1909 or 10; all played in different styles and all were living in different circumstances. But when interviewed about the blues in 1976 their remarks all showed how the expression of personal feelings was felt to relieve those feelings, and also how they relate to those of the wider community.

Many black people would have been, and still would be, offended by the idea that the blues singer 'spoke' for them, in much the same way that others would reject the spokesmanship of the preacher. Nevertheless, there did exist what almost amounted to a blues community. Its significance was in the processes of communal creation and participation in a shared culture, and within that world most singers regarded themselves as entertainers. But the idea that blues were the expression of deeply felt emotions made the music more than simply entertainment.

'The Devil's music – I don't think the Devil care for the truth, do you?' asks Henry Townsend. 'Because that's the brand – the Devil is a terrible thing, so he wouldn't like nothing that was real or something that was nice. There's a lot of things is taught and told to us that we all have to disregard now because we find it not to be true. I've been told things even about the Bible, and it's not in there, and people have sounded off terrible. And in later years I found out *that* wasn't true either. So, the truth is, I guess I stick to my blues as the blues, and I'm not afraid to play them because I'm scared that I'm gonna go to the burning place, whatever it is. I'm not afraid of that![16]

Henry Townsend's wife Vernell is also a blues singer and she too has met the inevitable complaints of the religious minded. Like her husband she has reflected on the subject; and like him she remains entirely unrepentant:

'I've heard old people say, down through the years, "Oh, that's the Devil's Music", and then they give you a Bible quote, you know. They'll say, "Because the Bible said 'Make a joyful noise unto the Lord!'", you know? They give you this reason. It *does* say that, but it doesn't say what *kind* of joyful noise to make to the Lord! The blues can be just as joyful as a spiritual.'[17]

Part Two

Charley Patton

'Charley Patton was a clowning man with a guitar. He be in there putting his guitar all between his legs, carry it behind his head, lay down on the floor, and never stopped picking!'[1]

This was how Sam Chatmon remembered his half-brother Charley Patton, perhaps the greatest and most influential of all the early Mississippi singers, sometimes called 'Founder of the Delta Blues'. Howling Wolf also remembered Patton:

'He was a nice guy, but he just loved the bottle – like all the rest of the musicians. He was a great drinker. I never did know him to do no gambling or anything like that . . ., but *drink*! I did know him to play good, and everybody liked him. He was a mixed-breed fellow, a light-skinned guy. He looked kinda like a Puerto Rican. He was from Will Dockery's place – that's a plantation out from Ruleville . . . He'd go from place to place around there.

'He used to play out on the plantations, at different one's homes out there. They'd give a supper – call it a Saturday night hop or something like that. There weren't no clubs like nowadays. Mostly on weekends they'd have them. He'd play different spots – he'd be playing here tonight and somewhere else the next night, and so on.'[2]

Howling Wolf was only a teenager when he first saw Charley Patton in the late 1920's, and although by then Patton's music was a little old-fashioned, it was to remain some of the best remembered and most inspirational of a whole generation. His singing was rough and intense or gentle and soft by turns, sometimes full of passion, sometimes warm and joyful. He could be tough and moody, or spritely and light, his guitar singing and moaning along with his voice, now a quiet, easy strum, now with the strings venomously snapping back onto the neck of the instrument. He could set up rocking dance rhythms with the bass strings droning and buzzing beneath delicately chimed runs in the upper register.

In some songs his words would slur and run into each other to the point of incoherence, snatches of a word slipped in here, a phrase there and all completely integrated into the guitar-playing with a sliding, shifting rhythmic pulse. Patton's strange pronunciation makes the transcription of his records difficult and sometimes impossible. Even his contemporaries often did not know what he was on about.

Son House, who often went around with Patton in the 30's and who is probably the greatest living exponent of the early Delta blues, told some interviewers:

'A lot of Charley's words . . . you can be sitting right under him . . . you can't hardly understand him.'[3]

Patton frequently played his guitar with a slide on the strings, using either a knife (like the Tutwiler musician that Handy saw in 1903), or the broken off neck of a bottle, slipped onto a finger of his left hand. In some of his songs he would complete the sound of a word with the slide, as in his erotic *A Spoonful Blues*.

> *(Spoken)* I'm got to go to jail about this spoonful,
> An' all a spoon, aw that spoonful,
> Women goin' crazy everyday in their life 'bout a . . . . . .
> It's all I want, in this creation is a . . . . . .
> I go home.
> *(Spoken)* Wanna fight,
>   'bout a . . . . . .
> Doctors dyin'
> *(Spoken)* Way in Hot Springs,
>   just 'bout a . . . . . .
> These women goin' crazy everyday in their life 'bout a . . . . . .[4]

On several of his records there are spoken interjections, asides and comments, sometimes made by Patton himself but also by friends in the recording studio. These little commentaries, though sometimes hard to catch, add to the rhythmic impetus of the music as pure sound and help give a feeling of depth. But they also add a sense of community, a feeling that Patton is singing to, or for somebody. When he was performing Patton was mainly an entertainer. Son House especially remembers the clowning, of which he was somewhat critical as he told Nick Perls:

'Charley, he'd try to make a record out of anything, you know, 'cause he'd love to clown . . . "Yeah baby" (imitated Patton) . . . and a lotta kinda stuff like that. We'd let him do all that part . . . He'd take all them old foolish songs and things . . . some of them would sound all right . . . some of them had a meaning to them

... some didn't. That's the way he played. He'd just say anything, the first thing he could think of ... "Hey baby" ... "Aw
sho" ... and all that old kind of funny stuff ... Oh yeah, we
often tell him, too. Say "Charley, you outta stop so much that ol'
foolish messin' around". "Oh man, all I want to do is get paid for
it. What's the difference?" I'd say, "Yeah, but it just sounds so
foolish and a lot of junk to it". Patton – "What's the difference,
man?" I'd say "OK, that's your little red waggon".[5]

Patton was very much the community entertainer, remembered
not only for his clowning but also for his drinking, womanising and
occasional brawling. Although he was frequently on the move,
always aiming to catch harvest time when people would briefly be
in the money, his life was that of an average plantation dweller. His
death certificate in 1934 described him not as a musician but as a
farmer. The date of his birth is uncertain, variously given as 1881,
1887, 1890, and even who his father was is open to doubt. It may
have been either Bill Patton, his mother's husband, or Henderson
Chatmon, the father of a huge family who were nearly all
musicians. Charley was born near Edwards, Mississippi, and
seems to have swopped around between his two 'families'. One
'father', Bill Patton, was apparently a part-time preacher and from
him Charley learned many religious songs, some of which he later
recorded. Son House enjoyed that:

'Nary a one of us wasn't sanctified, but we's making out like it,
you know to make a record ... We wasn't nothing but ol'
whiskey drinkers and blues players.'[5]

One of his religious songs *Prayer of Death* (Parts 1 and 2) was
issued on record as by 'Elder J. J. Hadley'.

> *(Spoken)*   The prayer of death. Tone the bell!
> Time to just toll the bell again.
> Tell them to sing a little song like this.
>
> Take a stand. Take a ... Take a stand,
> If I never, never see you any more,
> Take a stand. Take a ... Take a stand,
> I'll meet you on that other ...[6]

Musically Patton probably learned far more from the Chatmons
than from the Pattons. He had numerous brothers and half-
brothers by Henderson Chatmon and Anney Patton. Henderson
Chatmon was himself a fiddle-player – old songs like *Turkey in
the Straw* and *Liza Jane* – and almost all his children played
instruments. One son was Sam Chatmon, who remembered
learning music as a child.

'My father, he played in slavery time, when the white folks wan' it, he *had* to play. And when I was big enough to remember when he used to be playing round the house at times, I'd ask him, "Let me try!" He say, "No, you too small yet to play, too little, so you wait." So I climbed up side the house against the wall and got my brother's guitar, and I'd break a string on it, trying to pick it and tune it, and I'd crawl back up there and hang it back up. When he come in he say, "Someone's been handling my guitar!" Says: "It wasn't none of me." You see I lied all the way from a little child on up! So my daddy, when I did get big enough to play, I go to playin' a piece, and I'd make a mistake. I was playing a guitar. He said, "Bring me a fiddle here, let me show you how that go." And then me and him would sit down and play for maybe two hours.'[7]

All Sam's family were musical: 'Played guitar, violin, tenor banjo, and mandolin, piano, saxophone, clarinet, just anything more or less borrowed, hired or picked up, they played.'[7] Like the rest of his brothers, and like Patton himself, Sam often played for white people as he recalled in 1976. 'Mighty seldom I ever play for coloured, they didn't have nothing to hire you with.' He looked back on the kind of treatment black musicians received without rancour.

'Well, they treat you good in a way, and in a way they didn't. You, you was compelled to do just like you do when you go to your own master's house. You couldn't come in the front and when you get ready to go out you couldn't go out the front, you had to go round to the back and whenever they serve refreshments they serve everybody else and then you'd have to go out on the back porch and let them serve it to you out there.'[7]

The Chatmons were among the most prolifically recorded of all blues musicians in the 1920's and 1930's. Bo Chatmon, using the name Bo Carter, made more than a hundred sides for various companies, and the brothers themselves recorded nearly as many under various names like the Mississippi Sheiks (usually a vocalist with guitar and violin), the Chatman Brothers, The Mississippi Mud Steppers, or The Mississippi Blacksnakes. Their records were usually group sessions, employing more sophisticated chords and progressions than singers like Patton; they would play waltzes, the black bottom and two-steps. 'That two-step was an intelligent dance, a very nice dance the two-step was',[8] according to the Rev. Rubin Lacey who played with the Chatmons in the 1920's.

In fact to Sam's ears Patton's approach to music jarred:

'I didn't like the way he sang. He was my brother, but he just had a way – (*Sings*) "Saddle up my pony, hook up my black maaaaare . . ." I didn't like that! . . . Now he picks good, but he just brings that song out, like there's somebody choking to death.'[9]

The rougher, more earthy and emotional blues of Charley Patton seem to have been picked up while living with the older Chatmons. But the really crucial stage in his life was when he moved from the Edwards and Bolton area to Dockery's Plantation in the heart of the Mississippi Delta. Dockery's Plantation was established in 1895 by Will Dockery, and the Patton family moved there a couple of years later. It was white-owned and worked entirely by blacks, but it was efficiently run and well kept by its paternalistic planter. It was probably the best kind of life available to Mississippi's illiterate black farming population. Dockery's was near the small Delta towns of Ruleville, Drew and Cleveland, and also near another large white-owned plantation, Jim Yeager's.

In this fairly small area there were an astonishing number of first-rate blues singers of whom Charley Patton was only one. A process of group creation was established, with ideas and songs swapped and guitar patterns exchanged as they frequently played together in the plantation quarters, for house parties or for dances. The gathering of these many musicians in the Delta was part of the wave of migration bringing blacks to the area as tenant farmers and sharecroppers. Men like Patton were perhaps master musicians in the community, but they were not committed professionals. Some musicians would come just for the harvest, others would stay, but all were part of the generally fluctuating community.

In later years, one of Patton's most popular records was *Mississippi Bo Weavil Blues:*

> It's a little bo weavil she's movin' in the . . . Lordie!
> You can plant your cotton and you won't get half a cent, Lordie!
> Bo weavil, bo weavil, where's your native home? Lordie!
> 'A-Louisiana leavin' Texas anywhere I'se bred and born',
>   Lordie!
> Well I saw the bo weavil Lord a circle Lordie in the air, Lordie!
> The next time I seed him he had his family there, Lordie!
> Bo weavil left Texas Lord, he bid me 'Fare thee well', Lordie![10]

The boll weavil, a cotton eating insect, had entered Texas by the 1890's and had rapidly spread a wave of destruction through thousands and thousands of cotton-farming acres. By 1915 it had reached Mississippi, presenting a major crisis to the community. There were many early blues on the subject of the little boll weavil. He frequently appeared as a rather naughty little friend with whom some blacks seemed to identify in his destructive instincts and in his search for a home.

Life was already marginal, but the plight of the Southern tenant farmer and farm worker was worsened as planters reduced their acreage and changed to other crops. A second blow was the series of disastrous floods of 1915 and 1916, when enormous areas were devastated and many people, planters and tenants alike, were ruined. These were neither the first nor the last of the great Mississippi floods. In 1927, another flood savaged the area and became the inspiration for one of Charley Patton's greatest records *High Water Everywhere*, an agonised and passionate performance which sold many copies in the early 1930's and was one of the songs most identified with him. It is a profoundly serious work, which somewhat belies his reputation as a clown. Accompanied by doomy toning of the bass strings, with tension and water rising to the sounds of thumps on the guitar, his voice is strained, with a choking, cracking hoarseness. At moments he subsides into resignation punctuated by delicate strokes on the upper strings.

> Backwater at Blythville, doctor weren't around,
> Backwater at Blythville, done took Joiner Town,
> It was fifty families and children, suffer to sink and drown.
>
> The water was risin', up at my friend's door,
> The water were risin', up in my friend's door.
> The man said to his womenfolk:
>   'Lord we's better'd row'.
>
> The water it was risin'; got up in my bed,
> Lord the water it rollin', got up to my bed,
> I thought I would take a trip Lord out on a big ice-sled.
>
> Oh I hear, Lord, Lord, water upon my door,
> *(Spoken)*   You know what I mean? Same here,
> I hear the ice boat Lord went sinking down.[11]

It was songs like this and others with ostensibly rural themes like *Pony Blues*, *Down the Dirt Road Blues*, and *Banty Rooster Blues* (all recorded in 1929) that secured Patton's local popularity but also ensured that his influence spread beyond the range of merely personal contact. One of the many musicians showing deep infusions of Patton's style was slide guitarist Booker White:

'I never did meet Charley Patton. I met his brother though. I never did meet him but I was in the Mississippi Delta and his records sellin' like hamburger. That's the honest to God truth. I didn't never get chance to meet him. No more than just hearing his records.'[12]

While Patton and other record makers would sometimes sing about the world around them, of boll weavils or flood disasters, the bulk of their music was about the closer world of their personal feelings.

The principal theme of the country blues, and probably of all blues, is the sexual relationship. Almost all other themes, leaving town, train rides, work trouble, general dissatisfaction sooner or later reverts to the central concern. Most frequently the core of the relationship is seen as inherently unstable, transient, but with infinite scope for pleasure and exultation in success, or pain and torment in failure. This gives the blues its tension and ambiguity, dealing simultaneously with togetherness and loneliness, communion and isolation, physical joy and emotional anguish. In Patton's blues, even the sound itself has the feeling of tension, with damped down, 'dirty' toned, monotonously repeated bass figures giving a heavy emotional undertow, lightened by the sensously rising and sliding notes, driving and swinging with the joy of release.

Many blues singers consider the guitar a second voice; a Delta singer who left for St Louis in 1925, J. D. 'Jelly Jaw' Short, remembered Patton from his youth and told Samuel Charters:

'He used to play the guitar and he'd make the guitar say "Lord have mercy, Lord have mercy, pray, brother, pray, save poor me". Now that's what Charley Patton'd make the guitar say.'[13]

But Patton's blues speak with several voices simultaneously. In the words of his songs, with their impressionistic flow, picking up odd verses from anywhere, using traditional words or phrases from other songs, he shifts from snatches of direct conversation, asides and other people's replies, to pure narration and to his own thoughts and observations.

> When your way gets dark, baby, turn your lights up high,
> (Spoken) What's the matter with 'em?
> Where you see my man, Lordy, he come easin' by.
> I take my baby . . .
> (Spoken) Take her 'fore this brown I take my baby . . .
> Trouble at home, baby,
> (Spoken) Tryin' to blow me down.
> It wouldn't hurt so bad but the news all over this town.
> *When Your Way Gets Dark*[14]

In Patton's *Running Wild Blues* the focus changes from 'I' to 'he' to 'she' in a torrent of words turning a popular song of the time into a 'nonsense' jingle. The permutation of words could be endlessly extended, and in their rhythmic ebb and flow they take on the coherence of a dream.

> I'm runnin' wild, I'm runnin' wild, that mighty boy,
>   that mighty boy, he's runnin' wild,
> In all my dreams, in all my dreams, this mighty boy,
>   he's runnin' wild,
>
> He's runnin' wild, that mighty boy, that mighty girl,
>   that mighty girl, she's runnin' wild,
> She's all night long, she's on my mind, that girl of mine,
>   that girl of mine, she's runnin' wild,
>
> I'm runnin' wild, I'm runnin' wild, that mighty boy,
>   that mighty boy, he's runnin' wild,
> All night long, she's on my mind that girl of mine,
>   she's on my mind . . .[15]

As an entertainer Charley Patton expressed exuberance and joy, the desire to have a good time, get drunk, clown around; but the underlying sense of emotional reality which permeates his music give it depth and power. However he is remembered, whether as a clown and rowdy entertainer or as one of a number of influential musicians of his time, Charley Patton's records are still superbly moving blues performances. Songs about boll weavils or forgotten incidents in small Mississippi towns may be of limited interest, but Patton's blues, and those of his many contemporaries, transcend their limitations. They have a universality of feeling even when the words are incomprehensible or obscure. As the blues singer will tell you, 'blues is a feeling'.

Henry Thomas 'Ragtime Texas'

'These poor people could never travel when they were slaves; so they make up for the privation now. They stay on a plantation till the desire to travel seizes them; then they pack up, hail a steamboat, and clear out. Not for any particular place; no, nearly any place will answer; they only want to be moving.'[1]

The constant movement of blacks that Mark Twain noted in the 1880's could be paralleled in the lives of almost limitless numbers of blues musicians. Over and over again the theme of their songs was travel – 'I got to keep moving . . .', 'I got rambling, rambling all on my mind', 'I'm here today and tomorrow I may be gone'. In this respect the bluesman reflected a tendency to be found in American society at large and in black society in particular, where, especially since Emancipation, movement had symbolised freedom. Notions of 'boundlessness' have often been taken to be part of the American Dream, but the constant migrations, over long or short distances, over all parts of the Southern states and increasingly to the North were more a reflection of the arid and sterile quality of life for most poor blacks. Trapped into a kind of economic servitude by sharecropping, with few opportunities to break out of those limitations, travel could itself be an assertion of independence.

To the white outsider the endless and seemingly pointless travel was hard to understand and something to be regretted. A liberal planter from Mississippi, lecturing in 1901, believed the blacks 'a restless people. Ever seeking change, they sometimes wander far afield . . . they move but in a narrow circle, yet always in the same vain, aimless quest . . . Certainly, the plantation Negro, changes his residence far too often for his children to form local attachments or to develop anything akin to such a sentiment . . .'[2]

For some blacks movement might mean from one plantation to another in a ceaseless quest to find good soil, or a fair-minded boss; others were simply seasonal migrants going wherever there was work. But untold numbers were simply hobos, those almost mythological figures of American folklore among whom there were, of course, many musicians.

Odum and Johnson believed that the hobo singer loved idleness and shunned work:

'His songs are the most pathetic and plaintive of all, for he depends upon them to arouse pity and to gain the favors which he desires. He makes much of his hard times, his loneliness, his lack of friends and sympathy; yet he would not change his conditions if he could. He makes conditions of his own liking, and these things constitute his "good time".'[3]

Writing from the perspective of 1925, Odum and Johnson might well have regarded such a description apt for one of the earliest of blues singers we know about, Henry Thomas, who used the hobo nickname 'Ragtime Texas'. Thomas is of special interest because he was one of a handful of the oldest generation of blues singers to have made phonograph records. The first blues record was not made until 1920 when Mamie Smith's *Crazy Blues* paved the way for many hundreds of other performers. Most of these were only in their twenties when they recorded; the date of Henry Thomas' birth, 1874, means that he grew up through the entire period when the blues were developing as a clearly recognised and separate form. From his legacy of some twenty-three records made between 1927 and 1929, we get a glimpse of how the blues fitted into the cross currents of folk music.

'Ragtime Texas was a great big fellow that used to come aboard at Gladewater or Mineola or somewhere in there. I'd always carry him except when he was too dirty. He was a regular hobo but I'd carry him most of the time.'[4]

This was how a retired train conductor named G. T. Hardy (who used to work the passenger trains out of Dallas) recalled Henry Thomas to folklorist Mack McCormick. Hardy had many affectionate memories of the old wandering musician who played a guitar and blew the 'quills', or pan pipes made out of cane from a river bottom. In the days when Ragtime Texas was hoboing, 'that guitar was his ticket'. All he would do, if he couldn't ride for free inside the carriage, would be to jump into an empty gondola or box car, or onto the blind end of a baggage car. If all else failed, he would ride underneath the cars, on the truss-rods. But given a kindly conductor like Hardy, Thomas could usually find a place in the smoking car, or in the 'For Colored' coach at the back.

There was one occasion Hardy remembers when he noticed how there were less children than usual scampering up and down the corridors. Then, in one of the white coaches, there was Ragtime, playing away. 'I found him up there picking guitar, singing, playing that whistle business, and letting out *whoops* to where he had half a dozen youngsters dancing up at the front of the car.'[4]

McCormick says he has collected many such reminiscences. The trouble is it isn't always possible to tell if the stories apply to Ragtime or to any one of countless other hobos and musicians whose lives were essentially the same.

'Most of what they remembered was that there used to be a guitar-player hanging around every depot up and down the line. They described not one but dozens of men who used to hang around the domino parlour or some across-the-tracks tavern until train time when, with everyone else in town, they'd come over to the depot. Wherever the train stopped it was commonplace to look across the platform and see one or two musicians in the crowd.'[5]

McCormick has discovered from the family bible that Henry Thomas was born in Upshur County, Texas, one of probably nine children. His parents had been slaves, and even as free people were still pretty well trapped in the semi-feudal world of the Texas cotton economy. Henry himself is well remembered as having hated cotton farming. He upped and left home as soon as he could, earning his living with his guitar, or supported by some woman; sometimes he would settle in one of the small Texan towns, or head for the more exciting world of Dallas, or of Shreveport in Louisiana. But increasingly he drifted into the life of a hobo, up and down the line of the Texas and Pacific Railroad, through East Texas, up to Oklahoma, to Kansas City, and he even got as far as Chicago for the Columbian Exposition of 1893, and to St Louis for the World Fair of 1904.

Over and over again the theme of Henry Thomas' songs is travel; even in one of the two gospel numbers he recorded, *When the Train Comes Along:*

> When the train comes along,
> When the train comes along,
> I'll meet you at the station when the train comes along,
> I may be blind, I cannot see,
> I'll meet you at the station when the train comes along.[6]

He gruffly but cheerfully churns out the lines of the song, whanging away at the guitar in a kind of regular chunky beat like the rhythm of a train itself. His voice is neither particularly plaintive nor melancholy – it is the voice of a man who perhaps doesn't really expect to be listened to, just to rather hoarsely remind the milling crowds at the depot that there's some old guy who could do with the spare change in your pocket. The guitar-playing, though sometimes showing an impressive sensitivity and subtlety, is most frequently a heavy stomping strum, regular enough for the dancers at the country suppers at which he sometimes played. His *Old Country Stomp* is a typical old reel, a dance tune which even starts with square dance calls, before taking off into clusters of repeated lines where the words themselves become part of the rhythm:

> Get your partner, promenade,
> Promenade all around, now.
> Hop on, you started wrong,
> Take your partner, come on the train.
> I'm going away, I'm going away,
> I'm going away, I'm going away,
> I'm going back to Baltimore.
> Fare you well, fare you well,

Fare you well, fare you well,
Mistreated, mistreated Tom,
Mistreated since I been gone.[7]

Ragtime Texas was very much the songster, the musician who could provide a whole range of music – spirituals, country reels and songs drawn from the minstrel show tradition. One of his songs, *Honey, Won't You Allow Me One More Chance*, which inspired one of Bob Dylan's songs in the 1960's, was almost certainly drawn from a collection of coon songs published at the turn of the century:

I went home last night, the moon was shining bright,
Drinking, feeling dizzy about my head.
Well I rapped on the door, I heard my baby roar,
'Honey, I'm gone to bed.'
Get up and let me in.
'Oh, what was that you said? You know you haven't treated me right.
I've paid all this rent, you haven't got a cent.
You'll have to hunt a new home tonight.'
Honey, allow me one more chance, I always will treat you right.
Honey, won't you allow me one more chance?
I won't stay out all night.
Honey, won't you allow me one more chance,
I'll take you to the ball in France.
One kind favor I ask of you, just allow me just one more chance.[8]

The songster was more the residuary of popular themes and songs passed down than an individual creator. Henry Thomas' repertoire included snippets of dozens of songs known elsewhere, bits of work and prison camp songs, music taken from country dances, religious songs, the music played by countless similar white country musicians, and he was ready to perform for any kind of audience. Often in the middle of a song he would jump from one tune to another, adding snatches of different songs which would be well-known to his audience. If in the whirl of drinking and dancing anyone was bothering to listen to the lyrics they would not need the whole 'story' coherently set out; a reference here, a line or two there would be enough. This is a characteristic of many blues, the lashing together of lines or verses often almost totally unrelated to form an impressionist sweep and linked only by the overall mood of the song. A song composed in this way could be regarded as a singer's own (Son House even claimed a commonplace expression like 'Lord have mercy on my wicked soul' as his own).

Analysis of Ragtime Thomas' records reveals dozens of cross-references to lines of songs and tunes which crop up in early printed song collections, or in records made by other black and white artists. Two of his blues, *Don't Ease Me In* and *Don't Leave Me Here*, recorded in 1928 and 1929 respectively, are both pretty well the same melody and with only slightly different words. More interestingly, they both relate to a very popular theme, 'Don't leave me here, I'm Alabama bound'.

In different guises, the song *I'm Alabama Bound* crops up all over the place, and folklore collectors have found it in Texas, Mississippi and elsewhere. In 1939 Jelly Roll Morton claimed to Alan Lomax that he had made the song up himself in 1905, when he was in the Alabama barrel house circuit.

> I'm Alabama bound,
> Alabama bound.
> If you like me sweet baby,
> You've got to leave this town . . .
>
> She said, 'Don't you leave me here,
> Don't you leave me here.
> But, sweep papa, if you *just* must go,
> Leave a dime for beer . . .'[9]

In about 1904–1905 Roy Carew was living across the Mississippi from New Orleans where he worked in a factory.

'From Hylas, the office boy at the plant, I got my first impression of the blues. He had a choice assortment of fragments that he sang, some of which would not bear repeating. One of the better bits was the following:

> Why don't you be like me?
> Why don't you be like me?
> Just drink good whiskey boy,
> And let the cocaine be.

'The melody wasn't much and bore a similarity to *Alabama Bound*, to which Jelly Roll laid some claim, stating that the tune was picked up from him.'[10]

The first of Ragtime Texas' versions of the theme has the same basic melody with the chorus 'Doncha leave me here' replaced by 'Don't ease me in', the title he gave his song. That phrase was itself a folk expression cropping up in many a Texas prison.

Many of the old slave plantations were converted into the notorious 'County Farms', when the overcrowding of the jails after the Civil War led to a system of leasing out prisoners for work on either State projects or for private business men. The name of one of these men became locked into folk memory: Cunningham. He was one of the many in the late 19th century who used prisoners to work his sugar cane fields along the Brazos River bottoms.

> Don't ease, don't you ease,
> Ah, don't you ease me in.
> It's all night long, Cunningham, don't ease me in.
> I've got a girl, she's little and short,
> She leave here walking, loving babe, talking true love talk.
> Don't ease, don't you ease,
> Ah, don't you ease me in.
> It's all night long, Cunningham, don't ease me in.
> I was standing on the corner, talking to my brown,
> I turned, sweet mama, I was workhouse bound.[11]

Life in the Texas County Farms and Penitentiaries was almost unbelievably harsh and brutalized. Often inside for trivial offences or simple 'vagrancy', prisoners were repeatedly beaten and flogged and sometimes literally worked to death. Shackled together in chain gangs, perhaps up to 300 to a chain, these men – and sometimes women – would work sixteen hours a day, six or seven days a week, draining swamps, smashing rocks in the quarries, or building roads. They were watched over and driven on by guards on horseback armed with shotguns and whips and at night were locked into damp and dilapidated quarters, sometimes chained to their bunks. They were strictly segregated by sex and the dormitories never had the lights turned out. Yet paradoxically some specially trusted or privileged prisoners were allowed to have their lovers in overnight. In such conditions, the phrases 'Don't you ease me in' and 'All night long' had special significance.

Thomas' second version of the Alabama bound theme, *Don't Leave Me Here*, uses several of the same verses as *Don't Ease Me In*, but soon gets onto his favourite motif, the railroad.

> Don't leave, don't you leave,
> Oh, don't you leave me here,
> It's all night long, sweet papa, don't leave me.
>
> I'm going away, and it won't be long,
> Just ease your train, lovin' babe, I'm Alabama bound.[12]

It is only from the broad sweep of his records that we get much idea of Henry Thomas as a person; there is little beyond the image of an inveterate traveller, keeping himself to himself with a kind of gruff exterior and a fierce independence, always on the move. It is for others to make of him what they might, his patchwork songs tossing out a hint which might be him and then again, might not.

> Trouble in your time, I tired in your mind,
> Show me that woman you can trust.
> I done lying, lying down, my head to the wall,
> Show me that woman you can trust.
> Well the law's on your side, I'll never get a dime.

> I'll make it to my shanty if I can,
> If I can, if I can,
> I'll make it to my shanty if I can.
> Dog's on my track, man's on his horse,
> Make it to my shanty if I can.

> *Shanty Blues*[13]

Lead Belly

If the character of Ragtime Texas is still opaque and ambiguous through lack of detailed knowledge, the same may well be true of another blues singer of that early generation although much more is known about him. As the legendary Lead Belly, Huddie (pronounced 'Hue-dee') Ledbetter was perhaps the first major country blues artist to be acclaimed by the white world.

His enormous repertoire of folk songs, spirituals, prison songs, country reels, work songs, blues, ballads and even cowboy songs, was recorded for posterity by John A. and Alan Lomax working for the Library of Congress. He had spent many years on chain gangs in the ferocious penitentiaries of Texas and Louisiana – always for crimes of violence and assault – where he was discovered by the Lomaxes. He was recognised as the living repository of a dying folk culture: his songs were recorded and published; he appeared in concert halls and in folk clubs, and for many years was taken to be a 'typical' blues singer. To this day many of his songs, *Goodnight Irene*, *The Midnight Special*, *The Rock Island Line*, *Take This Hammer*, are sung wherever folk music is played.

But while to the liberal white world of the 1930's Lead Belly may have symbolised an oppressed people struggling to be free, to those blacks who knew his music he reminded them of times they wished to forget. By the time he had sung his way to freedom (twice he received official prison pardons having sung for the

Governor) and been launched on his career as a folksinger, his music was many years out of date, even evoking memories of the knotted handkerchief and the 'Yassuh Boss' of the slave plantation. The few records he made specifically for the black 'Race' market in the Thirties sank without trace.

Meanwhile the music of Lead Belly remains to be heard on dozens of records, and it still retains an extraordinary force and power. Whatever he is taken to 'symbolise', or 'represent', his music is that of a unique personality, and once heard it is impossible to mistake it for anyone else's.

Lead Belly was very much a man of his time, and it is not hard to see why people wishing to forget those times would prefer not to listen. Like Ragtime Texas, he grew up in the years the blues were emerging and was also primarily a songster. He was born on January 29, 1889 in Louisiana, but grew up just across the border in the State of Texas. The land of his childhood was a sparsely populated, almost frontier territory – Texas was only admitted to the Union in 1845 as a slave State and by the 1880's the population was still only about one and a half million of which only a quarter was black.

'We was living out in the country – which I was born dead in the country about 20 miles, and 30 and 40 miles from any kind of big town. Closest little place around us was 5 miles. We had to ride 5 miles to get mail and get it once a week. Read a newspaper once a week, and that was good . . . in that neighbourhood.'[1]

Communities were scattered and isolated – 'no white man in 20 miles' – and life was raw and the country still untamed. His sharecropper father, Wes Ledbetter, worked for a black owner until able to buy his own patch of land, 68½ acres of it at 2.50 dollars an acre. Wes and his half-Cherokee Indian wife Sally had to cut down the trees and burn the dense brush to clear the ground. Sometimes they would fight – 'My daddy used to knock Mama down if she disagreed with him'[2] – but in their own cut-off world, punctuated only by periodic trips to Shreveport with wagon loads of cotton, or visits from his uncles, there was a regularity in their lives and a stability that Huddie was probably never to find again.

All through his childhood and youth life meant cotton farming, which he plunged into with a ferocious energy, and country entertainments. He absorbed just about every kind of music: spirituals from his mother, jigs, schottisches, 'breakdowns', field hollers and shouts, work songs, children's game songs and lullabies. In this otherwise silent, almost sealed-off part of the world, work songs were a natural part of almost any activity. On his long walks to school he would sing to himself *Ho-Day, Who Ready*. When his uncle stayed the night, he would sleep in Huddie's bed, writhing and cursing and singing in his sleep to his oxen, and Huddie never forgot the song, with its cry 'Whoa God-Damn!', (an appropriate rhyme for the notorious 'Cunningham' of County Farm fame.)

> Whoa buck and gee by the lamb,
> Who made the back band gee Cunningham.
> Whoa Cunningham and Whoa Cunningham,
> Who made the back band whoa, Cunningham.[3]

While he absorbed the music of work, the hours of leisure were taken up with country dances, the 'sukey jumps'. He would take his 'windjammer' accordion or his guitar and ride over to play for the dancers.

> Jaw bone eat and jaw bone talk,
> Jaw bone eat you with a knife and fork . . .[4]

One of the first songs he heard was *Poor Howard*.

'Poor Howard was a poor boy; he went all around the plantations playing for the sukey jumps. He was the first man who started sukey-jump playing in the whole world. And when poor Howard was dead and gone, everybody sang this song:

> Poor Howard's dead and gone,
> Left me here to sing this song.
> Poor Howard's dead and gone,
> Left me here to sing this song.'[5]

Huddie's prowess as a prolific cotton picker – he could 'pick more cotton than any man in Caddo Lake County except my daddy' – and his reputation as the best entertainer in the area, began to be matched by a different kind of notoriety. He carried a gun given him by his father, 'only in self-defence',[6] and his massive physical self-confidence was liable to lead to fists flying and worse. Part lionised, part feared and part regarded as an unstable and dangerous influence in the community, by his late teens Huddie was already acquiring a reputation for drinking, womanizing and violence which was to dog him for the rest of his life. When he got a girl pregnant a second time and still had got no further than a common-law relationship with her, public outrage forced him out.

His first instinct was to head for Shreveport, where he'd been

when he was 'knee high to a duck', and get down to the notorious
Fannin Street. The street was a twelve-block conglomeration of
wood-frame buildings, brick houses and warehouses, and with
its countless dance halls, brothels and boarding houses, it was
the centre of round-the-clock entertainment for the town's black
population and for the farm workers in town for a good time with
'plenty gals and drinkin'. At heart it was a sleazy, violent and frequently murderous place, full of transient drunks and down-at-
the-heel prostitutes. Occasionally Huddie had been sent on
errands to Shreveport, once with 40 dollars – 'I was a big shot,
sure, when I had that 40 dollars' – and always his Dad said, 'Son,
don't go down on Fannin Street.' 'Nossir Papa,' he'd say, but
'that's just where I was going.'[7]

In later years he recorded a song in memory of his Shreveport
days at the turn of the century.

'When I was a boy, I put on long pants, and I'm going down on
Fannin Street, and I'm going in the barrelhouse . . .[8]

> My mama told me – my little sister too,
> Women on Fannin Street, son, they gonna be the death of you.
> Oooh, ooh, ooh.
> *(Spoken)* I didn't care.'[9]

It was at this point that Huddie really added blues to his
songster's repertoire. What he had been playing was fine for the
country suppers and sukey jumps around Caddo Lake, but in
Shreveport the rootless and violent customers in the drinking
palaces demanded the heavier, more aggressive music.

'When you played fast music that was ragtime – and when we
got barrelhouse, we got blues. Out in Alabama they need to sing
"Rag is in the bag, we got the blues – we're in the barrelhouse
now . . ." Then they come out on it with their low-down
dances.'[10]

In the 1930's and 40's Lead Belly's repertoire was probably
wider than that of any other black musician on record. He could
remember songs and tunes from every phase of his life. His
blues-playing sometimes gets forgotten in the breadth of his
scope, but he was capable of tremendous power with his
resonant twelve-string guitar and hollering voice. He gave his
own personal stamp to everything he sang. His guitar playing for
the blues laid emphasis on bass-heavy strums, a technique un-
copied elsewhere but which he himself adapted from watching
the barrelhouse piano-players on Fannin Street.

'I'd sit by the bass side with my guitar. That's where I got that bass – on Fannin Street. And that's what I wanted to play on guitar, that piano bass. I always liked to play piano tunes. I got it out of the barrelhouses on Fannin Street . . .'[11] 'Boogie-woogie was called barrelhouse in those days. One of the best players was called Chee-Dee. He would go from one gin-mill to the next . . . He was coal black and one of the old-line players, and he boogied the blues. At that time anybody could walk into a barrelhouse and just sit down and start playing the piano. I learned to play some piano myself by picking it out.'[12]

From Shreveport, Lead Belly started branching out to parts of Louisiana and Texas – Marshall, Longview, Tyler, Fort Worth and especially Dallas – sometimes working as a farmer or on the levees, but still playing his guitar or accordion, the piano and even the harmonica. Between about 1910 and 1916 he half settled down to married life as a sharecropper, but his footloose party-loving ways got the better of him and he kept heading back to his musical haunts. Dallas was the most exciting of all, with its Red Light area down Elm Street ('Deep Ellum') and 'the central track', as Central Avenue was called because there was a railroad down the middle. With barrelhouses, gin mills, dance halls and night clubs, the pickings were good.

It was in Dallas at some point around 1912 that Huddie met up with arguably one of the greatest male blues singers of all time, Blind Lemon Jefferson, who influenced his music profoundly. He claimed that they'd 'run together' for years around Dallas. 'He was a blind man and I used to lead him around. When him an' I go in Depot we's sit down and talk to one-another.' They frequently played together at the 'Big Four', an especially popular club near the terminal. 'De womens would come runnin'! Lawd have mercy! They'd hug and kiss us so we could hardly play.'[13]

Blind Lemon would sometimes play the guitar with a knife or bottleneck, and Lead Belly probably picked up that same technique from him. Later he was to record a surprisingly delicate and haunting version of the traditional blues *See See Rider*. With its gently stinging guitar slides, it is one of his most lyrical recordings.

> See See Rider,
> See what you have done.
> Made me love you,
> Now you done gone.[14]

Lead Belly's voice, with its massive delivery, could sometimes be strident in its power, but from Blind Lemon he seems to have learned delicacy and control as displayed in one of his finest and more melodic blues, *Black Girl*, a song often known as *In the Pines* and popular in both black and white traditions.

> Black girl, black girl,
> Don' lie to me,
> Tell me where did you sleep last night?
>
> In the pines, in the pines,
> Where the sun never shines,
> I was shiver' the whole night through.[15]

Blind Lemon went on to become just about the most successful and commercially popular of all the male blues singers of the 1920's. It was Lead Belly's tragedy that a series of violent incidents were to see him serving seemingly endless years in Texas and Louisiana penitentiaries, from about 1917 to 1925 and from 1930 to 1934.

In these crucial years he was able to add his magnificent chain gang songs and prison hollers to his song bag, and following his discovery by John Lomax his career as a folk singer began.

The barrelhouse circuit and the 'Piney Woods'

'He was ragged as a pet pig, wore a big smile on his face, and was a nice-looking brown skin fellow until you got to his lips – he had nice, fat, greasy lips.'

This was how Jelly Roll Morton described a barrelhouse pianist called Game Kid. In 1939 Jelly Roll recorded his memories of the early days of blues and jazz for the Library of Congress, illustrating his anecdotes with snatches of song, many of them wistfully sung blues, performed in his light, clear, but melancholy voice.

'Back in 1901 and 1902, we had a lot of great blues players that didn't know nothing but the blues.

> I could sit right down here and think a thousand miles away,
> Yes, I could sit right here and think a thousand miles away,
> I got the blues so bad I cannot remember the day . . .'[1]

The New Orleans trumpeter Bunk Johnson remembered Jelly Roll as one of the best in 1902: 'Jelly would sit there and play that barrel-house music all night – blues and such as that'.[2] He would play the honky-tonks where men from the levee went, 'some of whom didn't bathe more than once in six months and, I'll go so far as to say, were even lousy'.[3] And away in the dark there would always be an old broken-down piano and somebody playing the blues.

I'm a levee man,
I'm a levee man,
I'm a levee man,
I'm a levee man.

Captain, captain,
Let me make this trip.
I need some money,
To fill my grip.
Yes I need the money . . .[4]

Jelly Roll wasn't just playing in New Orleans. In the early 1900's and even later he worked the sporting houses, honky-tonks and barrelhouses in Mississippi, along the Gulf Coast to Alabama ('I'm Alabama bound . . .'), through Louisiana to Texas, or up river to Memphis, Tennessee. In these years of travel he encountered countless blues pianists, most of them largely forgotten and unrecorded, like Skinny Head Pete, Florida Sam, or Brocky Johnny – these men more or less made their living out of music, or at least, 'they didn't work, because they were kept up by women'.[5]

It was the world of the so-called barrelhouse circuit, where quasi-professional musicians could pick up the themes that ordinary working people were creating and add them to their repertoire of ragtime music and popular songs. For many of these pianists the blues was their main style; for others it would be just an occasional piece. Like the guitar songsters of the time, the pianists were often all-round, eclectic musicians.

'They played quitely anything. The sort of music I heard around there was the same sort of music I'm playing now,' commented Little Brother Montgomery who was born in Kentwood, Louisiana, in 1906, and who knew Jelly Roll in his childhood. 'Oh I played lots of numbers that were popular at that time, like *Mickey*, *Twelfth Street Rag*, *You Must Not Get So Musty 'Cause Your Water's On* – this is the tune we now call *Tin Roo Blues*, *Get Over Sal* – they call this *Walkin' The Dog*, *Tishomingo Blues* and *A Long Way to Tipperary*. So you see I can do more than play the blues . . .'[6]

Little Brother's father owned a honky-tonk, and dozens of musicians like Jelly Roll passed through, inspiring Brother to start playing by the age of five. He too has an almost inexhaustible list of long forgotten piano-players.

'I was playing in honky-tonks, barrelhouses; barrelhouses and honky-tonks the same thing. That's where people gamble, shoot dice, back there. They played Marnie, Cotch, you know, Poker and, you know, put the dice through the horn, they played every-thing. They work all the week, Saturday night they take a bath and they go to the juke, call it the juke, the honky-tonk, barrel-house, then they go down there and gamble until Sunday morn-ing. Well anyway they had somebody playing in the front, some-body be playing the piano, me or somebody else. I ran away from home when I was II years old. First job I had was 8 dollars a week room and board. My father had a juke, he had a honky-tonk and I heard the guys playing there, Jelly, I heard Jelly Roll Morton play for my father, Rip Tops, Papa Lord God, Son Framion and Loomis Gibson, Cooney Vaughn, different ones you know, they were grown, grown-ups, but they played. Charlie Mahana, No-leg Kenny, guy didn't have no legs, a piano player. We had a lot of great piano players back there.

'I left home when I was eleven and I went all around those places and played, and then I didn't get back home 'til I was fifteen, I stayed away four years the first time. Then I'd been going ever since, you know. I was riding, I wasn't paying my way, riding freight train, they call it hitch-kiking now, you know.

Ride freight, get in one of them cars where they keep the coal in a car-box, hobo, you know. Hobo on a V S and P T P to Santa Fe, the Illinois Central, Kansas City Southern, I get on, get in one of them coal cars and go to sleep you know. Wake up in another town.'[7]

Just as Lead Belly learned from men like Chee-Dee in Fannin Street, so the tradition was passed on. Unlike most of those honky-tonk pianists, Little Brother himself went on to record a number of magnificent piano solos and blues, pieces like *Shreve-port Farewell*, or *Crescent City Blues*. In a high, slightly nasal voice he sang blues of great poignancy accompanied by piano-playing of disciplined dignity and mellow seriousness.

> The first time I met the blues, mama, they came walking through
> the wood.
> The first time I met the blues, baby, they came walking through
> the wood.
> They stopped at my house first, mamma, and done me all the
> harm they could.
>
> Now the blues got at me, Lord, and run me from tree to tree.
> Now the blues got at me, and run me from tree to tree.
> You should have heard me begging, 'Mister Blues, don't murder
> me!'
>
> *The First Time I Met You (1936)*[8]

It was almost literally true that the first time Little Brother met the blues they were walking through the woods. His birthplace of Kentwood, Louisiana, was right in the heart of the forest belt of the South. This area, part of it called the Piney Woods, covered vast tracts of Mississippi, Louisiana, Alabama, Arkansas and Texas, and was a major contributor to America's timber industry. Kentwood was just one of many company towns in the South which by 1909 was producing nearly half of the nation's timber and large quantities of turpentine. Throughout the Piney Woods, lumber camps, logging, saw-mill and turpentine camps were set up around the little towns, usually connected by railroads along which hobos, wandering musicians and workers would ride.

The memories of some of the earlier jazz and blues musicians suggest that blues and boogie-woogie piano styles were developed in these camps. Bunk Johnson and Lead Belly heard boogie in Western Louisiana in the early 1900's. Richard M. Jones first heard it in 1906 in a railroad camp played by a man called 'Stavin Chain' (the name itself is that of a folk hero who crops up in a number of obscene folk songs and blues). Men like Stavin Chain would have been playing in the 'barrelhouse jukes' installed in the camps by the companies and where drinks could be bought. It was a tough and brutal world, prone to sudden outbreaks of violence, where the work was dangerous and unhealthy and accidents were frequent. The camps were often isolated deep in the woods as the trees got hacked back further and further, and the enforcement of law was rough and ready. The housing provided by the companies was primitive, fresh water and cooking facilities minimal.

'Oh they was rough' says Little Brother, thinking back to his logging camp barrelhouse days. 'They had some rough places. See those guys wearing them big gumboots up to here, you know, most of them carried them big pistols too, German Lugers. They kill somebody, you know, and then they stand on them, and studied gambling: "Put my money down . . ." And next morning the quarter boss would come – they'd do it on a Saturday night, the quarter boss he come, then they'd have a shooting, shoot it out with him too . . . Oh it was rough, but they always liked musicians, and if you could play they would always take up for you and go with you.'[9]

Although pianists were the chief entertainers on the circuit, some were guitar-players. One of these was Big Joe Williams, who was born in Crawford, Mississippi, in 1903. By the age of ten or twelve Joe had already started hoboing and rambling around the country to places like Mobile, Alabama, Biloxi, Mississippi, and to Pensacola, Florida. This established the pattern of his life which he kept up virtually until his death in 1982, settling somewhere for a while, and them moving on restlessly.

He started playing for country suppers and picnics: 'There be hundreds of peoples like through all those pastures you see peoples hollering "Poor Joe". I was "Poor Joe" then, and from that to Good Road camps, where they building rock roads. So every payday I'd be at the Good Road camps, you know, where they rollin' up them heavy dices and having a good time and drinking what they call "cat-whiskey" you know, some call it "corn" but it's "cat-whiskey" . . . and I was right on it like light. I'd probably be there this weekend, from there to the logging camp, a saw-mill, anywhere where they having a big time at, I was there.

'What'd all be happening there? Well they'd have fights 'n cuts 'n sometimes one of them'd kill somebody and never stop gambling – just sit on him and keep a-gambling, and back in them days they didn't pay no attention, 'n all like that, all in life. Plenty of fun back in those days, lots of fun.

'Piano and guitar, me and Little Brother Montgomery used to play right down here at a place called Electric Mill . . . They had a big camp there, piano and guitar, and, ah, the girls dance. I got sit on top of the piano and play my guitar and sometimes the women dance on top of the piano, all had a wonderful time. They shoot craps, dices, drink whiskey, dance, every modern devilment you can do the barrelhouse is where it's at . . .

'I travelled by highways and freight trains and buggies, every once in a while grab a horse and ride with him too! . . .

'I never, only way I worked might be at the end of a period to be in a job so I can be there at payday to play music. (*Laughs*) All through the Delta, I did the same thing. See, you go in, a good musician, and the boss man gets acquainted with you, and all the peoples, the hands like what you doin' and go tell the boss, 'He really good, we need him out here to play for our barrelhouse." He say, "Well, yeah, you just stay here and play," you know, like that, and he knew I wasn't goin' to do no work much and if he made me work I'd be going the next day!'[10]

Big Joe recorded blues for many companies. He worked in small bands and on minstrel shows even, and was commercially pretty successful in the late 1930's and early 40's with his very down-home music. He took to using an idiosyncratic guitar, a self adapted nine-stringer, which gave his playing a very full bass sound, with plenty of 'bottom'. His dextrous treble work and percussive style generated a beautifully controlled swing, while the generally tough sound of his guitar and the rough and hoarse quality of his voice gave his blues an almost primitive intensity. His songs range from the stinging Depression number *Providence Help The Poor People* to simple ditties of his personal life. He told Pete Welding in 1964:

'There was a place down there in Mecca, Mississippi. I used to have a woman down there called Pearl Binyon. I got tangled up with her, and another guy was giving me trouble with her, and so I just made that:

> Gonna pack my suitcase and move back to the Piney Woods,
> Cause I got a woman down there, boys, don't mean Poor Joe no good.

So that's how that came about.'[11]

In the world of the Piney Woods instability was generic to the whole way of life. The timber lands were rapidly being stripped by lumber companies. Trees were coming down far faster than any attempt at replanting so that by 1933 over 80 million acres of timberland had been laid waste. The hills and gullies were left scarred, with great ugly gaps where trees had been ripped out or felled, leaving the soil to be eroded by wind and rain. As soon as a timber or railroad company had reduced one bit of woodland to waste, the temporary rails were shifted, the camps moved and the saw-mills closed, leaving the employees with no work.

This was a situation well understood by blues singers like Elzadie Robinson who came from Shreveport, Louisiana, and who worked as an entertainer around Houston, Texas, before emigrating to the North. She regularly sang with a piano-player called Will Ezell who came from the barrelhouse circuit, and together they cut records in the 20's like *Barrelhouse Man* and *Sawmill Blues*. His style was a delicate ragtime-influenced blues which effectively complemented Elzadie's emotional singing of his *Arkansas Mill Blues*. Despite the raucous pleasures of Saturday nights, the realities of the lumber camps remained grim for most workers.

> I was lyin' in my bed this mornin',
>   an' heard the mill whistle blow like it was cryin'.
> I was lyin' in my bed this mornin',
>   an' heard the mill whistle blow like it was cryin'.
> Arkansas Mill has cut all that timber,
>   ain't no more work for that man of mine.

Listen, listen, how mournful that whistle did blow,
Listen, listen, how mournful that whistle did blow,
It blowed its last chirp, it ain't never gonna blow no more.[12]

Migration

'I got the blues so very bad until I want to get away from the old plantation and go for the city life. But I must realise that I am a farmer, so if I do go to Dallas, Texas, a great big town, I have to learn how to do something besides farming, because there is no farming there. So I have to be a real good person in order for people to accept me, and mostly a foot-stool for the public, in order for me to obtain what I am out after.'[1]

Curtis Jones happens to have been a blues pianist, but he was just one of countless blacks who took part in the restless move from country life to the cities. At first the movement might be small and fragmentary, little more than aimless hops from plantation to plantation and then sometimes drifting into towns and cities only to ease back into the countryside. But by 1920 a fundamental and irreversible shift had begun to take place within the black population.

In the 1890's as many as 80 per cent of black Americans lived in the rural South, but by 1920 that figure had dropped to 65 per cent and by 1950 there remained only 20 per cent. The shift was two-fold. At first the cities of the South started drawing in blacks from the surrounding countryside but more significantly hundreds of thousands of people started heading for the Northern States and the industrial cities. The mass movement of poorly educated, unskilled blacks, used to segregation and the Jim Crow laws of the South, meant that the issue of race was no longer a purely Southern question. The South had always claimed to know how to handle 'their' blacks, and the reaction of the white South to the growth of black enclaves within the Southern cities presaged the kind of problems that were to face blacks when they reached the North. One of the fastest growing cities in the South was Atlanta, Georgia, where by 1910 over a third of the population was black. In 1906, after months of racist agitation had created an atmosphere of tension, there occurred a vicious race riot lasting several days. An outraged and hysterical white mob, inflamed by loose and unsubstantiated press talk of assaults on white women, rampaged the streets, beating up blacks and destroying property. The city virtually ground to a halt in the frenzy during which many blacks were killed. In other Southern cities too blacks faced white resistance. In 1912 Louisville, Kentucky, became the first of several cities to enact legislation for the racial segregation of housing. The law designated certain areas as white only or black only, setting a legal sanction for the practical creation of city ghettoes. Other cities, including Richmond, Virginia and Atlanta followed the lead.

For blacks in the South urbanization meant little escape from segregation and intimidation, so that for many the North began to assume an almost religious and mythical significance as the land of freedom. The language used to refer to the North took on the same biblical flavour as it had during the campaign to abolish slavery – The Flight Out of Egypt, The Promised Land, Canaan. One group of Mississippians heading for Chicago even held a ceremony when they crossed the Ohio River, stopping their watches, kneeling down in prayer and singing the gospel hymn *I Done Come Out of the Land of Egypt With The Good News.*

The image they held of the North induced visions of unlimited wages and unbridled liberty, initially based on the stories passed on by porters and waiters working on the Pullman trains, or from the letters sent by friends and relatives already in the North.

'I am well and thankful to say I am doing well. I work in Swift's Packing Co. in the sausage department . . . We get $1.50 a day . . . Tell your husband work is plentiful here and he won't have to loaf if he want to work.'[2]

In 1919 men could easily earn up to 25 dollars a week in Northern cities and women from 12 to 18 dollars. In either case this was far above the kind of money farm workers got in the South, where they might make as little as 75 cents a day. The acute and observable contrast in economic conditions between North and South was a major factor in drawing blacks from the farms and workplaces where life was cheap and conditions degrading. As a child in Texas before the First World War, Curtis Jones had lived with his sharecropper parents.

'Sometimes you have a good year and sometimes a very bad year. But in my father's condition all of his years seemed to be very bad. The kind of shelter was a tumble-down log cabin where you had to stuff the walls with rags in the winter season to keep from freezing to death.'[3]

At first prejudice and discrimination in the North were strong enough for there to be no real escape from the South. There simply were no jobs available even though industry was expanding. America had become the land of dreams and hopes for the peasantry and poor of Europe, in exactly the same way as the

North was to become the Promised Land of the Southern share-cropper, and as long as the factories of Northern industry were manned by Europeans, there was little chance for the blacks. In the peak year, 1914, over 1,200,000 Europeans crossed the Atlantic and poured into the cities with their meagre bundles of possessions.

But 1914 was a turning point, for Europe, for America, and ultimately for the blacks. The outbreak of the First World War virtually halted immigration from Europe – down to 326,000 in 1915 and by 1918 to a mere 110,000. With the stimulus of war heavy industry boomed, and suddenly there was an acute shortage of labour in the North.

Until this point the migration of blacks had been a trickle, grabbing the few jobs available in domestic employment and the service trades. Opportunities had been mainly for women, as servants and cooks in white homes, and most enclaves of blacks in the cities were dominated by women. In 1900 virtually every city with a population of more than 20,000 blacks had a huge surplus of women over men, both in the North and the South. For every 100 men in Washington or in Baltimore there were 126 women; in New York, for every 100 it was 124; in Atlanta 143; in Memphis 103. Of the major cities only Chicago had a majority of men, with only 88 women to every 100. But with the sudden increase in demand for workers in the North, black men found themselves with the advantage. They changed from loitering around 'the ragged edge of industry' to gaining a foothold on the centre. In the period 1916–1919 the heaviest migration was to the key Northern industrial States of Pennsylvania, Illinois, Ohio, New York and Michigan.

With war-time labour shortages, migration became more purposeful and direct, without the gradual phasing from rural area to town to city in the South and then on to the urban North. People from the most heavily rural areas of the South, from Mississippi, Alabama, Georgia and Louisiana, now moved straight to the Northern cities and to jobs in steel mills, foundries, packing houses and stockyards. There was a pattern of movement along geographical lines: from the Eastern part of the South, the Carolinas and Georgia, they went to New York and Philadelphia; from the central Deep South of Alabama, Mississippi and Louisiana they followed the Illinois Central and the Gulf, Mobile and Ohio railroads to Chicago, Detroit and Cleveland. During the decade 1910–1920, almost all cities with over 25,000 blacks saw an increase in the black population of more than 50 per cent. The black population of Detroit increased a fantastic 611 per cent, Cleveland by 308 per cent, Chicago 148 per cent and Philadelphia and Indianapolis 59 per cent.

This period of migration was the first real opportunity for escape from the South. Before this time life for the sharecropper had presented no alternatives. Oppression was normality and the lack of education or knowledge of other possibilities narrowed any view of how life might be different. The growing awareness of the existence of a way out began to have a profound effect on thinking in the South. A preacher in Mississippi told an inquirer from the US Department of Labor studying the pattern of black migration in 1916–17:

'My father was born and brought up as a slave. He never knew anything else until after I was born. He was taught his place and was content to keep it. But when he brought me up he let some of the old customs slip by. But I know there are certain things that I must do and I do them, and it doesn't worry me; yet in bringing up my own son, I let some more of the old customs slip by . . . He says, "When a young white talks rough to me, I can't talk rough to him. You can stand that; I can't. I have some education, and inside I has the feelings of a white man. I'm going." '[4]

A factor in the growth of this new consciousness was the propaganda of more militant blacks in the North, particularly represented by the weekly newspaper the *Chicago Defender*, copies of which reached the South, sometimes with difficulty in the face of severe white disapproval. W. C. Handy was one who would smuggle copies and distribute them among the black folk. In 1916 the *Defender* thundered:

'Every black man for the sake of his wife and daughter should leave even at a financial sacrifice every spot in the South where his worth is not appreciated enough to give him the standing of a man and a citizen in the community.'[5]

In 1917 the paper instigated a 'Great Northern Drive', backed with articles, editorials, cartoons and even poems.

> Some are coming on the passenger,
> Some are coming on the freight,
> Others will be found walking,
> For none have time to wait.[6]

The response of the white South to agitation of this kind could be cruel. The *Atlanta Constitution* reported in October 1919:

'SUMTER NEGRO FOUND DEAD AFTER SPREADING PROPAGANDA'. The body was found with a rope round his neck after he had been 'circulating incendiary propaganda among negroes'.[7]

Whites were also profoundly disturbed by the activities of the labour agents from Northern business interests who touted for workers in the South. Many cities enforced prohibitively expensive licensing laws on these agents who offered free transport and high wages to the blacks they were able to contact. The South resented the loss of 'their' blacks. The Southern economy, under-capitalised, lacking in skilled labour and business experience, with energy and resources tied up in the stultifying and outmoded sharecropping system with its high-risk, low-turnover structure, was in no position to hold on to its cheap black labour. While some industry developed in the South – the iron industry in Alabama, tobacco in North Carolina, textile factories in Georgia, Alabama and the Carolinas – development was far behind that of the industrial North. Northern capital dominated the American economy, controlling the South to its own advantage and placing it in an almost colonial position. The South produced the raw materials or the half-finished goods while the North processed them, marketed them and pocketed the profits. Underdeveloped as an industrial, manufacturing economy, the South depended upon the vagaries of agriculture where a season's low cotton prices could depress the whole community. The ravages of the boll weavil and the terrible floods of 1915 and 1916 further weakened the South's economy. Alabama was especially hard hit, and it has been estimated that one in ten blacks left the State.

However high their hopes, and with whatever fear and trepidation they moved from the South with their few possessions and battered luggage, little in their experience of life can have prepared the blacks for the changes they would have to face in the cities. The journey would take them through country quite unlike the cotton fields or rice fields of their home territory. It could be a time of mounting anxiety, but also of excitement, with an eye constantly on every white person, always with that question in the mind, 'How should I react?' Would the Northern white man be in reality like the dreams had imagined him, or would he yell 'Get back Nigger!' just like in the South? Used always to judging every action by the presumed wishes of the white, it was strange having to behave according to one's own prerogatives. It was strange too to find white eyes no longer watching every move, ready to cast a command, or laugh with condescension and patronisation. Here in the North the black was all but invisible, no longer part of a small community, which, though fluctuating and unstable, had a regularity in the very narrowness of choice it offered. Now even a black face was a stranger to the migrant as, in old-fashioned and probably ill-fitting clothes, he or she stepped off the train in Chicago or Detroit. In the small towns and plantations of Mississippi no precise address would have been needed to find a friend or relation; but in the teeming and vast cities, with their endless blocks of tenements and two-storey frame houses, all looking bewilderingly alike in their decay and dilapidation, how could one find an uncle or sister? At the stations there were guides who for a fee would trace a relative or friend, but many were men of few scruples, hustlers in cities where hustling had become a way of life.

At first the housing that blacks moved into, in areas already recognisable as black enclaves, were not necessarily over-crowded. But as more and more migrants poured into cities like Chicago – more than 50,000 between 1916 and 1919 – the geo-graphical zone they inhabited hardly expanded. The density of population merely intensified, with people taking in more and more lodgers and several families sharing cooking facilities in 'kitchen-ettes'. Where overcrowding was at its worst, separate families would take turns to sleep in what they called 'hot bed' apartments.

Already in Chicago, one of the most important centres of blues activity from the 1920's on, there had existed 'de facto' segregation, where blacks were unable to have free access to housing where they wanted to live, and employment policies and practices restricted them in the jobs they could get. In the ghettoes a tradition had developed of self-help activities, welfare institutions, burial societies, churches and political organisations run by blacks and for blacks. Within this world, fired by news-papers like the *Defender*, a racial consciousness grew, with leadership and rhetoric generating the belief that the black com-munity's isolation was created by their own choice; that like the Europeans 'sticking together', their world was controlled by themselves.

Indeed, compared with the South where the planters controlled the blacks' housing, their employment, their political life and their whole welfare, crushing independence at every turn, a city like Chicago provided a semblance of dignity and self-determination. A black could choose where to live – as long as it was in the ghetto; where to work – as long as it was 'nigger's work'; what to read, where to spend leisure time, and enjoy all kinds of new freedoms. Black leaders, in politics, business and in journalism became heroes to the Race, simply because such figures could hardly exist in the South.

But the sense of solidarity within the community was fragile; the successive waves of migrants began to appear to those already settled as too loud, too uncouth, too irresponsible, altogether too embarrassing. For the settled and more prosperous élite with their concern for dignity and decorum, in churches with quiet, unemotional services like the white world they half sought to emulate, the emotionalism and ecstasy to be found in growing numbers of store-front sanctified churches was something to be viewed with disquiet. And if there were divisions in class and status within the black community, there were weaknesses too in its economic foundations. Black businesses tended to be small, underfinanced and unstable, with pitifully small access to white-controlled banking facilities. Municipal services were inferior to those of white Chicago, and job opportunities still restricted. There had indeed been a shift from employment in domestic service to factory work but the jobs available were still the least skilled, the ones with least possibilities of promotion, and the ones most liable to lay-offs. So the lives of black people in the Northern cities were still dominated by prejudice, poverty and ignorance, but in new ways. Rootlessness and insecurity were of a different kind from those in the old country communities. The ghetto could be cruel and violent, impersonal and competitive, giving a new dimension to the problem of finding a viable identity in a world still dominated by whites.

That the Northern whites could be as brutal and vindictive as the Southern, though usually at an impersonal distance, was brought home to blacks by the race riots which sporadically savaged the black community. There were 25 major white-initiated race riots within seven months in 1919, ranging from Texas to Washington and from Tennessee to Nebraska. But probably the worst riot was in Chicago: 15 whites and 23 blacks were killed, 600 blacks were wounded and a thousand families burned out. Over the following four years, with scant attempts by the Chicago police to control the problem, more than 50 black homes were dynamited.

'I came looking for deliverance,' says the musician Thomas A. Dorsey ('Georgia Tom'), who arrived in Chicago from Atlanta in 1916, 'and to get deliverance you just have to wait on the movements of providence.'[8]

Part Three

Crazy blues

'There's fourteen million Negroes in our great country and they will buy records if recorded by one of their own, because we are the only folks that can sing and interpret hot jazz songs just off the griddle correctly.'[1]

Perry Bradford, a hustling composer, band leader, pianist and singer, with a city-slick line in slang, pestered and badgered executives from the white phonograph recording industry, determined to get a black singer on disc with one of his songs. The man he finally persuaded was Fred Hagar of Okeh Records, a man who had apparently received threatening letters from Northern and Southern pressure groups warning him that to record coloured girls would lead to a boycott of Okeh phonograph machines and records.

'May God bless Mr Hagar, for despite the many threats, it took a man with plenty of nerve and guts to buck those powerful groups and make the historical decision which echoed aroun' the world. He prised open that old "prejudiced door" for the first colored girl, Mamie Smith, so she could squeeze into the large horn – and shout with her strong contralto voice:

> That thing called love – money cannot buy,
> That thing called love – will make you weep and cry.
> Sometimes you're sad – romantic and glad,
> The most wonderful thrill – you ever had . . .'[1]

As Perry recalled in his autobiography *Born with the Blues*, it was a happy moment, 'for I'd schemed and used up all of my bag of tricks to get that date; had greased my neck with goose grease every morning, so it would become easy to bow and scrape to some recording managers. But none of them would listen to my tale o' woe, even though I displayed my teeth to them with a perpetual-lasting watermelon grin . . .'[1]

February 14, 1920, was the date of this historic recording

session, when Mamie Smith cut *That Thing Called Love* and *You Can't Keep A Good Man Down*. This was the first occasion that a blues singer was recorded. Her first session was made with white musicians, and the songs chosen were much like any ordinary popular song of the day.

That Thing Called Love was commercially a success, the boycott of Okeh products never happened, and in a few months Mamie Smith was called back to make a further record, this time with black musicians. On August 10, 1920, the first blues proper was recorded by Mamie Smith and her Jazz Hounds, which included fine jazz musicians like Johnny Dunn on cornet and almost certainly Willie 'The Lion' Smith on piano. This too was another Perry Bradford composition, the famous *Crazy Blues*.

> I can't sleep at night,
> I can't eat a bite,
> 'Cause the man I love,
> He didn't treat me right.
>
> Now, I got the crazy blues,
> Since my baby went away.
> I ain't got no time to lose,
> I must find him today.[2]

'Why don't you all go and do something about the great Mamie Smith?' challenged the Texan pianist Victoria Spivey, recalling those early days. 'See, she was the first of all of us. Her and her Jazz Hounds. She was a beautiful woman too, and she could sing! Well I mean we all come along behind her. Mamie's the one that paved the way over there. Then we came behind her.'[3]

Crazy Blues was an astonishing hit, selling 75,000 copies in the first month, at a dollar a time. The fact that the singer was black gave the record a symbolic significance. The sales excitement it generated proved the existence of a large and unexploited market, and the production and sale of blues records started to accelerate rapidly. 'Can I remember?' said Victoria Spivey about the impact *Crazy Blues* made when she was little more than a child. 'By heaven I was singing it before I left Texas, in a way of speaking: (*Sings*) "And I got the crazy blues"'[4]

The record was a major breakthrough, a turning point in blues history. It was the moment the music ceased to be transmitted exclusively through local folk culture, with all the transcience of 'live' performances. From the time of Mamie Smith's first recordings it became possible for anyone in any part of the country to hear the same blues and hear it repeated in exactly the same way and as many times as the listener wanted, until the grooves of the disc were worn smooth. The many kinds of blues that had emerged would now gradually become fixed into various, more regular patterns, and the new forms themselves would in turn continue to interact with each other to produce still more variety.

To begin with, blues recordings were dominated by women singers who had come up through cabaret and vaudeville, and for many of them singing blues meant little more than adopting the material that was becoming fashionable. An early advert for a Mamie Smith record referred to her as a 'singer of "Blues" – the music of so new a flavor'.[5] In fact she had the clear voice and lightness of a popular singer, with little of the tension and slurred moaning of a country blues singer. Many of the early singers were characterised by this clear enunciation and diction, the style of performers used to projecting popular material with light jazzy dance bands. One of the earliest was the light-skinned Lucille Hegamin, who had a rich voice and a neat, rather jaunty, style of singing. One of her biggest hits was *Arkansas Blues* which was recorded by one company and eventually issued on eleven different labels.

> Ain't got no time to lose,
> I'm tired and lonely, I'm tired of roaming.
> I long to see my mammy in my home in . . .
> I got the Arkansas blues![6]

Composed by Anton Lada and Spencer Williams, *Arkansas Blues* had a catchy tune, and the jazzy accompaniment of the Blue Flame Syncopaters gave it a good bounce. Like many of the early women singers, with their popular song orientation and lightness of touch, Lucille Hegamin and Mamie Smith seem to reflect a feeling of joy and hope in keeping with the expectations of the black migrants newly arrived in the cities. Lucille Hegamin herself was described in an early record catalogue as 'the South's favorite – cyclonic exponent of dark-town melodies'.[7] Indeed she had come from the South – she was born in Macon in 1897 – and by 1914 was in Chicago. Billed as Georgia Peach, she sang 'nearly all the popular ballads and ragtime tunes of the day', at cabarets and night spots. She told Derrick Stewart-Baxter:

'I was a cabaret artist in those days, and never had to play theatres, and I sang everything from blues to popular songs, in a jazz style. I think I can say without bragging that I made the *St Louis Blues* popular in Chicago; this was one of my feature numbers.'[8]

Here was the ideal background for the breezy hopefulness of people coming to the big city with confident tunes about missing mammy at home in Arkansas. Despite the poverty and over-crowding of the swelling ghetto, Chicago could spell hope and stimulation.

Lil Hardin, the jazz pianist who, according to singer Alberta Hunter, 'played a mighty blues',[9] arrived in Chicago with her family from Memphis in 1918.

'I made it my business to go out for a daily stroll and look this "heaven" over. Chicago meant just that to me – its beautiful brick and stone buildings, excitement, people moving swiftly, and things happening.'[10]

Alberta Hunter was herself an immigrant to Chicago. In 1908 she ran away from home at the age of eleven and got a job as a cook, sending her mother two out of her six dollars a week plus board. As she got a bit older, she started hearing stories about girls making as much as ten dollars a week in night clubs. She went looking for such a job and got one in Dago Frank's 'where the sportin' girls hung out'.[11] Alberta made a career for herself in night clubs and cabarets and was another of the first to sing blues on record.

The club and cabarets where singers like Lucille Hegamin and Alberta Hunter started singing were part of the explosion of black entertainment that happened in Chicago in the War years and after; they were part of the glamour and excitement which helped draw people like a magnet. By the 1920's Chicago was in the mainstream of the jazz age, with some of the greatest names playing and recording there – names like King Oliver, Louis Armstrong, Johnny Dodds, Jelly Roll Morton. The Chicago of the 20's has now become part of America's mythology, with Prohibition, the rise of gangsters like Al Capone, speakeasies, gangland killings, bootlegging, the air of lawlessness, fast cars and tommyguns, a jazz band in every club, everything bright lights and speed. Deplored but eagerly explored, it has been written about and portrayed in dozens of Hollywood movies. For some Chicago was to become the essence of America, the melt-ing pot of nationalities and races, a city of opportunities for people of energy, or nerves, a city for the big gesture and extravagance and the big personality like the notoriously and outrageously corrupt Republican Mayor Big Bill Thompson, who worked hand in glove with the liquor racketeers and the rest.

Something of the flavour of those flamboyant times is conveyed by Little Brother Montgomery's memories of his own circle of musicians in Chicago, especially his father's old friend Jelly Roll Morton.

'Jelly Roll Morton was the biggest, you may say propaganda dough-papa in the world. He was the greatest somebody. He used to walk up to us on 31st, at Dickerson Music Store, on 31st and State, and there would be a lot of us, me and Will Ezell and Charlie Spand, you know, different ones, and sometimes Fats (Waller) would be in there, Clarence Jones would be in. They had a piano in there, and we was drinking that two bit moonshine, two bits a half a pint, you get a whole half pint for a quarter. We'd been in there and old Jelly Roll would throw somebody ten or 20 dollars, you know, "go get them poor devils some more moonshine", and then somebody would go round there and get it. "I'm all you piano-players have got," he said, he was all our God. He had a thousand dollar bill in his pocket all the time, you know, and a ·38 nickel-plated pearl handled 'Special', and he had diamonds all up his shirt, his teeth, everywhere else, on his things. He said he was all our God. "I'm all you musicians have got." He couldn't be playing the piano but, he'd have all the money, we wouldn't have none, so we let him *be* our God, you know, (*Laughs*) But he kept a pocket full of money all the time, he had them two 400 million dollar automobiles, he parked right behind the others, and then people would walk up and say "Jelly Roll must be in there".'[12]

What is less often remembered of the city is the appalling squalor and poverty of many people's lives, the sheer marginality and instability of their existence. A survey was prepared for the Chicago Council of Social Agencies, *The Hobo: The Sociology of the Homeless Man* by Nels Anderson, based on conditions in 1921 and 1922. It revealed that the number of homeless men in Chicago ranged from 30,000 in good times to 75,000 in hard times, of which probably a third were permanent residents, living in lodging-houses and hotels. In any given year between 300,000 and 500,000 seasonal workers and migrants passed in and out of the city, some seeking and finding work, others becoming down-and-outs.[13]

Chicago had something of the quality of a frontier town, rapidly expanding as an industrial community, a centre of transport, of commerce and of employment, drawing in people by the thousands and spewing them out again in an endless flow. Some settled to regular work, others found a thousand hand-to-mouth ways of hustling a living.

This was the background against which blues and jazz reached a high point of popularity. Many women singers fronted bluesy jazz bands, from the thin-voiced and sophisticated cabaret performer Alberta Hunter with Lovie Austin on piano, to the tough and throaty Bertha 'Chippie' Hill with King Oliver's band at places like the Palladium Dance Hall.

Nevertheless the recording world took some little time to catch up with the singers closer to the folk roots. There was still a tendency to go for the more sophisticated and vaudeville styles and mainly those readily available near the main recording centres. With their stagey background, their material often had carefully contrived lyrics and a well-ordered, dramatically presented scene, like Sister Harris' *Don't Mess With Me* (1923).

> Miss Lestrange Sarah Brown was the most classical gal in town
> She met honorable Rupert Paul dancing at that Wang Wang Ball.
> He took her home that night, she gave him a kiss,
> But when he went too far she up and told him this:
>
> 'Don't mess with me, don't mess with me,
> You work fast that's very true,
> You're in the right church but in the wrong pew,
> Don't mess with me, you better run along an' let me be,
> I've got a razor that's got a nasty blade,
> Just pass on circus, I've seen your parade,
> 'Cause I done picked the ground where your body's gonna be found.
> Don't mess with me . . .'[14]

Showbiz blues 1: The tent shows

'Dance, have a stage up there and dance', said Sam Chatmon, remembering the tent shows of his youth, 'and clowns, all like that – man, they'd have a big time in some places! They called them the Nigger Minstrels, and the Ringling Brothers, they had a big show. They had plenty elephants and lions, all like that. The show was just a street carnival – the one I'm talking about. They'd show sometime one night or two nights and then they'd take down and move to the next town.'[1]

While in the cities like Chicago cabarets and dance halls gave work to blues singers, a bigger breeding ground for blues entertainment was to be found in the longer-established world of travelling black show business.

Following the Nigger Minstrel traditions, numerous shows travelled the South and Mid-West, playing for the small towns and plantations. Many of them employed blues singers, both men and women, as part of their bonanza entertainment, bringing colour, extravagance and all kinds of fun – comics, jugglers, dance-routines, wrestlers, ragtime, cakewalk, trapeze artists and wire-walkers. Some blues singers found work with the 'second' companies of the big circuses, sometimes following the main show and sometimes touring separately providing entertainment for all-black audiences. But it was mainly the minstrel shows that spread the blues, in many different companies endlessly on the move, from Florida to Texas, Oklahoma to Mississippi, with names such as Tolliver's Circus and Musical Extravaganza, the King and Bush Wide-Mouth Minstrels, the Georgia Smart Set and its rival the Smarter Set, and Pete Werley's Cotton Blossoms Show. Pre-eminent in the field and best remembered of them all were Silas Green's from New Orleans, which started in 1910, and their chief rivals the famous Rabbit Foot Minstrels, organised by F. S. Wolcott from Port Gibson, Mississippi.

The minstrel and carnival shows would perform in huge tents carried in trailers or sometimes their own railroad cars which could be detached from trains and slipped into sidings. As the roustabouts and canvasmen rigged up the tent, a brass band would go parading round the locality 'ballyhooing' to drum up an audience, with performers perhaps waving and mugging from atop the back of an elephant. They would play for all kinds of people at levee camps or plantations, or set up outside small towns. Changing facilities might be in a tent or in the rail car, where they also sometimes slept. Ethel Waters recalls sleeping in a stable because 'the colored people in Lexington (Kentucky) wouldn't let carnival show girls into their homes, so we couldn't get a room . . . Baby Jim, the show's fat man, had to sleep in the stable, too, but for a different reason. He weighed between four and five hundred pounds. Like all carnival fat men, he was supposed to be the fattest in the world. In all Lexington there was no house with a door big enough for Baby Jim to get through, and no bed strong enough to hold his weight.'[2]

At this time Ethel Waters was appearing as one of 'The Hill Sisters, Featuring Sweet Mama Stringbean, Singing *St Louis Blues*. She was one of the first women to record blues, but hers was the pure-toned, sweet-voiced variety; she later became a very fine jazz singer before entering a career as a movie actress. She came from a rancid and decrepit slum in Chester, Pennsylvania, and was born in 1901 after her mother had been raped at the age of twelve. Her childhood was lonely and isolated in a crowded world surrounded by the sights of groping and fumbling sex in back alleys (she would keep watch while her friends experimented).

'In crowded slum homes one's sex education begins very early indeed. Mine began when I was about three and sleeping in the same room, often in the same bed, with my aunts and my transient "uncles". I wasn't fully aware of what was going on but resented it. By the time I was seven I was repelled by every aspect of sex.'[3]

She was always a leader in street gangs, stealing and hell-raising, and well acquainted with the local prostitutes. She had much affection for these women and respected them for the way they supported whole families and sometimes even their accidental children through college. Her neighbourhood was not exclusively black; there were plenty of whites, 'Hunkies and Jews, and some Chinese'. The whores, black and white, worked together, lived together and slept together.

'There was no racial prejudice at all in that big melting pot running over with vice and crime, violence, poverty and corruption. I never was made to feel like an outcast on Clifton Street. All of us, white, blacks, and yellows, were outcasts together and having a fine time among ourselves.'[4]

Ethel felt isolated from her aunts and her mother because while 'they discussed people and things that happened with considerable intelligence and insight',[5] they appeared to care little for her. It was in the world of showbiz that she found solace, especially in the camaraderie of being on the road with a tent show.

'I liked being in the carnival. The roustabouts and concessionaries were the kind of people I'd grown up with, rough, tough, full of larceny towards strangers, but sentimental, and loyal to their friends and co-workers. The carnival work was colorful and a new experience. But I didn't like it when it rained. It was bad underfoot in the tents because no planks were put down.'[6]

Tent show stages were usually made of boards on a folding frame, set up at one end, sometimes lit by candles, but more usually with gasoline mantle lanterns which later gave way to somewhat unreliable electric lamps powered by portable generators. Occasionally the shows would be done 'in the round' with four groups of dancers facing each quarter of the audience. Virtually all the famous and great women blues singers of the 20's passed through the rough apprenticeship of the tent show routine. Barnstorming from settlement to township and from State to State gave them the chance to learn their trade as entertainers. The discipline and control of the early blues records reflects the formality of tested professional performance. The blues was taken into a new relationship with its black folk cultural origins; the blues singer – at least the women singers of the 20's – was no longer an ordinary member of black society singing the songs of the working people or playing for the local dances. They were set up on stage, watched and listened to from afar, using every trick and stage device to 'present' their songs. The audience was in a more clearly detached position, and if not exactly passive (crowds would wildly cheer, groan, shout and stomp), they were no longer participants on a near-level basis. In fact blues had come close to creating a star system not unlike the world of white showbiz.

Not that blues was the only element in black minstrelsy and carnivals. The chorus girls, the comedy acts, the entertainers of every kind were there too, with jazz musicians bluesy and not so bluesy.

Ma Rainey

'Ma, there are two things I've never seen,' vaudeville performer Billy Gunn once told Ma Rainey. 'That's an ugly woman and a pretty monkey.' 'Bless you, darling,' was her reply.[1]

Gertrude 'Ma' Rainey was one of the greatest and most loved blues singers of all time. Her blues were rough and earthy, profound in depth and with a warmth which transcended mere words. She would moan 'hmmmmmmmm', and the audience would moan with her.

'She looked too ugly for me', recalled Little Brother Montgomery. 'Boy, she was the horrible-lookingest thing I ever see!'[2] But to her old pianist Georgia Tom Dorsey, Ma Rainey was 'lovely, congenial'. 'Well, I couldn't say she was a good-looking woman,' he adds, 'and she was stout. But she was one of the loveliest people I ever worked for or worked with. She called everybody "honey" and "darling", "baby" and so on. If you got in trouble and wanted to borrow some money or something from her, and you go to her for it, she wouldn't call you "darling", "babe" or "baby"! She said, "What, what did you do with your money? All right, here it is . . ." She's just that kind of person.'[3]

She was an extraordinary-looking woman, ugly-attractive with a short, stubby body, big-featured face and a vividly painted mouth full of gold teeth; she would be loaded down with diamonds – in her ears, round her neck, in a tiara on her head, on her hands, everywhere. Beads and bangles mingled jingling with the frills on her expensive stage gowns. For a time her trademark was a fabulous necklace of gold coins, from 2.50 dollar coins to heavy 20 dollar 'Eagles' with matching gold earrings. Every night she would sleep with the necklace still on, but one night a sneak thief whipped it while she was sleeping on a train and in disgust she replaced it with cheap imitation pearls. Sometimes she wore a glittering beaded headband, and regularly swished a great big frothy ostrich feather fan.

On stage she would have a huge eagle backdrop, and would appear out of a big box made to look like a phonograph, blowing kisses. At the time when Lon Chaney's silent movie *The Phantom of the Opera* was doing the rounds, her show once started with someone in a balcony bellowing 'The Phaaantuhm!' as her five-piece Georgia Jazz Band assembled in the pit. All round the theatre the chorus of voices then joined in, 'The Phaaantuhm – the phaaantuhm', rising to a crescendo as the stage curtain rose to reveal the giant replica of a Victrola, bathed in blue light. From inside the cabinet came Ma's moaning voice, the enormous doors then swung open, and there she was, resplendent in her sequined black dress and her shimmering jewellery.

Ma had a deep and rich contralto voice, sometimes softly moaning, sometimes a roaring shout, but always with an underlying seriousness and melancholy. Many of the songs she sang were her own, but she also drew on material from professional music writers. Whether or not they were her own songs made no difference: her blues were always deeply rooted in the experiences of the poor in the Deep South. Typical was *Chain Gang Blues*, with words by Charles Parker and music by Spencer Williams, which she recorded in 1926.

> Many days of sorrow, many nights of woe,
> Many days of sorrow, many nights of woe,
> And a ball and chain, everywhere I go.[+]

Ma Rainey came from Georgia – she was born in Columbus in 1886 – and despite, or perhaps because of, her involvement in minstrel and tent shows since the turn of the century, she was deeply aware of the realities in the lives of her audience. *Chain Gang Blues* reflects her commitment to the themes which her audience could understand. The chain gangs in Georgia, using women and children, could even be seen working in the streets of a city like Atlanta.

> It was early this mornin' that I had my trial,
> It was early this mornin' that I had my trial,
> Ninety days on the country road, and the judge didn't even
>   smile.[+]

Of all the so-called 'Classic' blues singers, Ma Rainey was the most rural and Southern in her style and in her appeal. She very rarely toured much north of Virginia and it was some time before she worked a city like Chicago, and then only after the blues became a commercial success. The first time she herself heard the blues was in a small Missouri town in 1902. She told folklorist John Work that a girl came to the tent and began singing a song so strange and poignant that she decided to use it in her act as an encore.

She worked just about all the famous minstrel and tent shows, Tolliver's, Al Baines', Silas Green's and the celebrated Rabbit Foot Minstrels. By 1915 she was billed with her husband Pa Rainey as a song and dance act, 'Rainey and Rainey Assassinators of the Blues'. Lucien Brown, a musician who recorded with Ma, recalled her husband:

'Well "Pa" Rainey was an *old* minstrel man. He had a whole outfit . . . tents and I don't what all . . . but he was an *old* man; that's why they called him "Pa" . . . and from that she picked up the name "Ma".'[5]

In the 1920's she was mainly running her own shows, going round with emblazoned railroad cars, or her own home-made house-trailer made out of an old car chassis and canvas top. They would carry around about four trunks of scenery, including her own drop with a picture of the Paramount record label on it. Little Brother Montgomery remembers that Ma Rainey always had a suitcase full of money, in 50 and 100 dollar bills – '"I got this from my man",' she'd say.[6] Laura Dukes, who was herself a tent show performer recalls someone once asking Ma, '"Ma, do you have any money?"' Ma replied, '"Honey chile, what you talking about? I got a roll big enough to choke a ox!"'[7]

Ma's Paramount records were copiously advertised, and at one point Paramount ran a competition, asking for a suitable name for *Ma Rainey's Mystery Record*. The winning entry was *Lawd, I'm Down Wid De Blues* by Ella McGill of Jefferson, Indiana. Ma, or 'Madame' Rainey as she preferred to be called, was Paramount's biggest selling star in the early 20's. Paramount had been operating as a subsidiary of the Wisconsin Chair Company since 1917 and by 1923, when Ma first recorded for them, her popularity helped make them one of the biggest and most important of the 'Race' labels – as black records were beginning to be called.

Ma's chief support was in the South, the heartland of her 'folk', and even when she used the most advanced and sophisti-

cated musicians on her records – and she worked with men like
Louis Armstrong, Coleman Hawkins and Fletcher Henderson –
she still retained her down-home style and feeling. She also
recorded with more rural accompaniments, with a banjo, kazoo,
tug, jug and washboard, as when she recorded with the 'Tub Jug
Washboard Band'. As her pianist, Georgia Tom composed many
of Ma's songs, some 'deep moanin'' blues and other gloriously
good-time romps. Either way they were blues of the rural South,
what Tom himself called 'low-down blues, that's all I could
say!'[8]

> Black cat on my door-step, black cat on my window sill,
> Black cat on my door-step, black cat on my window sill,
> If some black cat don't cross me, some other black cat will.
>
> Last night a hoot owl come and sit right over my door,
> Last night a hoot owl come and sit right over my door,
> A feelin' seemed to tell me I'd never see my man no mo'.
>
> I feel my left side a-jumpin', my heart a-bumpin', I'm mindin' my
>   P's and Q's.
> I feel my brain a-thumpin', and I've got no time to lose.
> Now I'm just superstitious, tryin' to overcome these blues.
>
> *Black Cat Hoot Owl Blues* (1928)[9]

The country quality of Ma's singing didn't appeal to everyone;
one who didn't like her was Little Brother: 'I didn't hate her, she
was all right, but I never cared too much for her. I seen her a lot,
you know, she always sounded flat to me. When she sings, she
sang flat. She had a big mouth too (*sings*) "Eh Bo Weavil, don't
sing them blues no more", I never did like that kind of
singing!'[10]

On the other hand Victoria Spivey, herself a big blues star in
the 20's and 30's, loved Ma Rainey.

'Oh Lord, don't say anything about Ma. All her gold hanging
round her tight. Ma was a mess. Ain't nobody in the world ever
yet been able to holler "Hey Bo Weavil" like her. Not like Ma.
Nobody. I've heard them try to, but they can't do it. "Hey Bo
Weavil". All right. 'Cos bo weavil he was eating up everything
down South. That worm would eat up all the food and everything. And she holler "Hey Bo Weavil, you been gone a great
long time". Now there was two *meanings* to that. I was such a
smart little hip chicken, I knew just which bo weavil she was talking about. Oh I was clever!'[11]

Whatever their location in time or place, Ma Rainey's blues, like those of all the great blues singers, transcend their limitations to speak of human warmth.

> You'll find me wrigglin' and a-rockin',
> Howlin' like a houn' . . . [12]

In 1935 she retired from life on the road and spent her last years running two theatres she had acquired in Columbus and Rome, Georgia. Deeply involved in the Congregation of Friendship Baptist Church where her brother was deacon, she died in 1939. Her death certificate listed her occupation as 'housekeeping'.

Showbiz blues 2: The theatres

'Every Friday night they had a Midnight Ramble', says Laura Dukes about the Palace Theatre on Beale Street, Memphis. 'They had it so they had one night for the white and one night for the colored people. That's when the girls, I don't know, look like they half-stripped you know.'[1]

If black showbiz was parallel to white, it was nowhere more apparent than in the world of theatre. At first blacks could perform in segregated white theatres, like on the Western Vaudeville and the B. F. Keith-Orpheum circuits. These chains of theatres would book in Negro acts which blacks could watch from the segregated peanut galleries. But soon the growing tide of black talent, and the size of the black audiences piling into the growing cities in the South and North demanded more facilities: there was clearly money to be made. In 1907 a man from Memphis started a small circuit of theatres in the South, the success of which led to the establishment in 1909 of the famous, and infamous, Theatre Owners' Booking Agency variously known as TOBA, Toby Time, or Tough On Black Asses. These white-run theatres provided pretty squalid working conditions; often there was no backstage and on the smaller stages, no wings. In some, artists would dress underneath the stage behind thin partitions, come out through the orchestra pit and climb precariously up a ladder, hoping to get on stage before the lights came up. The Monogram Theatre in Chicago was so cramped there wasn't room to stand upright when changing costume and, being right next to a railway line, every time a train passed performers had to stop singing or telling their jokes till the noise died down.

The TOBA theatre hired either independent acts or complete companies, with bands, chorus girls, comics and every kind of vaudeville routine, the show running for perhaps a week before moving on to another city. None of the theatres paid travelling expenses so artists would seek to avoid schedules with long distances involved. It could be a gruelling and humiliating life for the lesser performers, often harassed by white theatre bosses like the notorious Charles P. Bailey of the 81 Theatre on Decatur Street, Atlanta. Bailey was a vindictive and arrogant 'czar' in his own theatre, and his authority ran outside it: he would issue passes for the black artists to break Atlanta's curfew regulations (like most Southern cities at that time, Atlanta banned blacks from the streets after a certain hour).

Soon most cities with a black population of any size had a Negro theatre – the Pastime and the Beale Avenue Palace in Memphis, the Lyric in New Orleans, the Lyceum in Cincinnati, the Dream in Columbus, Georgia, the Koppin in Detroit, the Bijou in Nashville, the Booker T. Washington in St Louis and others in Florida, Arkansas, Missouri and Alabama. Not every theatre was a TOBA outfit; there were independents in New York, Washington and elsewhere. But all featured the women blues singers alongside their jugglers, snake-charmers, high-kicking 'High Brown Chorus Girls', 'Sepia Lovelies' and quick-fire comedy routines.

Georgia Tom Dorsey, who used to go out on the road regularly with Ma Rainey in the 1920's now looks back on those days with a mixture of pride and rueful amusement.

'I got the band together and we travelled all over the country, except California. Got stranded in many places and got to the point somewhere we were so broke – you know some of the houses didn't draw – we'd have to slip out and eat. You let another actor know you got money, you're supposed to divide with them. So another fellow and I we got up about 4 o'clock in the morning, slip out to a little restaurant and eat and come back, go to bed and wouldn't have to buy anything for anyone else! But it has been rough, it had been tough, and yet all the glory that all of the actors, musicians receive is duly for them. They should have, should have had it a long time ago.'[2]

Black audiences were sometimes cruelly demanding. If they didn't think much of a performance they would maintain an impervious independence running up and down the aisles, yelling greetings to friends and even breaking out into fights. But for the best-loved blues singers the emotional rewards could be enormous, appearing in glamorous revues, heading their own companies, singing and moaning the deepest and most emotional of blues. Spellbound audiences would greet the end of a song with whoops and shouts, exultantly screaming for more, applauding wildly and stamping their feet. At such moments the blues stars became virtually racial heroines, symbols of success and glamour, dressed in resplendent outfits, decked in sequins and dazzling jewellery, disappearing for a quick-change to re-appear in yet another sumptuous gown. In a society which denied black people the dignity of human equality, denied them the means to even strive for it, the trappings of riches and success were symbols of great potency. That the successes of the great blues singers like Bessie Smith, Ida Cox, Ma Rainey and many others were based on their own intimate knowledge and experience of the blues culture of the poor and dispossessed made the symbolism even more profound.

Bessie Smith

While Ma Rainey was the Mother of the Blues, the greatest of them all was the Empress, Bessie Smith. Ma's appeal and popularity was mainly 'down-home' in the South, but Bessie's empire extended throughout the black community, from the rural South to the urban North, from the roughest share-cropper's phonograph to the sophisticated New York theatres. Her audience even included white Southern record buyers and radio listeners and segregated white theatre-goers. She was 'taken-up' and fêted by white intellectuals who were seldom conscious – as she was – of their own patronisation and con-descension. Her status as one of the biggest stars in black show business meant that she could command a certain respect even from Southern theatre owners; but always the courtesy she got was good treatment 'for a black person'.

'Bessie knew this of course, but she went along with the game – unless somebody gave her trouble. Then, it didn't make any difference whether they were white, black, Southern or Northern, she'd give them a tongue-beating or she'd beat up on them with her fists,'[1] recalled a contemporary.

She was a fighter with both men and women, punching to the floor Clarence Williams, a notorious hustler in the music busi-ness who tried to screw her contractually, or fighting with her husband's mistresses and endlessly brawling with her husband himself. She had a tempestuous temper and enormous physical courage. On one occasion a bunch of white-robed Ku Klux Klansmen were starting to collapse the big tent she was per-forming in. When the gang of prop boys she had collected to stop them backed off, she ran to within ten feet of the Klansmen, put one hand on her hip, clenched the other, bawled an obscenity at them and yelled: 'I'll get the whole damn tent out here if I have to. You just pick up them sheets and run!' A further string of abuse finally drove them away. Then she walked back to the prop boys. 'And as for you, you ain't nothin' but a bunch of sissies.'[2]

Bessie came from a very poor family in Chattanooga where she was born in 1894 in what she called 'a little ramshackle cabin', with five surviving brothers and sisters. By the time she was eight or nine both parents were dead. Nearly half the 30,000 population of Chattanooga was black, and many of them were unemployed. The background of Bessie's life as a black woman was a second-class citizenship, segregation and squalid poverty. Despite all her subsequent success and acclaim as a money-making hot property, she never forgot who she was and where she came from.

Bessie's big-hearted generosity was one of the things re-membered by Victoria Spivey, who had tremendous admiration for her as a performer too, "'cos you never missed a lick. She never missed a lick and she had full control at all times. Full control . . . She was a beautiful woman, and I tell you one thing about her, I ain't gonna brag her too much; she'd get you tall, and she'd throw away a lot of money, and she'd drink her liquor: *and she'd give you her last dime.* And she'd pick up many a scally-wag on the highways and on the road and gave them oppor-tunities and breaks in life.'[3]

Many regard her 1928 record *Poor Man's Blues* – made before the Great Depression of the 30's – one of her most moving achievements. Many of her songs were written by professional writers, but this was her own composition, delivered with an icy control, and a slow passionate anger.

> Mister rich man, rich man, open up your heart and mind,
> Mister rich man, rich man, open up your heart and mind;
> Give the poor man a chance, help stop these hard, hard times.
>
> While you're living in your mansion, you don't know what hard
> times mean,
> While you're living in your mansion, you don't know what hard
> times mean;
> Poor working man's wife is starving; your wife is living like a
> queen.
>
> Please listen to my pleadin', 'cause I can't stand these hard
> times long,
> Aw, listen to my pleadin', can't stand these hard times long;
> They'll make an honest man do things that you know is wrong.

Now the war is over, poor man must live the same as you,
Now the war is over, poor man must live the same as you;
If it wasn't for the poor man, mister rich man, what would
you do?[4]

Bessie identified with the poor and dispossessed; inspired by the 1927 Mississippi floods, which covered 20,000 square miles and eventually made 200,000 homeless, her *Back Water Blues* takes the point of view of a victim.

Back Water Blues caused me to pack my things and go,
Back Water Blues caused me to pack my things and go,
'Cause my house fell down, and I can't live there no mo'.

Mmmmmmmm Mmmmmmmmmm, I can't move no more,
Mmmmmmmm Mmmmmmmmmm, I can't move no more,
There ain't no place for a poor old girl to go.[5]

To this day Bessie Smith has remained a symbol of resistance to defeat and oppression. Ruby Walker told Bessie's biographer Chris Albertson:

'Bessie wasn't fooled by those Southern crackers smiling at her. She wasn't scared of those white people down there. Not Bessie – she would tell anybody to kiss her ass. Nobody messed with Bessie, black or white, it didn't make no difference.'[6]

One of the most pernicious and dehumanising effects of white racism has been for gradations of skin colour within the black population to take on characteristics of a caste system. The closer the colour was to white, and some blacks could 'pass' as white, the more attractive they were felt to be even among black people. Bessie herself always stood up for blackness, while all around her people sought to appear white. She was 'a *big* woman with that beautiful bronze color and stern features. Stately, just like a queen,'[7] according to Zutty Singleton. Mezz Mezzrow said she was 'tall and brownskinned, with great big dimples creasing her cheeks, dripping good looks – just this side of voluptuous, buxom and massive, but stately too, shapely as an hour-glass, with a high-voltage magnet for a personality.'[8]

She made no concessions to the pretensions of others, remaining resolutely herself but also gaining the reputation as 'a rough-and-tumble sort of person', or 'a kind of roughish sort of woman'. Even those who admired her tremendously as an artist felt a certain unease. May Wright Johnson, a singer whose husband James P. Johnson often played piano for Bessie, remembers her as 'terrific and there's been nobody since that could sing the blues like Bessie Smith. She would come over to the house, but, mind you, she wasn't my friend. She was very rough.'[9]

The blues have always tended to be associated with roughness and a lack of 'class'. Harry Dial was a jazz drummer in St Louis in the 20's whom Mamie Smith wanted in her band. He knew of the famous blues singers like Bessie, Clara Smith (no relation), but never thought of the blues as special music.

'As far as we were concerned, they were all just blues singers, and we didn't pay them no mind. They didn't mean anything to us at all, because we heard that all day and night. Every kid on the block was singing or whistling, and it was going on all round us, next door, upstairs, across the street, down the alley, everywhere . . . it wasn't anything special to us. The one girl we did think was great was Ethel Waters. She always came along with some good tunes, and she didn't just sing the blues . . . She always had good material that we thought was classy. That, in our opinion, placed her above the average blues singer. We also thought she was a more attractive woman than the other blues singers. She had everything in her favour and she outlasted all of them . . . that speaks for itself. She was the class of that era, she really was . . .'[10]

Sometimes rough, sometimes aggressive, often drinking heavily, Bessie's marriage to Jack Gee, after a blissful beginning in 1923, brought her unending cycles of fighting, remorse, feeling sorry for him, and mainly pain.

> I cried and worried, all night I laid and groaned,
> I cried and worried, all night I laid and groaned,
> I used to weigh two hundred, now I'm down to skin and bone.
>
> It's all about a man, who always kicks and dogs me aroun',
> It's all about a man, who always kicks and dogs me aroun';
> And when I try to kill him, that's when my love come down.
>
> *Please Help Me Get Him Off My Mind*[11]

Bessie's marriage ended in separation, and at times before and after she had many affairs, ranging from those of friendly affection to others which were passionately sexual, with both men and with women. There were undoubtedly periods of happiness and many good times, drinking and partying when the 'funk is flyin''. Apart from a brief period just before her tragic death in a car crash in 1937, when she found an emotionally supportive and affectionate relationship with an old Chicago bootlegger friend Richard Morgan, the pattern of her life was one of personal anxiety and turmoil, even at the height of her professional success.

Had a dream last night that I was dead,
I had a dream last night that I was dead,
Evil spirits all around my bed.

The Devil came an' grabbed my hand,
The Devil came an' grabbed my hand,
Took me 'way down to that redhot land.

Fairies an' dragons spittin' out blue flame,
Fairies an' dragons spittin' out blue flame,
Showin' their teeth 'cause they was glad I came.

Demons with they eyelids drippin' blood,
Demons with they eyelids drippin' blood,
Draggin' sinners to that brimstone flood . . .

Blue Spirit Blues (1929)[12]

As a performer her singing was incomparable; moving, powerful, sensuous, earthy, and she was also an actress of some depth, a comedienne and an agile dancer. While she could be tough, ill-mannered, crude and 'irresponsible', Bessie Smith was passionate and full of big-hearted generosity and kindness, yearning for acceptance on her own terms. If her personal life was frequently a disaster zone, it never hollowed out her extraordinary spirit.

I'm a young woman an' ain't done runnin' round,
Some people call me a hobo, some call me a bum,
Nobody knows my name, nobody knows what I've done,
I'm as good as any woman in your town.
I ain't no high yellow, I'm deep yellow-brown,
I ain't goin' to marry, ain't goin' to settle down,
I goin' drink good moonshine an' run these browns down.
See that long lonesome road – don' you know it's gotta end,
An' I'm a good woman an' I can get plenty men.

Young Woman's Blues (1926)[13]

In the words of Little Brother Montgomery, 'She was one of the greatest all-round singing: she just had a woman's voice of singing anything. She sung, she didn't care, she had a bluesy voice. She was the greatest in her time, you know, back then, Bessie Smith.'[14]

Women's blues

'Wow – but Bessie Smith spills fire and fury in *Hateful Blues* on Columbia Record 14023D,' read an advert in the *Chicago Defender* in July 1924. 'Talk about hymns of hate – Bessie sure is a him-hater on this record. The ways she tells what she is going to do with her "butcher" will make trifling fellows catch express trains going at sixty miles an hour. The music is full of hate too. You can almost see hate drip from the piano keys. Fury flies off the violin strings. Every note is a half-note. No quarter for anyone.'[1]

The first blues records were made almost entirely by women. Examining the catalogues of three major 'Race' record companies in 1926, the folklorists Odum and Johnson commented: 'The majority of these formal blues are sung from the point of view of woman . . . upwards of seventy-five per cent of the songs. Among the blues singers who have gained a more or less national recognition there is scarcely a man's name to be found.'[2]

From the beginning, women had been important in the blues. Back in 1902, Jelly Roll Morton remembered the Tenderloin District of New Orleans where the prostitutes 'in their little-girl dresses were standing in the crib doors singing the blues'.[3] He particularly remembered the pianist with the missing fingers with whom trumpeter Bunk Johnson also worked, and recalled:

'I knew Mamie Desdoumes real well. Played many a concert with her singing those same blues. She was pretty good looking, quite fair, with a *nice* head of hair. She was a hustlin' woman. A blues-singing poor gal. Used to play pretty passable piano around them dance halls on Perdido Street. When Hattie Rogers or Lulu White would put it out that Mamie was going to be singing in their place, the white men would turn out in bunches and them whores would clean up.'[4]

Dr Edmond Souchon, who came from a privileged and prosperous white family in New Orleans, remembers the songs of a servant in his household called Armotine. When she was doing the cooking – this was about 1901–2 she would sing for hours.

'Her deep contralto was clear and soft, with a rhythm that often made me stop playing to listen and pat my foot. Her songs were an admixture of Creole folk songs, church hymns and up-to-date hits of the late 90's or early 1900's.'[5]

One of the many songs she sang was a version – yet another – of *Alabama Bound* with the sexual imagery of rural life.

> I'm Alabamy bound, I'm Alabamy bound,
> I'm Alabamy bound.
> And if you want my cabbage patch,
> You gotta hoe the ground.[5]

Another of her favourite songs was the one associated with the bluesy and dirty-toned Buddy Bolden Band.

Ain't that man got a funny walk,
Doin' the 'Ping-Pong' 'round Southern Park.
Nigger man, white man, take him away,
I thought I heard them say.[5]

Black women seem to have played a lesser role in the early days of rural and country blues. It was usually the men who moved around, deserting sharecropping to go on the road, making a living with music, while the women were left behind to raise the children. This is not to say they didn't sing or play the blues; there were many, like Josie Bush who lived in Drew, Mississippi, with Willie Brown – one of Charley Patton's greatest musical companions when Patton was at Dockery's. Josie could apparently perform blues just as well as Willie. Patton himself frequently sang and played with women, one of them being his last wife Bertha Lee with whom he recorded in 1934. But the pattern of country life seems to have been such that women played a subsidiary role, mainly following the men who were regarded as the master entertainers for plantation dances or parties.

Nevertheless, women did play an important part in spreading rural musical culture, passing on songs and especially the feeling of the blues. T-Bone Walker, himself a blues star in the 1940's, recalls:

'I think that the first thing I can remember was my mother singing the blues as she would sit alone in the evenings in our place in Dallas, Texas . . . I used to listen to her singing there at night, and I knew then that the blues was in me, too.'[6]

It was in the world of professional entertainment that women really came into their own. While few women lived as independent migratory farm workers, or as hobos, or as wandering musicians on the barrelhouse circuit, the world of minstrels and vaudeville entertainment gave them the chance to establish the blues at the forefront of black culture.

The importance of the women singers in blues history can hardly be overstated. It was the women who were the first big stars, and the names of singers like Ma Rainey and Bessie Smith have become symbols both of black pride and of America's contribution to popular culture as artists in their own right.

The women singers frequently worked with jazz bands which, in contrast to the greatest isolation of the male country blues singers, provided a visible display of togetherness. For the new and struggling migrants desperately trying to create a new community in the cities, the singer and her band represented shared communal feeling, half as entertainment and half as public ritual and celebration. She became almost a priestess preaching before her congregation, drawing on the manner, style and emotionalism of the Deep South churches.

'The blues? Why the blues are part of me,' said Alberta Hunter. 'To me, the blues are – well, almost religious. They're like a chant. The blues are like spirituals, almost sacred. When we sing blues, we're singin' out our hearts, we're singin' out our feelings. Maybe we're hurt and just can't answer back, then we sing or maybe even hum the blues. Yes, to us, the blues are sacred. When I sing:

> I walk the floor, wring my hands and cry,
> Yes, I walk the floor, wring my hands and cry . . .

what I'm doing is letting my soul out.'[7]

The Church was the dominant and most stabilising institution in the rural South, an outlet for emotions and a bastion of status within the community. While on the one hand many churchgoers condemned the blues as sinful, the music of the Church itself was not unlike them, as T-Bone Walker tells us:

'Of course, the blues come a lot from the church, too. The first time I ever heard a boogie-woogie piano was the first time I went to church. That was the Holy Ghost Church in Dallas, Texas. That boogie-woogie was a kind of blues, I guess. The preacher used to preach in a bluesy tone sometimes. You even got the congregation yelling "Amen" all the time when his preaching would stir them up – his preaching and his bluesy tone.'[8]

Georgia Tom Dorsey started out as a blues musician but in the 30's he became an important and innovative composer of gospel music. The move from one kind of music to the other never bothered him:

'There's always been a beat as you call it in the church. If they didn't have a piano organ, they did it with their feet, pat their feet, pat their hands. There are moaning blues that are used in spirituals, there are moaning spirituals that are used in blues. Blues is a good woman feeling bad, and a good spiritual is something that lifts the heavy heart.'[9]

Women had always played a big part in the black church and many singers came from religious households. No-one could have been more 'secular' in private life than Bessie Smith, but even at the height of her career she would always try to get to church on a Sunday when on tour, and she often sang hymns around the house. Everyone who saw her perform agrees that her movements and vocal style evoked the fervour of a Southern Baptist Church. The guitarist Danny Barker:

'If you had any church background, like people who came from the South as I did, you would recognise a similarity between what she was doing and what these preachers and evangelists from there did, and how they moved people . . . Bessie did the same thing on stage. She, in a sense, was like people like Billy Graham are today. Bessie was in a class with those people. She could bring about mass hypnotism. When she was performing you could hear a pin drop.'[10]

Several of Bessie's generation did in fact turn to religion, and Ethel Waters, after a long career as a jazz singer and film star, came to sing religious songs for the Billy Graham Crusade.

Not only were women the pillars of the Church but also the main strength of black families; many families had a female head, whether mother, aunt, eldest sister or whatever. Under the extreme pressure of economic disintegration, a family break-up usually left the woman in charge, facing the acute social and economic problems on her own. So for the newly striving city communities both North and South, perhaps some saw in the women blues singers the stability of the maternal figure; certainly the record companies thought so. Columbia called Martha Copeland 'Everybody's Mammy'; Paramount called Ma Rainey 'Mother of the Blues'. These were the 'Classic Blues' singers, a term loosely applied to the women singers from the tent shows and vaudeville tradition, and those who worked with jazz bands. Many of them had warm enveloping voices, and while they had the moaning quality of Southern country blues, their style had little of the rambling inconsistency of the male singers. The women projected strength and power, and their blues were more formal – a formality made necessary through working with larger bands.

Ida Cox was one of the biggest stars of the 20's fronting her own extravagant shows, rich with the symbols of success. Among her many themes, she often gave womanly advice to her listeners.

> Girls, I'm gonna tell you this, ain't gonna tell you nothin' else,
> I'm gonna tell you this, ain't gonna tell you nothin' else,
> Any woman's a fool to think she's got a whole man to herself.

But if you get a good man and don't want him taken away from
you,
Girls, if you get a good man and don't want him taken away from
you,
Don't ever tell your friend woman what your man can do.
    'Fore Day Creep (1927)[11]

There seems little doubt that many of the Classic Blues sentiments were aimed directly at the women in the audience and
there could be close identification between audience and singer.
The white intellectual Carl Van Vechten saw Bessie Smith in
1925 at the Orpheum Theatre at Newark where 'the black and
blue-black crowd, notable for the absence of mulattoes, burst
into hysterical, semi-religious shrieks of sorrow and lamentation.
Amens rent the air, little nervous giggles, like the shattering of
Venetian glass, shocked our nerves. When Bessie proclaimed,
"It's true I loves you, but I won't take mistreatment any mo'," a
girl sitting beneath our box called "Dat's right! Say it,
Sister".'[12]

Though there was inevitably great rivalry and competition between performers there was often also an underlying sense of
solidarity amongst the women stars. This seems to have been
particularly true of Victoria Spivey, who had many good friends
in the music business to the end of her life: 'Ida Cox was another
good old soul . . . I was so crazy about Ida Cox, heck, I walked off
my act out there, where, where was that? Omaha, Nebraska. I
walked off of my act out there and joined Ida Cox's band, her
show, and travelled round with her for about a month and a half,
just to be near her. Ah, I used to love those women, just like that.
I loved Sara (Martin), I never did live too close to Clara (Smith),
yes, I got close to her because one day I got sick, Koppin
Theatre, Detroit, and she taken my place for me, that's close
enough, that helped up the spot for me.'[13]

Despite their importance as breadwinners and heads of
families, black women faced what has been called the 'double
jeopardy' of being not only black but also female. Historically,
America has been not only white dominated but also male
dominated, socially, economically, institutionally, and even con-
stitutionally (women didn't get the vote until 1920). In the caste
structure of American society white men were on top, followed
by white women, then black men, and right at the bottom black
women. Consigned to the roles of mammy or whore by white
society, they were economically exploited, sexually assaulted, or
otherwise abused by whites.

So even though black women were at least able to work in a higher proportion than white women, the range of work they could do was restricted not only by their own lack of education and skills, but also by prejudice against blacks and by the prevailing male ideas of what women could do and were worth. They were forced to accept the lowest paid jobs out of sheer economic necessity, vainly struggling to keep their families together, and even when doing the same job as men they were paid even less for it. On top of this, just as the poor whites in the South had the social reassurance of being at least 'superior' to the niggers, many black males found refuge in the belief that men were superior to women, leaving black women little better off than the 'slaves of slaves'. With black families already teetering on the brink of economic disaster, the tensions and personal conflicts this could produce were enormous. Because black women could often get work as cooks, maids, or wet nurses when their menfolk couldn't, the reverse side of this coin was that they often came to accept the notions that black men were lazy, shiftless and irresponsible.

> There's nineteen men livin' in my neighbourhood,
> There's nineteen men livin' in my neighbourhood,
> Eighteen of them are fools an' the one ain't no doggone good.
> *Dirty No-Gooder's Blues* – Bessie Smith[14]

The prevailing sense of irony in the blues, the 'laughin' to keep from cryin'', the 'good woman feelin' bad', and the feeling of hope in pain clutched with pain in hope, prevents it being seen one-dimensionally or simply as 'protest' music. As a music of feeling, feeling known to be shared by others, the blues is an evocation and exploration of both personal and communal responses to the surrounding world. In as far as anger, outrage and protest are in themselves reactions to things unacceptable, the blues can adopt that stance, but usually with a cynical eye on the consequences.

> If my captain ask for me,
> Tell him Abe Lincoln set us free;
> Ain' no hammer on this road
> Gonna kill poor me.
>
> This ol' hammer
> Killed John Henry,
> But this hammer
> Ain' gonna kill me.

I'm headin' for my shack,
With my shovel on my back,
Altho' money what I lack,
I'm goin' home.

Section Hand Blues – Sippie Wallace (1925)[15]

Down-home humour and bluesy irony are themselves strat-
agems for survival, and survival in turn becomes a form of self-
assertion and resistance.

Now my hair is nappy and I don't wear no clothes of silk,
Now my hair is nappy and I don't wear no clothes of silk,
But the cow that's black and ugly, has often got the sweetest milk.

Now when a man starts jivin' I'm tighter than a pair of shoes,
When a man starts jivin' I'm tighter than a pair of shoes,
I'm a mean tight mama with my mean tight mama blues.

Mean Tight Mama – Sara Martin (1928)[16]

In the Classic Blues not every subject is viewed with irony. The
young Victoria Spivey, who started recording at the age of sixteen, often touched on violence and disease in her songs. Her
bitter *T.B. Blues* of 1927 was a much adopted and adapted theme
at a time when inadequate and segregated medical facilities were
the rule in the South (once after a car crash Ethel Waters was
found by a white man whose initial, laughing reaction, before
reluctantly helping her was to say 'the more dead niggers there
are the better I like it'[17]), and tuberculosis was rampant in the
damp, overcrowded slum tenements of the North. Interviewed
by Paul Oliver in 1960, Victoria Spivey said:

'I had been lookin' at people who had the T.B. in part of the
country, and at that time if you had the T.B. nobody would have
no part of you; they put you away in hospital and you was just
doomed then, you gonna die. So I figured it was a nice thing to
write about.'[18]

Yes, he railroaded me to the sanatorium,
It's too late, too late, but I have finished my run,
This is the way all the women are done when they get the dirty
    TB.

Yes, I run around for months and months,
From gin-mill to gin-mill to honky-tonk,
Now it's too late just look what I've done done, now I've got the
    dirty TB.

Dirty T.B. Blues (1929)[19]

Victoria Spivey was one of the greatest surviving women blues singers of the 20's. She had the tough moaning style of her native Texas, with a distinctive and hard angular voice. She worked with many of the finest musicians of her era and, backed by a six-piece jazz band which included Louis Armstrong, her 1929 record *How Do You Do It That Way?* is an ironic observation of loneliness, her acid voice cutting through the warmth and vibrancy of the band.

> Oh, when the river runs flowers are bloomin' in May,
> And if you get good business how do you do it that way?
> Street-walkin' women they are happy and gay,
> But I'm never happy,
> How do they get that way?
>
> I want a man to be near because he brings good cheer,
> But the men don't like me, they don't seem to care,
> Now they come an' go, to an' fro every day,
> But I can't make them like me –
> How do you do it that way?[20]

As in all blues of whatever style or period, the Classic Blues' main theme was the sexual relationship, with almost every possible feeling represented: pain and regret, hate and apathy, fear, longing, hope and resentment, contempt, love, warmth or ambivalence, passivity, submissiveness and aggression. In some, like in a 1929 record of Mary Dixon's, the message was unmistakable – *You Can't Sleep In My Bed.*

> What's the matter with you, stop your whining around,
> What's the matter with you, stop your whining around,
> Find some other place to lay your lazy bones down.
>
> You're too big to be cute and I don't think you're clean,
> You're too big to be cute and I don't think you're clean,
> You're the damnedest-looking thing that I have ever seen.
>
> What you got in mind ain't gonna happen to-day,
> What you got in mind ain't gonna happen to-day,
> Get off my bed, how did you get that way?
>
> You'd better be done when my man comes in,
> You'd better be done when my man comes in,
> Stop shaking your tail, 'cos I don't know where you've been.
>
> Now a dog like you must have too much bread,
> Now a dog like you must have too much bread,
> Come out of my room, you can't sleep in my bed.[21]

Blunt and fairly unsympathetic rejection of former lovers is not uncommon, as in Ida Cox's *Worn Down Daddy Blues* (1928).

> You ain't got no money, you're down and broke,
> You're just an old has-been like a worn out joke,
> So I'm through with you, and I hope you don't feel hurt.[22]

Many blues take for granted the necessity of secret relationships. Ironically, Sara Martin's *Strange Loving Blues* (1925) takes its inspiration from an early children's hymn.

> Little drops of water, only grains of sand,
> Little drops of water, only grains of sand,
> Every sensible woman should have a back-door man.[23]

One of the more overt sexual blues was Clara Smith's *Whip it to a Jelly*. The song itself was frequently performed at a rollicking tempo, but Clara, who excelled at emotional slow-drag blues with her rich and mournful voice, holds the tempo right down, backed by ominous bass figures on the piano, giving the poignant feeling that all, regrettably, is fantasy.

> There's a new game, that can't be beat,
> You move most everything 'cept your feet,
> Called 'Whip it to a jelly, stir it in a bowl',
> You just whip it to a jelly, if you like good jelly roll . . .
>
> I wear my skirt up to my knees
> And whip that jelly with who I please.
> Oh, whip it to a jelly, mmmmm, mmmm
> mmmm, mmmm, mmmm, mmmm . . .[24]

Women's domination of the blues ended with the 1920's. Today interest in the period is often primarily concentrated on the jazz accompanists and there has been a tendency to deride the style as too contrived, too artificial and too close to vaudeville music. Classic blues are often contrasted to more 'authentic' forms of blues, usually taken to mean rural blues, and especially *male* blues.

Despite having many qualities specific to their time and era women's blues of the 1920's still have much to offer a society that continues to keep women's own history partly hidden from itself.

Part Four

The men start recording

'You've always had certain people who looked down on blues as far as I can remember, the gut-bucket blues, the backwoods blues. You have certain people who look down on them, even though they listened to blues at home – they'd listen to Ma Rainey, Bessie Smith, Mamie Smith, Clara Smith. That was more respectable. You find people have always been discriminate, classify themselves that way. Now it's true they were singing the same words – Ma Rainey, Bessie Smith and them, singing lots of the same lines but they were singing them differently. They were singing by arrangements and we were singing by whatever came to us first.' (Johnny Shines)[1]

Once Mamie Smith had made the breakthrough for 'Race' records, it was bound to happen eventually that the great underground reservoir of backwoods blues should be drawn on, and that meant the almost limitless numbers of men working on the levees, playing in plantations, or knocking out the blues on turpentine camp pianos. The ceaseless and restless movement of people had carried every kind of blues like spores in the wind, bringing every day a new growth. The black community had never been monolithic; even in the dire days of slavery there had been hierarchies of status and aspiration. Now the stratification and diversification of class was multiplying in complexity, and for every locality or area a different kind of blues could be heard – and in some places nothing but the blues. Johnny Shines again:

'See different places, different areas throughout the country liked different things. Some places didn't like nothing but the blues. Now, when you get back on the farms and places like that, you don't have to play nothing but the blues. You could play the same number all night, as far as that's concerned – as long as you played it fast and slow.'[1]

The Race market was showing there was demand for almost every conceivable kind of black music, and it was inevitable that a straight, undiluted male country blues singer should be recorded. The stranglehold of the Northern studios had been broken in 1923 when the first of many 'field recordings' was made. Equipment would be carried down to the South and temporary studios set up, in hotels, in hired halls, in schools, and queues of performers would be wheeled in – vocal quartets, pianists, guitar players, harmonica players, virtually anyone who had what passed for a song. The first recording of a male country blues singer seems to have been by a twelve-string guitarist called Ed Andrews who was recorded for Okeh in Atlanta in March or April 1924. Sylvester Weaver, a smoothly skilled musician from the city of Louisville, Kentucky had recorded two melodic guitar solos for Okeh in New York the previous November (which were probably the first recordings of blues guitar) but it was Ed Andrews who was almost certainly the first man to *sing* rural blues on record.

> Give me whiskey when I'm thirsty, water when I'm dry,
> Give me whiskey when I'm thirsty, water when I'm dry,
> I want it while I'm livin' – doggone it when I die.
> *Barrel House Blues* (1924)[2]

But the first commercially successful male singer was Papa Charlie Jackson, recorded later that year by Paramount. They were chiefly a mail order company, advertising heavily in the *Defender* and other papers, and they saw the sales potential of the South from the response they were getting. In their promotional *Paramount Book of the Blues* of 1927, they described Papa Charlie as 'a witty – cheerful – kindhearted man – who, with his joyous sounding voice and his banjo, sang and strummed his way into the hearts of thousands of people'[3]. His photograph shows him as a tall, elegant, long-featured man, dressed in a smartly-pressed tweed suit. He was a sophisticated all-round entertainer, with comic songs, vaudeville and minstrel-sounding material as well as blues, and in many ways he reflected the same outgoing spirit as the early cabaret women singers – the feeling of hope and ex-pectation of blacks first escaping the landlocked constriction of the South into the main stream of urban America.

'Charlie and his records took the entire country by storm, and now – people like nothing better than to come home after a tiring and busy day and play his records. His hearty voice and gay harmonious strumming on the banjo causes their cares and worries to dwindle away, and gives them a careful frame of mind, and makes life one sweet song.'[3]

He recorded some of the earliest versions of country blues standards, like *I'm Alabama Bound, Salty Dog, Spoonful* and *Shake That Thing*, but his stock in trade was his sophisticated six-string banjo-playing, full of complicated multi-patterned picking and a freely melodic sense of rhythm.

Papa Charlie's relaxed and sophisticated musicianship make him comparable to another of Paramount's most commercially successful bluesmen – Blind Blake. And just as the ease and charm of the early women singers was to give way to more personalised and disquieting blues, so Blind Blake conveyed far more than Papa Charlie the atmosphere of urban disenchantment and of disintegrating hopes. If the women singers with their bands came to seem like preacher and congregation, standing for the shared burdens of the struggling community, the male singers conveyed a sense of isolation. Blind Blake's musical sophistication was in his phenomenally fluent guitar playing; but all-pervading was a feeling of tired defeat.

> Packing up my duffle, gonna leave this town,
> Packing up my duffle, gonna leave this town,
> And I'm gonna hustle to catch that train southbound.

> I got the Georgia blues for the plough and hoe,
> I got the Georgia blues for the plough and hoe,
> Walked out my shoes over this ice and snow.

> *Georgia Bound*[+]

Blind Blake seems to have settled in a Chicago tenement block in the 20's, but all his life he was 'a travellin' man, staying alone and doing the best I can'. Much of his commercial success was in the South, and while his music was his living he still shared the life of working people. Bill Williams who was a similarly facile guitarist remembers seeing Blake on the 'camps' near Bristol, Tennessee, in 1921.

'I was working on the good road, what you call a road gang, out from Bristol. We used to live in the camps – under canvas. You know – we had a lot of tents and stuff, few little wooden houses, which they put up in the ditch beside the road we was making. And I never will forget the time. It was a Saturday night and it was raining. And this woman told me "there's a man wants to see you". So I went to the door and there was this feller, he was soaking wet, water streaming off him. And he had big thigh boots on – boots right up to here. And he was carrying a guitar, and he was blind. He'd come to the camps by himself, all the way from Bristol. Didn't have nobody with him. And he says, "You

Bill Williams?" I told him, yes. "You a guitar-picker?", and I says, "Yes, I am." "Well, I'm a guitar-picker too." That's all he said, and he come in and sets down to play, and man, he could really play. And then, every Friday and Saturday night he'd come to the camps to play for the boys, and we'd play together.'[5]

Blake's singing was warm and relaxed, with none of the harshness of some country blues; his voice was quiet, slightly wistful, giving his blues the feeling of self-deprecating irony. The Paramount adverts talked of his 'famous piano-sounding guitar' and it had a regularity of tone and precision which gave his music a soft lyricism especially in his slower blues:

> When you see me sleeping, baby don't you think I'm drunk –
> *(Spoken)*   No, I'm not drunk, not a bit of it.
> When you see me sleeping, baby don't you think I'm drunk,
> I got one eye on my pistol and the other on your trunk.
> *(Spoken)*   Play that thing low and lonesome, boy.
> *Early Morning Blues*[6]

By his own personal geographical ramblings and especially through his records, Blake had a tremendous impact on blues in the South. He himself probably came from Jacksonville, Florida, but through many parts of the South East, through Georgia and the Carolinas, traces of his outgoing 'rag' guitar playing can still be heard in other musicians. It is impossible to calculate the exact importance of the new mass media in shaping new traditions and creating new styles; for every musician chance or good fortune brought into the recording studio, there were countless others who were not recorded, many of whom were probably equally as good and just as creative as the ones recorded. But records would often pin a style to an individual name, personalising in the process a technique which might in fact have been commonplace. Nonetheless, Blind Blake was without doubt one of the most highly regarded of the early male blues singers, with an influence surpassed by only a few.

One man who probably did have an even greater influence was another blind singer, recorded by Paramount slightly before Blake. Blind Lemon Jefferson, as Son House remarked, was 'one of the crack-batters in record making'.[7]

Blind Lemon's records sold in all parts of the country, in the Northern cities as well as in the South. For the poor blacks of the city ghettoes as well as for the sharecroppers and levee camp workers of the South he was unbeatable. His cousin Alec Jefferson remembered him playing for country suppers in Waxahatchie, in Texas.

'Of course, my mother didn't let me go to them country suppers often. They was rough. Men was hustling women and selling bootleg and Lemon was singing for them all night. They didn't even do any proper kind of dancing, just stompin'. They'd go down to the station and get him in the afternoon. He'd start singing about eight and go on until four in the morning. Sometime he'd have another fellow with him, playing a mandolin or a guitar and singing along, but mostly it would be just him, sitting there and singing all night.'[8]

Blind Lemon is almost the archetype of all bluesmen, living the rough life that is grimly portrayed in his songs, full of fluid images of violence and death, the transience of relationships, endlessly on the move, but at the same time full of humour and rugged independence. While all around the universe of his vision there is decay and social collapse, Lemon's blues have a force and resilience, sometimes in their themes of lust and sexuality but also in their ability to enter into another man's shoes, to see things from his point of view. He was able, as the St Louis singer Henry Townsend said, to 'take sympathy with the fellow'.[9]

> I wonder why they electrocute a man after the one o'clock hour of the night,
> I wonder why they electrocute a man after the one o'clock hour of the night,
> Because the current is much stronger, then the folkses turn out all the lights.
>
> 'Lectric Chair Blues[10]

Despite the regular claims that 'everyone knew him', his character remains obscure. The only existing photograph of him reveals a certain defiance; a stoutish figure in a suit and tie, with a thick-lipped round face, blankly wearing wire-rimmed glasses he is playing a guitar almost flat on his lap. A sense of independence is confirmed by Victoria Spivey writing in *Record Research* in 1966.

'Blind Lemon was a medium size brownskin who kept himself neatly dressed. He was erect in posture and his speech was lovely and direct to the word. He had no glasses when I first saw him. A young man who was very attentive to him acted as his guide. Although he was supposed to be completely blind, I still believe he could see a little. If he couldn't he darn sure could feel his way round (the old wolf!! Smiles!!). Lemon never let his misfortune of sight press him. He could let you know that he was just as much a man as anybody. One of his most common expressions was "Don't play me cheap" – and people liked him and respected him.' Sam Chatmon met Blind Lemon in Atlanta, Georgia: 'He was all right, but sometimes he'd be sort of crabbish. The fellow's blind, got a way of speak things, you know. If that fellow didn't lead him exactly right, why he'd raise sand! Well, I was used to all that.'[12]

Lemon was an itinerant musician, still remembered all over the South. He was born on a farm at Couchman, Texas, in 1897. By 1920 he was already a big name and his fame spread with his journeyings into Oklahoma, Louisiana, Mississippi, Alabama and anywhere else where there was work and money, following the cotton harvest and playing at country picnics or in beer-joints in the small towns and cities. He was incalculably influential on other musicians, and that influence even crossed the colour line. The white Kentucky mountain musician Roscoe Holcomb said, 'Up till then the blues were only inside me; Blind Lemon was the first to "let out" the blues.'[13] It was Lemon's guitar-playing that impressed Delta bluesman Howling Wolf: 'What I liked about Lemon's music most was that he made a clear chord. He didn't stumble in his music like a lot of people do – *plink*.'[14]

He was especially remembered in Dallas, Texas, where Lead Belly worked with him, and which was a centre of intense blues activity in the 20's, with several singers being recorded there. T-Bone Walker claimed the blind singer was a very good friend to the family, coming over every Sunday, playing his guitar and drinking home-brew corn whiskey.

'I used to lead him around a lot. We'd go up and down Central Avenue. They had a railroad track, and all the places were like clubs, beer joints you know. They wouldn't sell no whiskey no way . . . He had a cup on his guitar and everybody knew him, you know, and he used to come through on Central Avenue singing and playing his guitar. And I'd lead him and they'd put money in his cup . . . I was really crazy about him. My whole family was crazy about him.'[15]

Despite marriage to a girl called Roberta around 1922–23, and the birth of a child a little later, Lemon kept travelling and the young Victoria Spivey remembers working with him in house parties and joints in Galveston, Texas, making a lot of money.

'Wasn't nowhere to play in them days. We didn't have no nightclub at that time, playing in Texas. We had picnics, parties. I'm going to tell you the truth. Those whiskey houses, why, they were bootleggers. You go there and ball and after those good-time women. I didn't know what they were then, but I know now, from what I'm looking at now. Those women got there, steal all that money, everything. They had pimps and they bring all that money to whatever house their pimp was at. I've had the top of the piano loaded up with 20 dollars, silver dollars from one end to another, them "bo" dollars. And they just tip you and you play on. "Hey little Moma," they just go, "Play me *I ain't got no more baby.*" "Play me this." "Play me this." Broads coming in trying to show another broad she made more money than she did last night. "Hey Daddy, here Daddy." . . . "What she give that man all that money for?" Pretty soon I knew exactly what they were doing.[16]

The world Lemon conjured up in his blues was full of 'bad liquor', 'wild women', 'easy riders,' 'heavy-hip mamas', 'dirty mistreaters', or even a 'fair-made woman cunning as a squirrel'. He was frequently 'worried and bothered' or had the 'low-down worried blues'.

> I got the blues so bad, it hurts my feet to walk,
> I got the blues so bad, it hurts my feet to walk,
> It have settled on my brain and it hurts my tongue to talk.
>
> *Lonesome House Blues*[17]

These are the stock 'literary conceits' of the bluesmen, and the currency was well established by the time Lemon started recording. In fact the first Paramount advert for one of his records, in 1926, called it 'a real, old-fashioned blues, by a real, old-fashioned blues singer'.[18] No doubt many people disapproved of his blues for their overt sexuality – 'the way she bucks on her hips it would make a panther squall'[19] – and for their sometimes less than elevated sentiments:

> I done swallowed some fire, taken a drink of gasoline
> Put it up all over that woman and let her go up in steam.[20]

But within the seemingly one-dimensional framework of 'feelin' lowdown in mind',[21] Blind Lemon showed all the extraordinarily expressive range of the country blues. He had an immediately recognisable sound, which stamped his own individuality on material of every kind, whether his own or drawn from blues tradition. He had a high and lonesome voice which he accompanied with complex and irregular guitar patterns – sometimes a soft strum followed by loping single-string runs, sometimes suspending the rhythm and holding it back while he sang, or toning out sound effects to underline his words. He could play regular-timed dance rhythms (despite Son House's claim that there 'couldn't nobody never be lucky enough to dance by his music'[22]), but mainly he used the guitar to answer to his vocal, flicking out little runs as he hollered, sighed or hummed. The total effect is a constant reminder of a very conscious artistry which distances his work from the simplicity of just 'having the blues'; his great achievement was in coherently articulating a view of the world, a view which went beyong simply feeling low down, and embraced attitudes which went beyond the pathos and pain of his sound. This, and the lonesome quality of his voice, convey a strong sense of self, an awareness of existing as an individual.

Lemon presents himself sometimes as mistreated, sometimes as a drunkard, sometimes as a man of aggression, but frequently with humour.

> Now I'm sittin' in my kitchen, mosquitoes all around my screen,
> Now I'm sittin' in my kitchen, mosquitoes all around my screen,
> If I don't arrange to get a mosquito bomb, I'll be seldom seen.
>
> I believe I'll sleep under a tin tub just to let them bust their bad
> old bills.
> I believe I'll sleep under a tin tub just to let them bust their bad
> old bills.
> Well mosquitoes so bad in this man's town, keep me away from
> my whiskey still . . .
> *Mosquito Moan*[23]

And in presenting himself as sexual man he had a range of imagery that went from the lamenting series of *Black Snake Blues* and *Black Snake Moans:*

> Um-um, black snake crawling in my room,
> Um-um, black snake crawling in my room,
> Yes, some pretty mama better get this black snake soon.
> *That Black Snake Moan*[24]

to the sweetness of his 'long distance well and it's blowin' oil that's all'.

> Ain't nothin' to hurt you, sugar ain't nothin' that's bad,
> Ain't nothin' to hurt you, honey ain't nothin' bad,
> It's the first oil well that your little boy ever had . . .
> *Oil Well Blues*[25]

Alongside songs of death, electric chairs and hanging, Blind Lemon repeatedly turned to images of imprisonment:

> Got a red-eyed captain and a squabblin' boss,
> Got a mad-dog sergeant, honey, and he won't knock off.
> *Prison Cell Blues*[26]

and hence to images of freedom.

> So nice to be where it's sunshine, I mean snow or rain,
> It's so nice to be where it's sunshine, I mean snow or rain,
> Because I can't go gay-cattin' and carryin' a ball and chain.
>
> *Lock Step Blues*[27]

Blind Lemon's blues created a world of humour, dreaming, occasional violence, the spectre of death and imprisonment, drinking and partying, a sexuality that veers from lust to distrust to pleasure, and continual harkings on the unreliability of women. Lemon himself appears as the one fixed point in a universe of random instability, and his comments on the nature of the world have the quality – and he is not unique in this – of folk proverbs. In 1929, on one of his last records *That Crawlin' Baby Blues*, he extended his vision to an area of experience seldom touched on by the blues, the effect on a baby of an atmosphere of casual promiscuity and family instability. But there is a shifting of identity within the song: is the singer himself perhaps the crawling baby?

> Heard a baby cryin', what do his mama mean,
> Heard a baby cryin', what do his mama mean,
> He's crying 'bout his sweet milk and she won't feed him just the cream.
>
> Crawled from the fireplace and stopped in the middle of the floor,
> Well he crawled from the fireplace and stopped in the middle of the floor,
> Says 'Mama, ain't that your second daddy standing there in the door?'
>
> Well she grabbed my baby, spanked him,
> I tried to make her leave him alone,
> Well she grabbed my baby, spanked him, I tried to make her leave him alone,
> I tried my best to stop her and she said,
> 'This baby ain't none of mine.'
>
> Some woman rocks the cradle and I declare she rules the home,
> Woman rocks the cradle, I declare she rules the home,
> Many a man rocks some other man's baby,
> Fool thinks he's rockin' his own.
>
> Well, it was late last night when I learnt the crawling baby blues,
> I said it was late last night when I learnt the crawling baby blues,
> My woman threw my clothes out doors and now I got the crawling baby blues.[28]

Field recordings

The Race record market boomed in the years 1927 to 1930, with blues and gospel records being issued at a rate of ten a week, more than double the figure for 1925. This meant endlessly scouring the country for new talent. All the recording companies had their talent scouts in the field – musicians, record store proprietors, whites and blacks in all parts of the country would be constantly recommending some new singer or group. Some were brought up North to record, but increasingly it was a matter of going down to the location with portable equipment.

There could be problems on the road. In some parts of the South the new carbon microphones in use since 1925 for electrical recording had to be kept in ice because in hot weather the humidity made them crackle. Then there was the way so many country musicians tended to play – some of them stamped their feet so vigorously as they sang that the engineers had to make them take their shoes off, or stuff pillows under their feet to stop the vibrations affecting the recording.

Even in the regular studios in the North there had always been difficulties, especially with jazz bands. In 1925, when the Western Electric system was in its infancy, a sound engineer recording Bessie Smith once insisted on suspending a conical tent over the singer and her six-piece band to get the correct acoustics. They had just completed a 'take' of *Yellow Dog Blues* when the whole thing collapsed. From under the canvas the Empress of the Blues emerged, cursing and swearing.

But in general the major record companies soon had the correct procedures mastered and had far better facilities in their custom-built studios than could be provided in make-shift circumstances down South. This is how Henry Townsend described the set-up at 666 Lake Shore Drive in Chicago when he was brought there from St Louis by Columbia in 1929:

'Yes, they had something like a small glass wall, I mean it wasn't a glass wall, but small glass in a wall between the musicianers and themselves, and the equipment stand, and they had signal lights down there for cues, a red and a green, and of course it was a pretty good size place the musicianer's part, but the engineers' place was a small place, you know, and it was on the lake front there in Chicago. Course now I think they had several studios, this particular one I was in, I think they had several different departments that they worked in; big bands, I guess, had some place else'.[1]

Field recording sessions could be exciting and nervous occasions. When some white musicians were auditioned by T. G. Rockwell for Okeh Records in Avalon, Mississippi, they recommended their friend Mississippi John Hurt and a session was fixed up for him in Memphis. Many years later, after his 're-discovery' in 1963, John was asked what it had been like:

'I remember a great big hall with only Mr. Rockwell, one engineer and myself; it really was something. I sat on a chair and they pushed the microphone right up close to my mouth, and told me not to move after they had found the right position. Oh I was nervous and my neck was sore for days after . . .'[2]

The hazards of field recording were not only technical; there were also difficulties in finding locations. During one company's trip to Dallas they first tried to rent a room in a hotel but were refused: the management would not allow blacks on the premises. Next they tried setting up in a church, but that led to a near riot when the congregation found out what kind of music they were performing and the gear had to be scrambled out a back door. The next day they tried their luck in a roller-skating rink. 'It was the noisiest damn place in the world'[3], and when drunken skaters started brawling with the musicians and forcing the engineers up against a wall at knife point it was clearly time to move on again. They eventually used a banqueting hall.

During the glorious boom years of blues recording, before the Depression of the 1930's knocked the bottom out of the market, there were five leading companies manufacturing records for the Race market, issuing them under seven main labels – Columbia and Okeh; Paramount; Vocalion and Brunswick; Gennett, and Victor. Paramount were the market leaders and they steadfastly stuck to their system of talent scouting in the South while still recording their artists in their Northern studios. All the others meanwhile made frequent trips to the South, and in the peak years for country blues, from 1927 to 1930, between them they set up seventeen sessions in Atlanta, eleven in Memphis, eight in Dallas, seven in New Orleans, as well as in several other places like San Antonio, Texas or Birmingham, Alabama. While the world of professional show-biz – the tent shows, theatres and cabaret circuits – provided the bulk of women singers, the male artists were to be found in more haphazard circumstances. There were some entertainment circuits, especially the medicine shows, the touring groups touting custom for cheap patent and herbal cures around the rural areas. But the main sources of musicians for recording were the cities.

Nearly every city in the South had its black section, with a 'main stem', the street where the action was. Garish, sordid, bizarre they might be, but for people whose lives were crimped and cramped at every turn, the pleasures of Dallas' Elm Street, Shreveport's Fannin Street, Atlanta's Decatur Street or Memphis' Beale Street, were an outlet of no little significance for black people. In these streets they could create their own communities – more or less – or at least seek their pleasures away from the eyes of the bossman.

When he was interviewed in 1976, 93-year old Gus Cannon, who was sometimes billed as one of The Beale Street Boys, looked back with pained nostalgia at the heyday of Beale, now deeply scarred by urban renewal.

'Oh, you know that was our street! Yeah! But it, it don't look like Beale Street now. They tore down so it just don't look like it to me, down in Memphis'.[4]

Because street-action blues were the everyday backdrop to the lives of the inhabitants, places like Decatur or Beale Street have now taken on a romantic, almost legendary glow, not only for blues historians but also for some of the participants, the people who spent their prime working them. But none of these great musical centres could have existed without the network of shabby neglected back streets just off them, where the poor huddled and struggled through their marginal lives. The fact that life in the cities represented more freedom and more opportunity for poor and ill-educated blacks than the country could offer, gave their blues an added poignancy. Some bluesmen lived and settled in the cities while others passed through, going back to the country. By word of mouth, or by chance hearing, the record company scouts and representatives could pick them up and bring them into their temporary studios.

Atlanta

The field recording sessions in Atlanta were mainly held for white hillbilly music, but it was a good location for blues too. The city itself was a pivotal communications centre, connecting the Deep South to the Atlantic coast and the cities of the North East. Its commercial growth meant that work opportunities were more varied and only about a quarter of the black population had to take labouring jobs. Country migrants were drawn in not only from Georgia itself, but also from neighbouring Alabama and the Carolinas, and despite the backlog of racial tension inherited from the race riot of 1906 and the revival of the Ku Klux Klan in

1915, the black population grew from over 60,000 in 1920 (out of a total of 190,000 plus) to 90,000 out of 270,000 in 1930. Some sections of Atlanta became almost entirely black, which gave some refuge from the sweltering financial and spiritual oppression that afflicted much of Georgia.

But it was scarcely possible to escape entirely the reminders of white supremacist feeling; the K.K.K., anonymously hooded and stirred by the excitement of flaming crosses, held their Klonventions on Stone Mountain overlooking Atlanta. The singer and one-man-band Jesse Fuller once unknowingly worked for a Ku Klux man in a bottle supply factory in Atlanta. By chance he saw the man's hood behind the counter.

'He had me cleaning up and I saw his hood. I didn't want to be part of this trouble. I got my money and left. He treated me alright while I was with him. I just didn't want to be around any more.'[1]

Fuller said in an interview in 1965 that he didn't have too much trouble with whites in Georgia because he wouldn't mix with them. But contact was sometimes unavoidable, as when he had a shoe-shine stand. A white man got on it and said, 'If you gonna shine shoes, white man don't wanna see no negroes on the stand.' Jesse Fuller replied that it was his stand and he'd use it to shine whose shoes he wanted. 'Listen to him sassing you out, by golly,' said another white, and they started punching and beating him. When Jesse hit back still more whites piled in and pulled guns on him.[2]

On this occasion there was no shooting, no lynching or castration, but for blacks this was the climate in which they lived in Georgia, never quite knowing when an incident might occur. Georgia Tom Dorsey, who left Atlanta for Chicago in 1916, said that 'down there, in small towns there, if a white man came walkin' down the street and it was a narrow path, I'd have to get out and let him pass'.[3] Tom prefers not to talk about the Jim Crow laws. 'I try to forget it', he says with a melancholy smile. 'It was nasty as far as I'm concerned!' He talks about his boyhood and days spent happily playing with the white boys who lived across the road from him: 'Nobody bothered us, they come to my house and played with me.' But he also remembers the atmosphere in Georgia which he calls 'a feeling someone was pressing, eventually to make the financial gain, that the black man wouldn't get a chance to do so well financially.' Tom's father was working on a farm 'for 40 or 50 cents a day' until the whole family all moved to Atlanta.[4]

Jobs, better pay, and the attractions of city life brought thousands of blacks into Atlanta where they huddled in those sections where they could get accommodation, in the narrow dirt-track streets of shabby wooden-frame houses. With the extra money and more leisure time, the pickings were ripe for musicians too. Their stamping ground was the famous Decatur Street, the noisy and colourful business and nightlife section, full of barber shops, saloons and taverns, and the 81 Theatre, where Charles P. Bailey bossed the scene (people claimed the theatre circuit initials T.O.B.A. stood for 'Take Old Bailey's Advice'). The singers would hang around either the pool hall on one side of the theatre or in the barber shop on the other, or they would go 'serenading' up the street for tips. Soon after he arrived in Atlanta, Tom Dorsey worked at the 81. 'As a boy I sold pop, ginger ale, red rock at the 81 Theatre. And I got a chance to meet all the stars, all of the performers that came to the theatre to play. And there they'd want a pop or something, a cold drink on credit until payday, and I got a chance to know them all! I stayed round that theatre, I'd hang around the theatre and I learned a lot. And I learned blues, I could play piano, and I think it payed off very well to me.'[5]

By the early 1900's Atlanta had become one of the 'sportingest' towns in the South. The young Perry Bradford was there and claimed there was 'mob-rule' by black and white gangsters in 'bell-bottom pants' and tailor-made 'Plymouth Rock' suits, carrying 'gats'. The brothel area of Cortland Street was run by three white pimps, Fashion-plate Charley, Pretty-boy Redmond and George Jones, while the black gangsters Handsome Harry, Lucky Sambo and Joe Slocum had their thumbs on Decatur Street.

'They controlled all the wild bar rooms which started rolling at five a.m. and closed at midnight. Anyone who knew their way around could always get a belly-full of corn whiskey at Walter Harrison's, Henry Thomas' and Lonnie Reid's joint until daybreak. It was a tame Saturday night in the notorious Decatur Street section if there were only six razor operations performed, or if only four persons were found in the morgue on Sunday morning.'[6]

Before the World War there were plenty of low-down blues piano-players, like Tom Dorsey, then known as 'Barrelhouse Tom'; but the scene gradually changed and the pianists moved on. Tom himself went to Chicago – 'looking for money, man, good money'[7] – and started his career as 'Georgia Tom', working with Ma Rainey and then having Race hits of his own with the 'Guitar Wizard' Tampa Red.

While Tom's old friends moved on and away from Atlanta, a whole crop of new musicians started working Decatur Street, bringing with them the sounds of the rural outlands. Atlanta became a melting pot of blues styles, making it ideal as a source of talent for the record companies. Not only were there the blues of the arid-earthed and poverty-stricken Alabama and parts of Georgia, but also the more delicate and sensitive styles of the so-called Piedmont area. This stretched roughly from Atlanta in the South up to Richmond, Virginia, a plain flanked by the Appalachian mountains in the West and the marshy coastlands of the East and covering parts of North and South Carolina. Much of this area was tobacco country, and there was in any case a richer diversification of agriculture as opposed to the dependence on cotton which left so much of the Deep South so permanently on the edge of economic disaster. Accordingly, the poverty of Piedmont was less severe and with a lower density of black population the whites seemed that little bit more prepared to live in racial harmony.

It seems too that there was more contact between the black and white musical traditions, with the result that the Piedmont blues has a lighter, more outgoing quality compared to the 'black' blues of, say, the Mississippi Delta. There is a world of difference between the driving urgency of a Son House, with his slurred moaning and tense, slashing bottleneck guitar, and the delicate slide work of a Blind Willie McTell.

McTell, who was born near Thomson, Georgia in 1898, could be heard in Atlanta off and on until the 1950's. His range of music was phenomenal, from sensitive slow blues, to quick-fingered twelve-string guitar 'rags', minstrel show songs, religious pieces and even white 'hillbilly' music. A travelling man, he was intermittently recorded from 1927 to 1956, sometimes disappearing only to pop up again, always maintaining the defiant independence of a professional musician. He broke recording contracts as easily as he flipped from style to style, using names like Georgia Bill, Blind Sammie, Pig 'n' Whistle Red, Barrelhouse Sammy and his own name. In the 1930's he was mentor, friend and musical companion to numerous other singers like Curley Weaver, Buddy Moss, Ruby Glaze and his wife Kate McTell, all of whom were on records with him. He was even recorded for the folk archive of the Library of Congress, for which John Lomax paid him ten dollars.

Willie McTell sang with a clear melodic and flexible voice, with an occasionally nasal quality which gave his blues bite. His resonant twelve-string guitar-playing was full of shifting bass rhythms and his slide work flowed with the lightness of his voice, answering his words or extending the feeling. The records he made in the 1920's were some of the most poignant of all those made in Atlanta. His *Statesboro Blues* has a quiet, almost aching magnificence:

> Wake up, mama, turn your lamp down low,
> Wake up, mama, turn your lamp down low,
> Have you got the nerve to drive Papa McTell from your do'?

> My mother died and left me reckless, my daddy died and left me wild,
> Mother died and left me reckless, daddy died and left me wild,
> No, I'm not good lookin', but I'm some sweet woman's angel child.[8]

Blind Willie McTell was just one of the many Atlanta musicians recorded in the 20's. A bunch of them who played Decatur Street were known to everyone as Peg Leg Howell and His Gang. The leader was one of the older musicians in town, being already thirty-five when he reached Atlanta in 1923. Peg Leg gained his name in 1916 when his brother-in-law got mad at him and shot him in the leg; it had to be amputated, forcing him to quit farming. Peg Leg usually worked Decatur Street playing his own guitar together with another guitarist, Henry Williams, and a way-out fiddle player called Eddie Anthony. Sometimes other players would join them with guitars or mandolins and Decatur Street would echo and ring to their raucous little band. They generated a wailing excitement, singing together with extrovertedly exaggerated voices and with Eddie Anthony's 'alley fiddle' scraping away at blues, rags, stomps and even old coon songs like *Turkey in the Straw*. It was in this street that Peg Leg was discovered by a Mr Brown who worked for Columbia Records.

'I was out serenading, playing on Decatur Street and he heard me and taken me up to his office and I played there. He first heard me playing out on the streets,' Peg Leg recalled in March 1964.

'My first record was *New Prison Blues*. In 1925 I had been in prison for selling whiskey and I heard the song there. I don't know who made it up. As for selling the whiskey, I would sell it to anybody who came to the house. I bought the moonshine from people who ran it and I sold it. I don't know how they caught me; they just ran down on me one day. I got paid fifty dollars for my first record. And I got royalties too – they came in twice a year. After the record came out, I used to sing different places around Atlanta, different places where I went. I mostly played along the streets.'[9]

Peg Leg Howell was one of the first Atlanta musicians to be recorded, and his music reflected a patchwork of old work songs, traditional verses and his own material. Apart from the stomps and country dance music he played with his gang, Peg Leg recorded some fine solo blues, slow, rough and introspective. Coming from a street-singing cripple, a bootlegger and ex-prisoner, Peg Leg's blues must have seemed the incarnation of the Devil's Music. In one of his first records the Devil even makes an appearance.

> My friends has turned against me, smiling in my face,
> My friends has turned against me, smiling in my face,
> Since I been disobedient I must travel in disgrace.
>
> I cannot shun the devil, he stays right by my side,
> I cannot shun the devil, he stays right by my side,
> There is no way to cheat, I'm so dissatisfied.
>
> Ain't nobody wants me, they wouldn't be in my shoes,
> Ain't nobody wants me, they wouldn't be in my shoes,
> I be so disgusted, I got those low down rambler blues.
>
> *Low Down Rounder Blues* (1928)[10]

Peg Leg's recording career came to an end before the Depression, but he kept playing in and around the city until the death of his friend Eddie Anthony in about 1936. 'After Eddie Anthony died I just didn't feel like playing any more.'[11] He lost his other leg through diabetes in 1952 and was found living in absolute poverty by George Mitchell in 1963.

Decatur Street wasn't the only place a musician could get work in Atlanta. Robert and Charlie Hicks worked a drive-in stand in a prosperous suburb, cleaning car windscreens and serving barbecued ribs, an occupation which gave Robert his recording name of Barbecue Bob. Both brothers arrived in the city in the early 1920's and lived fast and carelessly. Barbecue Bob was one of Columbia's most popular country blues artists, playing a twelve-string slide guitar in a fast rhythmic style, alternating between bass chords and ringing treble bottleneck. His brother also played a twelve-stringer, sometimes recording as Charley Lincoln, but also providing insane laughter on one of his brother's records as 'Laughing Charley'. Bob's style was straightforward, confident and assertive and he was a regular seller for Columbia. In 1927, when he started recording, Columbia pressed an initial 20,850 copies of his first number, *Barbecue Blues*.

> I'm gonna tell you now gal, like t'gypsy tol' the Jew,
> I'm gonna tell you now gal, like t'gypsy tol' the Jew,
> If you don't want me – it's a cinch I don't want you . . .[12]

Even in 1929, when the American economy began its descent into the Depression, Columbia were pressing about 6,000 copies of Barbecue Bob's records (compared with 9–10,000 for Bessie Smith). But as the economic collapse hastened in 1930, pressings of Bob's records were down to 2,000. He stopped recording in that year and about a year later he died of pneumonia aggravated by influenza at the age of twenty-nine. His brother 'Laughing Charley' went to pieces and took to heavy drinking, never to record again.

Death and the Depression were breaking up the 20's Atlanta scene – even though the musicians were nearly all young men. A superb young harmonica-player Eddie Mapp, who started recording at sixteen or seventeen, was only twenty when he was murdered in the street in November 1931. Barbecue Bob dead, his brother drinking, Peg Leg Howell back to selling moonshine – the heyday was over.

> You've started in moochin', but your moochin's in vain,
> You've started into moochin', but your moochin's in vain,
> Be careful with yourself, you'll get a ball and chain.
>
> Lard and bacon goin' to a dollar a pound,
> That lard and bacon goin' to a dollar a pound,
> Cotton has started to sellin' but it keeps goin' down and down.
>
> Just before election, you was talkin' how you was goin' to vote,
> Just before election, you was talkin' how you was goin' to vote,
> And after election was over, your head down like a billy goat.
>
> Hard times, hard times, sure got hard times now,
> Hard times, hard times, we got hard times now,
> Well just think and think about it, we sure got hard times now.
>
> *We Sure Got Hard Times Now* – Barbecue Bob (1930)[13]

Memphis

> When I get back to Memphis, you can bet I'll stay,
> When I get back to Memphis, you can bet I'll stay,
> And I ain't gonna leave until the Judgement Day.

I love ol' Memphis, the place where I was born,
I love ol' Memphis, the place where I was born,
Wear my box-back suit and drink my pint of corn.
Lord, if I just had the railroad fare! It would be *right* like that!

Going Back to Memphis – Charlie Nickerson and the Memphis Jug
   Band (1930)[1]

As one of the most thriving blues cities in the South, Memphis
was an ideal site for field recording. You could catch barrelhouse
pianists, country guitar-pickers, bottleneck guitarists, male or
female singers and any variety of 'jug band' musicians. All would
be available in Memphis or pretty close by – playing the joints
along the legendary Beale Street, in gambling halls and pool
rooms, serenading up and down the street or set up in the open
air in Handy Park, playing for business conventions in plush
hotels, for 'classy' white dances, at political rallies, or out in the
country playing at fish fries, picnics or plantation hops.

Memphis was one of the most exciting cities in the South in
the 1920's, a magnet for blacks raised in the country, a city of
hope and expectation of a better and less cruelly demanding life.
At the centre of the cotton economy it served parts not only of
Tennessee, but also of Arkansas and Mississippi. The Rev.
Robert Wilkins, himself a blues singer in Memphis in the 1920's
and 30's, as a small boy used to make the long trip to and from
his home in Hernando, Mississippi.

'We would drive a waggon or buggy to Memphis; it was but
twenty-two miles. I hauled five bales of cotton on a two-mule
team from Hernando to Memphis to the cotton shed there on
South Lauderdale (Street). Then I come up here on Front
Street and pick up freight to take back to the merchandise
store.'[2]

Close to the river front there were cotton warehouses and
dozens of sample-rooms, the Cotton Market and Exchange,
dating back to when the Mississippi was the main means of
transport and, as an old-timer recalled, 'them niggers used to
load the packets down on the levvies: up one gangplank they'd
run, with a load so big you couldn't hardly see the man under it,
and down the other to get another load and a-singing all the
time.'[3]

By the 1920's river transport found itself competing with the
railroads, especially the Illinois Central, the Louisville-Nashville
and the Southern, and with Highways 49, 51 and 61 where the
sight of even blacks driving Model-T Fords was increasingly

common. River, rail or road, all were rich in the mythology of the blues – the singers hoboing, 'riding the rods', walking and rambling in the restless search for escape from segregation. Memphis was for many a launching pad for the journey to the North, and many who got there were soon on the move again, while others would stay or drift in and out of town. In the process, Memphis developed its own rowdy, lawless and violent reputation. Roustabouts, boatmen, levee workers – who had to keep the levees built up to protect the city from the river – rail-workers, pullman porters, cotton farmers, drifters, gamblers, musicians, hustlers and prostitutes, all mingled on Beale Street. The harmonica- and guitar-playing leader of the Memphis Jug Band, Will Shade talked to Paul Oliver in 1960 about the old days:

'Sportin' class o' women runnin' up and down the street all night long . . . git knocked in the head with bricks and hatchets and hammers. Git out with pocket knives and razors and so forth. Run off to the foot of Beale and some of them run into the river and drown. Roustabouts on the boats would come in at three and four and five in the mornin' when the boats come in. The *Katy Adams*, they used to call that a woman's boat, a woman's boat on the water. All the women would follow that boat . . . jest pay fifty cents for cabin fare and ride that boat from Memphis down to Rosedale and that's the way they made their money . . . They used to wear their money twixt their legs, hung on a sack tied round their waists . . . and they had so much money, when they got back to Memphis they be humpbackedted, they couldn't straighten up.'[4]

By the time Major R. Raven-Hart, an Englishman, saw Beale Street in 1937, it had already long achieved an almost legendary notoriety. Whatever the realities of its violence, the razor fights, ice-pick killings, shootings and stabbings, and its background of impersonal and commercial sex, it was virtually a tourist attraction.

'We visited Beale Street (really Beale Avenue, but never so called) in the later afternoon, but it is definitely the sort of place that one must be taken to, and by someone of colour. Later in the year, and all through the winter, white visitors are catered for by the "Beale Street Ramblers", whose show admits both races; but at the moment all the drinking-places and cabarets were negro, and (so a large and friendly policeman told us) they do not welcome visitors, especially of the tourist type like ourselves. I do not blame them at all.'

The Major's 'friendly policeman' showed them round some of the landmarks of this 'Main Street of Negro America'.

'This was the Hole-In-The-Wall, where they played craps all night and all day – but you never won anything on account of the fines – whatever you did, you were fined for it, spitting on the dice, or dropping them on the floor – and if you did win you never got away with the money. And this was the Monarch Club, poker mostly, where the boss once shot a nigger for knocking another one down – didn't allow no fighting in that club – but the nigger shot back when he was half dead, and they both died. And the bar here was where Wild Bill shot it up and killed half a dozen. And Fatty was shot there too, and ran out with five bullets in his back, and a nigger undertaker after him, and when he fell down that nigger sat right on his body till his own car came, so's not to lose the burying of him: a big funeral it was.

'And here's where we got Koen for beating up a white woman at a party; she ran out on the street stark naked and him after her, and then he got into the basement here and we broke up the floor and threw tear-gas bombs down, and he got shot when he didn't surrender . . .'[5]

In the early 1900's the Monarch ('The Castle of Missing Men') had already established itself the favourite of country people, with crap shooting, no closing time and barrels of whiskey on the counter. You could get any kind of moonshine, or dope, like reefers and cocaine. The man killed in the incident recounted to the English Major was Bad Sam who for years had been the bouncer. There were regular killings and he would just dump the bodies outside. The Monarch was one of a string of joints run by the 'Czar of the Memphis Underworld' Jim Kinnane – celebrated in one of Robert Wilkins blues *Old Jim Canan's*. He and his brother Thomas also had the Hole-In-The-Wall (a 'rough joint' according to pianist Sunnyland Slim), the Red Light and the Blue Light. At one of Kinnane's places you could bump into Razor Cuttin' Fanny. 'Everytime you see her if you didn't give her that piece of bread and side of fish she cut your throat.'[6] Or down at the Panama there was Mary the Wonder, a voodoo lady. At the Vintage there was prize fighting, at the Midway the sound of rolling blues piano. The favourite haunt of musicians was probably Pee Wee's, which like many of the Beale joints was run by an Italian, W. C. Handy used to hang out there in his Memphis days before the First World War and he knew plenty of blues musicians. The cloakroom was stacked with horns, guitars, violins, bull-fiddles and banjos, and anyone could just pick an instrument and play. A band leader or singer wanting a musician would get one either there or, in the 1920's, at Howard Yancey's office on Beale. Yancey managed most of the jug bands and his office served as a meeting place where people came asking for engagements.

A rather more superior source of employment for the jug bands was the extraordinary Mayor of Memphis, 'Boss' Crump. E. H. Crump had made his name in 1908 trying to stamp out vice on Beale Street, a campaign which had brief success; for a while heads were kept low but soon the joints were jumping again:

> Mr. Crump don' 'low no easy riders here,
> Mr. Crump don' 'low no easy riders here,
> I don't care what Mr. Crump don' 'low,
> Gonna barrelhouse anyhow;
> Mr. Crump can go catch himself some air.[7]

But memories of Crump's efforts, which included passing a law forbidding Negroes to be on the streets after midnight, were enshrined in black memories. One of the most popular bluesmen in Memphis, Frank Stokes, who had a fairly long recording career with Dan Sain as the Beale Street Sheiks, used to sing:

> 'Fore Mr. Crump got here,
> Things went very well,
> Now that he's in town,
> Its like burning hell . . .[8]

From his first term in office in 1909, the Crump political machine came to run not only the city but virtually the entire State of Tennessee for well on forty years. The State, like all the so-called 'Solid South', was dominated by the Democratic Party in a proportion of about two-to-one against the Republicans, who were tainted by the memory of Lincoln as the party who freed the slaves. Through the voting weight of Shelby County, of which the population of Memphis is the heart, the Crump machine could make or break any candidate in the Democratic party simply by swinging the mighty Memphis vote. It is said that when a Pope died two blacks were overheard discussing it.

'Who was he?'

'Oh, a big fellow very important – in a county east o' heah.'

'He died, you say? Who do you reckon Mr Crump is goin' to put in his place?'[9]

Crump's was the era of the great urban bosses, like Curley in Boston, Pendergast in the amazingly corrupt Kansas City, or

Hague – 'I am the law' – in Jersey City. It is a surprising feature of his career that Crump never made a public speech yet, with a population of which 40 per cent was black, he had a keen eye for the publicity gesture which would keep Memphis happy. He had a hand in the creation of Handy Park in 1931 to honour the great composer of *Memphis Blues*, and there would be free boat rides for cripples and organised possum hunts. Each year there were huge picnics at the fairgrounds where jug bands sometimes played; at one such event in the 1940's 30,000 free frankfurters and 1,600 gallons of lemonade were distributed while Crump strolled around tossing firecrackers to the kids under pennants saying 'Thank you Mr Crump'. Memphis could thank Crump for a fairly well-run city, with better public services than many in the South, but at a price. As Crump took his seat on a campaign rostrum, a black politician commented:

'There he sits, ladies and gemmun, and though his skin is white his ole heart's as black as yourn or mine.'[9]

Through ruthless application of a poll-tax he constricted the political influence of the black population and for the duration of his office the democratic process was stifled. Political opponents would find it difficult to find printers to publish campaign literature, or arenas whereby to make public speeches; then too, Crump would take out abusive press adverts against his opponents – 'donkey', 'vulture', 'treacherous', 'venomous', 'no more right to public office than a skunk has to be foreman in a perfume factory'. In the 1940's when the liberals were leading the fight against the poll-tax, writers from the Nashville *Tenessean* got some of the same treatment. One was accused of 'ventosity' and 'a foul mind and wicked heart'; another was called 'unworthy, despicable, a venal and licentious scribbler . . . with the brains of a quagga' and he was compared to a 'wanderoo'. A third was said to have a 'low, filthy, diseased mind', full of 'ululation', and the three together were 'mangy, bubonic rats, yellow to the core'.[9]

Crump was no fool. As a leading investment banker with financial strength in real estate and insurance he had the support of the Memphis establishment. The Crump machine worked by providing jobs for the faithful and the kind of government the establishment required. His legacy was equivocal; on the one hand he was proud of what he had done for Memphis in bribing people with good government, and 'who could want anything better than that?' But as John Gunther remarked, 'out of laziness and fear, participation in the American process passed Memphis by, and for this civic infantilism Mr Crump is alone responsible. Stanley Baldwin once wrote that dictatorship is like a giant beech tree – very fine to look at, but nothing grows underneath.'[9]

In fact something did grow beneath the Crump Machine: jug band music. It didn't originate in Memphis, but became the city's hot music in the 1920's and on into the 1930's. As early as 1905 the first organised jug bands were appearing in Louisville, Kentucky, and soon they were a regular feature at Kentucky racetracks. They started off as bands using cheap household containers like earthenware jugs as well as the more conventional instruments. Around Louisville the jug bands were mainly rag-time and popular dance-orientated using saxophones, trom-bones, cornets and pianos. It was the rougher, bluesier bands which hit Memphis when Will Shade – partly inspired by the records of Louisville's Earl McDonald's Dixieland Jug Blowers – set up the Memphis Jug Band.

The jug was a cheap alternative to a double bass, giving out a low-pitched buzzing sound when blown at different angles – an easy, not to say corny technique, taken for granted for years. You could do it with bottles, coal-oil cans, or anything which would resonate when blown across the top of the neck. Other 'primitive' instruments were paraded, like kazoos – little submarine-shaped instruments which worked on the comb and paper principle. It gave a rasping sound when you hummed through it, rather like a poor man's trumpet. Another favourite was the home-made bass. 'Some people call it a garbage can', said Will Shade, 'but I calls it streamline bass.'[10] Basses like this could be made with a broom handle, a piece of string and any kind of washtub. There were all kinds of tub, jug and washboard bands, or skiffle, jook and spasm, bands, in a line stretching back to the New Orleans street urchins' Razzy Dazzy Spasm Band which was playing at the turn of the century. The tradition of improvising instruments goes back to slavery time when all sorts of objects and utensils were used for rhythmic accompaniments to the juba 'pat', while the dancers slapped their thighs and other parts of their bodies, or the ground, each slap having a different tone. As a child in Florence, W. C. Handy used to make rhythms by scraping a nail across the jawbone of a dead horse and experimented with the sound effects of broom handles, fine tooth combs, and teeth rattling with 'the thumb of our right hand on our goozle or Adam's apple, yelling at the time:

Went down the river,
Couldn't get across,
Paid five dollars for an old gray horse.[11]

In the jug bands some of the instrumentation would be used for purely visual effect and general lunacy ('the white folks like to see us get drunk'[12]), but the serious use of a jug could give an eerie 'bottom' to the sound of a slow blues, especially when combined with the mournful and wailing sound of a harmonica.

By the 1920's the harmonica, or 'mouth harp', already had a fairly long ancestry in black folk culture. Again Handy in his childhood:

'Sometimes we were fortunate enough to have a French harp on which we played the fox and the hounds and imitated the railroad trains – harmonica masterpieces.'[13]

Fox chases, the sounds of baying and yipping hounds and train imitations seem to have been the standard fare and lots of people could do them. There were various fine harp-players recorded as solo or lead artists in the 20's, like the tiny De Ford Bailey, a hump-backed Nashville shoeshine 'boy' (any black of whatever age would be a 'boy' to the whites) who was the only regular black performer on the white country music show 'Grand Ole Opry' on Nashville's WSM Radio. His signature tune was *Pan-American Blues*, a blasting performance like an on-rushing train. They claimed to treat him as a mascot, but for him that meant 'I wasn't getting but four or five dollars a night, and they kept me standing at the back'.[14]

There were other solo harp-blowers in the 20's, like Jaybird Coleman and George 'Bullet' Williams of Alabama, and both developed a highly vocalised tone of harmonica, with strange buzzing and wailing sounds. Coleman (who is said to have been managed by the Ku Klux Klan in 1929) had echoes of the field holler in his singing, and he added responses on the harp, creating weirdly masked and distorted effects when he mingled both voice and harp sounds. Bullet Williams also had impressive technique on his small group of recordings like *Frisco Leaving Birmingham* and *The Escaped Convict*, both from 1928. In 1976 he was affectionately recalled by one of his old companions on the road, the unrelated Big Joe Williams:

'Once, at time I had one partner, one buddy, I only had one buddy could keep up with me, and I guess you've read about him, George 'Bullet' Williams. He's disappeared many years, 20 years, 30 years ago. He had a little mistake – drunk in Jackson –

and I think they put him in the pen (?) and I ain't never located him. Harp playing guy he was, called him "Hounds on the Harp".[15]

It is the crying sound of the human voice which carried the instrument beyond the train imitations and the sound of fox chases. Blues musicians play the harp with cupped and fluttering hands, dragging out the notes, then damping them down, squeezing and opening the sound as the tongue and lips work over the reeds, blocking or half covering them to dirty the tone and bend the notes. Of all instruments perhaps the harmonica comes closest to the essence of the blues, the simple expressiveness of the human voice, putting into sound the feelings that are beyond words.

Blues harp was a central feature of several of the jug bands playing not only in Memphis. There were similar small groups in Dallas, Atlanta, Birmingham and elsewhere but the best remembered were from Memphis – Jed Davenport's Beale Street Jugband; Jack Kelly's South Memphis Jug Band, which featured the bluesy violin of Will Batts rather than harp; Gus Cannon's Jug Stompers and the most commercially successful of them all, the Memphis Jug Band.

Will Shade was paid a regular retainer by Victor Records, and he dominated and organised the Memphis Jug Band through a recording career lasting from 1927 to 1934. He had a large and fluctuating line-up. Some of the musicians were briefly members only to move on to solo careers of their own, like singer-guitarist Furry Lewis, while others just played intermittently. There were so many musicians who occasionally played in the Memphis Jug Band it was sometimes possible to make up two separate bands to play at different dances at the same time. At other times when work was slack they might work the streets in ones and twos. Although in group composition the Memphis Jug Band might have been haphazard, musically they were anything but. Will Shade, a perfectionist who tirelessly rehearsed the band, was in firm control both in liaising with the record company and as the musical ideas man. He made sure his was a precision outfit. Before a recording session each musician knew exactly what to do and when to do it, and while the results were often full of spontaneity, they were never sloppy. 'Play that thing man, you know that's all my peoples all together there!'[16]

Many of their songs were harmony vocals, producing a strong element of wistfulness in the slow blues and good-time raucousness in the fast dance tunes. Often group members would interject remarks and instructions.

'Benny, you a fool with that thing!'
'Son, you play that thing . . . just listen to that harp!'
'Wonder what is that now? Oh, it's *Move that thing*, ain't it?'
'Play it again – you ain't played it but once!'[17]

Dance tunes, waltzes, minstrel songs, songs of lyrical melodiousness, harp-blasting breakdowns, rocking mandolins, strutting guitar rhythms, the Memphis Jug Band could do them all, on demand, for any occasion; but they excelled at slow blues, like their famous *Stealin', Stealin'*, where the group vocals are perfectly integrated in a melancholy lilt, with Will Shade's bluesy back-up harp-playing weaving in and out of the lines, following the words.

> Stealin', stealin', pretty mama, don't you tell on me,
> I'm stealin' back to my same old used-to-be,
> Now put your arms across me like the circle round the sun,
> I want you to love me, mama, like my easy rider done;
> If you don't believe I love you, look what a fool I've been,
> If you don't believe I'm sinkin', look what a hole I'm in.
> Stealin', stealin', pretty mama, don't you tell on me.
> I'm stealin' back to my same old used-to-be,
> I'm stealin', stealin', pretty mama, don't you tell on me,
> I'm stealin' back to my same old used-to-be . . .[18]

Of all the jug bands the greatest was perhaps Gus Cannon's Jug Stompers which featured the wonderfully expressive harmonica of Noah Lewis. Gus Cannon described Lewis to researcher Bengt Olsson, who has done an enormous amount to document blues activity in the Memphis area.

Gus met Noah near Ripley, Tennessee, in 1910: 'Lawd, he used to blow the hell outa that harp. He could play two harps at the same time . . . through his mouth and nose, same key and same melody. Y'know he could curl his lips 'round the harp and his nose was just like a fist. Noah, he was full of cocaine all the time – I reckon that's why he could play so loud and aw, he was good!'[19]

His playing was so strong and loud he could play with brass bands at frolics in the country around Henning, Tennessee.

Gus and Noah recorded together in the Jug Stompers in the late 1920's. With the clip of banjos or guitar underpinning the slowly rhythmic group sound, Noah Lewis' harp-playing had a magnificently controlled grace and melancholy strength, sometimes taking the lead but also drifting and floating back into the ensemble-playing to mingle with the kazoo or Cannon's oilcan 'jug'. Lewis was also one of the group's singers, and he sang with a sad, almost choking voice.

> The judge he pleaded, clerk he wrote it down,
> Clerk he wrote it down indeedy,
> The judge he pleaded, clerk he wrote it down,
> If you get jail sentence, you must be Nashville bound,
> Some got six months, some got a solid . . .
> Some got one solid year, indeedy,
> Some got six months, some got one solid year,
> But me and my buddy got lifetime here . . .[20]

Gus Cannon himself, who was born in 1883 ('They started to raise me in Mississippi, but the rope broke . . .'[21]), is one of the oldest blues musicians on record. He could play the fiddle, but by the 1920's was mainly a banjoist and a tremendously popular performer on the travelling medicine shows. The bigger ones were almost on the scale of tent shows, but many just sold off the back of trucks or wagons. Gus travelled with several different shows off and on from 1914 to 1929. He told Bengt Olsson:
'Dr Stokey out of Clarksdale, Mississippi, was the first doctor I went out with. It was a good show . . . comedians . . . oh, they'd cut up . . . dancers and me and ole Elijah Avery, he was a guitar and banjo player . . . good too. Had all that cork on our face . . . made us look even blacker . . . shit . . . painted our mouths white . . . made 'em look big . . . I had to have a shot of liquor before the show. If I didn't it seemed like I couldn't be funny in front of all them people. When I had one it seemed like them people was one and I would throw up the banjo in the air and really put on a show. Y'know, the doctor would advertise his stuff and I'd run out there in the audience with soap, tonics . . . oh, all kinds . . . say, "Hold your hand up if you want it!" . . . after a while: "Sold out, doc!" and he'd give me some more medicine . . . one bottle for a quarter; three for a dollar! Ha, ha . . . that was a fast talking devil. I'd sell that and we'd go on with the show.'[22]

He was a fine blues singer in his own right and started recording as Banjo Joe in 1927 with Blind Blake, including an incredible performance on slide banjo. As leader of the Jug Stompers from around 1928 to 1930 he was at his peak, holding the band together with perfect musical control and giving it a haunting blues quality. But some of the band's material had much of the flavour of the 'Doctor' show.

> I 'member the time just before the war,
> Colored man used to hunt him out chips and straw,
> But now, bless God, old marster dead,

Colored man plumb fool about feather bed,
Eeh, wee, my dear Nancy, over the road
I'm bound to go . . .

Feather Bed (1928)[22]

Gus had richly justified pride in his abilities, especially given that he had no education and had to get along on what he called 'mother wit'. Three years before he died in 1979 he gave one of his last interviews, when he was 93 and partially deaf. He talked about his music and where he got his ideas. 'Oh, I usually lyin' in bed, dream of things. I dream, I get up, git my banjo and try to play whatever's on my mind. Then I wouldn't forget it. That's the way I learnt. Ain't nobody learnt me nothing, but I hear the other fellows play something that I like I go home see could I play it. But when I got old now can't remember back there, can't remember like I used to. 93, so I think I'm doing pretty well. I done put out something of it, it help me to live on. So I hope you all hear it, I'm giving you what I got. I don't know, I may be dead tomorrow but you got what Gus Cannon put out.'[24]

One of the bigger medicine shows, travelling with a tent and even employing a pianist, was the Red Rose Minstrel Show. The Albino barrelhouse pianist Speckled Red was with the show along with the balding, jovial songster Jim Jackson. 'They sold what they call *Gen Sing*,' recalled Red. 'It had some kind of alcohol in it. Good for anything. Fact it wasn't good for nothin'. Sold different kinds a' soaps, some kind of medicated soap. Oh they made plenty money! Don't need to worry 'bout that. He sold plenty medicine.'[25]

Jim Jackson was a 'name' in Memphis with his line in minstrel songs and simple blues. He recorded one of the biggest hits in the late 1920's with *Jim Jackson's Kansas City Blues Parts 1 and 2* which sold it tens of thousands. It was so popular it was remade in Parts 3 and 4, to be followed by two parts of *I'm Gonna Move to Louisiana* using exactly the same tune! Jackson was well-known around Hernando in North Mississippi, where in the early part of the century a whole clutch of guitarists were playing, like the immensely popular Frank Stokes, Elijah Avery (of Cannon Stompers fame), 'Guitar pickin'' Buddy Taylor, and Robert Wilkins. Stokes was a regular feature of the street serenading scene in Memphis, but also played the back country suppers and picnics. As Lincoln Jackson told Bengt Olsson:

'In 'em days we had what you call moonlight picnics you know. They'd last for three days straight! Out in the woods y'know;

lotsa shade and ain't no-one gonna bother you out there. People come in buggies or horseback from miles aroun'. In the nite we'd lite rags with oils so everythin' be fine . . . barbecued hogs, goats an' chicken; had lotsa moonshine whiskey an' crap games. Man, we had ourselves a time. That's the kind of occasion Frank'd play for us.'[26]

Stokes, who was described by another of Olsson's informants as a 'good ole choked-up singer', survived to the age of 90 after a career hardly dependent on his brief spell of recording between 1927 and 1929.

No more dependent on records was Robert Wilkins who turned away from the blues in 1936, to devote himself to religion. 'It was just a sudden thing,' he told Pete Welding. 'Look like something appealed to me and I heard it; said "Don't do it no more".'[27] But in his day as a bluesman he was one of the most expressive of singers, with a voice which dipped and ran to the fluent lines of his melodic guitar. His records certainly helped get him work whenever he wanted it around 1928 and he played 'pig stands', sporting houses, hotels, house parties, white children's parties, college dances and even police parties – 'nothing there but captains and polices and sergeants'. Sometimes he'd just drop in a police station and play in the lobby.

'I never did have any trouble with them. Sometimes I'd meet them late at night, on the streets and they'd stop me – some that didn't know me – and I'd tell them where I'd been playing, and they'd want to know what I could do with a guitar to play for white people's parties. And I'd tell them I'd play most anything they'd want to hear. They'd just tell me to strike it, so I'd strike them a couple of pieces. He'd maybe hand me a dollar and drive on off.'[28]

His records of 1928–35 have a relaxed ease, but the touch of vibrato in his voice gives his performances an introspective intensity.

> I'll certainly treat you just like you was white,
> I'll certainly treat you just like you was white,
> That don't satisfy you, girl, I'll take my life.
>
> I love you girl, I will tell the world I do,
> I love you girl, I will tell the world I do,
> And that's the reason you treat me like you do.
>
> *Falling Down Blues* (1929)[29]

Not all of the blues singers recorded in Memphis necessarily made the city their regular base. Several sessions were arranged by the white owner of a music store in Jackson, Mississippi, H. C. Speir, who was a talent scout for all the major companies. Some sessions he fixed in Memphis, others in the North, but he was intimately involved in the recording careers of some of the greatest of all the Mississippi singers – Charley Patton, Tommy Johnson, Ishmon Bracey, the Chatmons, and on and on in an almost inexhaustible list.

Tommy Johnson and Ishmon Bracey recorded in Memphis in sessions also involving Charlie McCoy and the magnificent Rosie Mae Moore. With his few but popular records, Tommy Johnson spread a reputation as one of the finest and most influential of all the country bluesmen. He had come under the spell of the great cluster of musicians at Dockery's Plantation before the First World War – not only Charley Patton, but other musicians too, both recorded and unrecorded, like Willie Brown and Josie Bush, Dick Bankston, Ben Maree, Henry Sloan and Tommy's brother Ledell. This ferment of musical creativity had a profound influence on Johnson even though he explained his musical talent to Ledell by saying he'd 'sold himself to the devil'.[30]

In his wandering career, and with a succession of 'wives', Tommy Johnson made a big impact on the city of Jackson in the 1920's where there were many superb blues singers. With a more self-conscious awareness of musical excellence, these were far closer to being professional or semi-professional musicians than the casual back country musicians of the Dockery days. They would serenade the streets, or play dances for the white folks – waltzes, two-steps, the black bottom, ragtime, blues – anything the customers wanted. They formed a friendly community, with Charlie McCoy, several of the Chatmons – who were to become tremendously popular in the 1930's – Walter Vincent, Rubin Lacy, and many others. As the Rev. Rubin Lacy told Tommy Johnson's biographer David Evans:

'Lots of people would come in there to Jackson, in and out, just didn't live there. If he could play anything, naturally we boys that lived there would always welcome other musicians. Naturally you couldn't tell what you could learn about them . . . Just come on to Jackson, and we got together and got to playing good music.'[31]

H. C. Speir of course was quick to pick up most of the best talent for recording, and one of these was Tommy Johnson.

Tommy's style betrays comparatively little of Charley Patton's influence. His voice is clear and high with repeated use of a gentle falsetto which owes nothing to the rough incomprehensibility of the older man. The guitar playing too, while using some riffs clearly related to the Patton-Willie Brown style, has a more regular beat, with a characteristic series of bass patterns, almost 'walking-basses', picked up by numerous guitarists over the next thirty years. Charlie McCoy accompanied Johnson to produce a beautifully integrated guitar combination, with a series of repeated progressions of a haunting persistence. In the main Johnson's songs used traditional verses, but the classical purity of his performances made them definitively his own. Among the records he made in Memphis are blues everafter associated with his name.

> I asked for water, and she gave me gasoline,
> I asked for water, and she gave me gasoline,
> I asked for water, and she gave me gasoline, Lord, Lordy, Lord.
> Crying, Lord, 'I wonder will I ever get back home?'
> Crying, Lord, 'I wonder will I ever get back home?'
>   Lord, Lordy, Lord.
> *Cool Drink of Water Blues*[32]

Another of H. C. Speir's finds was the rather aloof, enigmatic and detached figure of Skip James, who was on the Jackson scene in the 1920's but seems to have kept himself very much apart. His recording career was brief and, with the Depression beginning to bite, not commercially successful.

> Sing this song and I ain't gonna sing no more,
> Mmmmmm . . .
> Hard times will drive you from door to door[33]

Like Rubin Lacy, Ledell Johnson and Ishmon Bracey, Skip turned to the Church and it was not until the folk revival of the 60's that he sang the blues again. Although his blues are part of a small but flourishing local tradition in his native Bentonia, Mississippi, the icy precision of his playing and the self-conscious artistry of his music set him apart making him appear both highly individual and even idiosyncratic. His piano-playing in particular, with tumbling cascades of notes and unpredictable pauses, freezes comparisons with others. His aloofness, almost amounting to arrogance, and his own acute awareness of the seriousness of his music, were part of an introspective and philosophical nature.

'This world is fulla people seekin' the advantage of other people . . . Now this type of person don't care about anything and the least thing he get, he'll make out with it. He don't have no sympathy for those that are tryin' to do right and be honest . . . You go to Dallas, Texas; there's a place where you can pay fifty cents and see anything you want. Some guys there would sell their brothers. Crimes against nature: make you sick to your stomach.

'I never did seek for those things, but it's a good idea sometimes to experience things because heap of times everybody ain't gonna tell you exactly how things are. You might think or say, "Aw, I don't believe that humans would do things like that". Well, you take your fifty cents then you go there and you'll see things you may not think are existing in this world.'[34]

Whether with piano or with guitar, Skip James' blues are eerily intense; the taut line of his voice, sometimes smoothing into falsetto, and the studied effects of his instrumental accompaniment make his records some of the most impressive of all the Mississippi country blues.

> I would rather be dead and six feet in my grave,
> I would rather be dead and six feet in my grave,
> Than to be way up here, honey,' treated this a-way.
>
> And the old people told me, baby, but I never did know,
> The old people told me, baby woman, but I never did know,
> 'The Good Book declare you got to reap just what you sow'.
>
> When your knee bone achin' and your body cold,
> When your knee bone's achin' and your body cold,
> Means you just gettin' ready, honey, for the cypress grove.
>
> *Cypress Grove Blues*[35]

Part Five

The Depression

The Great Depression of the 1930's devastated America; it was a material, spiritual and emotional disaster directly affecting the lives of millions of people. Within the space of a few months, from the end of 1929, the nation faced almost unparalleled social dislocation as banks collapsed, savings were wiped out, factories shut down, mortgages were foreclosed and economic failure followed failure. Shocked and uncomprehending, people shuffled in bread lines, took what food they could get from soup kitchens in the streets, before starting back on the hopeless task of finding a job. All over the country there were aimless and dispirited wanderers, transients endlessly leaping onto passing freight trains to take them anywhere there might be work, sleeping rough in makeshift shanty towns, or wrapped in newspapers wherever they could find a place to lie. There were blacks and whites, people who had once been prosperous, others who had always been on the edge of disaster, some with good education, others with none, old people and especially young people, all joined the ranks of the unemployed and the dispossessed. For some such privation was nothing new, hard times had been normality even in the prosperity of the 20's, but for others the blow was numbing, leaving them floundering for pride and self-esteem in a world which appeared to be closing in and collapsing.

There had been tremors and warnings before but the disaster really began with the Wall Street Crash of 1929. At first the effect of the sudden and dramatic collapse of stock market values was limited to the world of finance in which bankers and brokers hoped for the establishment of a 'more secure technical position', but when 40 billion dollars were wiped off share values in the last quarter of 1929 it became inevitable that the disaster would spread. More than 5,500 banks and over 100,000 businesses failed by 1932; a quarter of the railroad companies were bankrupt and everywhere factories were closing down. Workers had their wages cut or working hours shortened, but many were simply fired. Between 1929 and 1932 America's national income was halved and unemployment reached grotesque proportions. In the spring of 1930 there were 3 million out of work, rising to 4 million by the autumn; by the end of 1931 there were 7 million and still the worst had not been reached. Gloom and despondency were sometimes relieved by hopes that all would be well if only that elusive 'confidence' could be restored to the business world. But by the autumn of 1932 unemployment had reached 11 million; the following year statistics simply broke down and while roughly a quarter of the work force were out of work the exact figure could have been anything between 12 and 15 million.

A disaster of this magnitude was quite inconceivable to those of the 1920's who had felt that 'the business of America is business'. In that decade expansion of industry and the growth of commerce had seen the national income almost double. There was apparently unparalleled prosperity and faith in financial and economic institutions was boundless. It was believed that business success was the reward of individual effort and was a sign of almost righteous merit, while failure was thought to be caused by personal inadequacies of character. Alongside the faith in 'rugged individualism', it was also believed that the accumulation of wealth at the top of society would bring benefits to all, that wealth would 'trickle down'. It was generally agreed that government intervention in the economy would be positively harmful to the generation and spread of wealth and so there was little concern for social or structural reform. 'Sound' opinion held it as axiomatic that people could either raise themselves by their own efforts or else they would benefit from the general prosperity.

The flaw in this belief, and the ultimate cause of the collapse of the economy, was the sheer scale of poverty and the dislocating effect of a widening imbalance in the distribution of wealth.

The gulf between rich and poor was so great that the 36,000 wealthiest families had incomes that equalled the total combined income of the 12 million poorest families. The living conditions of these 12 million families, or 42 per cent of the population barely reached the level of subsistence. Poverty was so great in rural areas that many homes had neither running water nor electricity. In Mississippi only 2 per cent of farm homes had running water and a mere 0.5 per cent had electricity.

In the context of this scale of deprivation and want, the

expansion of industrial and manufacturing capacity outstripped the market's ability to support it, supply exceeded demand and the edifice collapsed. The growth of mass industry meant that sectors of the economy were so locked into dependence on each other that failure in one part brought disaster to another, till the whole structure started to fall like a house of cards. Prosperity and industrial expansion had been based on the ruthless use of mass-production techniques, with moving assembly lines and time and motion studies bringing economies of scale. Economic power became concentrated in the hands of the large corporations and industrial giants; the automobile industry alone had 3,700,000 workers directly or indirectly dependent on it for their jobs. Mass-production, while seeming to offer unlimited possibilities of expansion, was however totally dependent on there being a mass market; as some industrialists like Henry Ford were aware, purchasing power had to keep pace with production. It was the failure to maintain this purchasing power on the part of the population that was the central flaw in the mounting orgy of stock market speculation that preceded the Crash, for while in the 1920's corporation profits and share dividends both rose by over 60 per cent, real wages only rose 11 per cent. Nor was that the only problem in the development of a mass market. While the mechanization of industry, and to an extent agriculture, was increasing manufacturing capacity and worker productivity, it was also pushing people out of jobs. With American agriculture already depressed in the 1920's, the economy was further weakened by a decline in world trade as country after country sought to protect itself behind tariff barriers in order to keep out foreign goods. With markets shrinking and purchasing power not increasing rapidly enough there were signs of trouble well before the Crash. 'Something is happening in Chicago,' warned the *Chicago Defender* in early 1929, 'and it should no longer go unnoticed. During the past three weeks hardly a day has ended that there has not been a report of another firm discharging its employees.'[1]

A familiar pattern was beginning to manifest itself; blacks, always the last to be hired, were the first to be fired, but the omen of hard times for all, black and white, was ignored.

Poverty was nothing new for blacks even in the Northern cities where work and comparative prosperity had continued to draw blacks from the South throughout the 1920's. During that decade a further 773,000 had been lost to the South through migration. But for all the jobs in the steel mills, stockyards, food processing

and packing factories, and for all the improvements in democratic and political rights, poverty was the foundation of life for
the black ghetto. In 1928, well before the Crash, Blind Blake was
already proclaiming:

It's a hard time, good man can't get no dough,[2]

while for Big Bill Broonzy, another Chicago-based blues singer,
it was:

Starvation in my kitchen, rent sign's on my do'.[3]

As Georgia Tom remarked, 'I don't know what brought on the
Depression, I don't know: I didn't feel so depressed for I didn't
have a thing to start with.'[4]

In one eighteen-month period rents trebled for one small
section of the black ghetto in Detroit where 15,000 people were
crammed in virtual shanties. A common answer to the problem
was the widespread tenement institution of the House Rent
Party which flourished in all the cities of the North under a
dozen different names, Too Tight parties, Too Terrible parties,
Chitterlin' Rags, Calico Hops, Kados, Skittles, house shouts,
house hops, Juggles and Struggles, Stomps, breakdowns and
boogies. When rent day was due, you 'pitched a boogie', inviting
the neighbours round and charging an entrance fee of perhaps a
quarter and a jug of gin.

'They call them house-rent parties,' recalled Little Brother
Montgomery, 'and they call them Blue Monday parties. Just like
you've got a house, he got one, she got one. You know, Tuesday
night we'd be over to Miss Lumpton, and next time we'd be over
to Miss McGee, and then all the people from that party would go
patternise (*patronise*) the other person. The gang at this party
they'd be at the next party.'[5]

Like Little Brother, Georgia Tom used to play piano at the
Chicago rent parties:

'I had a circuit, I had a place to play every night. If you got 50
cents, or 35 cents a night for playing piano for 3 or 4 hours you
had good money. They'd have to raise this rent money and they
would have these house-rent parties to raise their money. I got in
with a bunch there, so I walked round dressed up in the day and
played at night. It wasn't much, they give you a little something,
best you got was all that you could drink, all you could eat and a
good-looking woman to fan you, that's about the best you'd get.'[6]

Born of acute poverty, the rent party was also an outlet for the
frustrations and neuroses of overcrowded ghetto life. With music

provided by pianists like Speckled Red, or countless others, the success of such parties led to some apartments being run on semi-permanent lines as Good-Time Flats or Buffet Flats, where prostitution, gambling and bootlegging flourished, bringing the ghetto further into the racketeer's web of police bribery and protection money.

When the Depression hit the cities another community institution which helped relieve poverty and distress was the Church. Many of the little store-front churches set up 'thrift shops' selling shoes and clothes at minimal prices. The charismatic religious leader Father Divine established a chain of co-operatives providing meals free or for 15 cents in restaurants and coal at cost from coal yards. Shoeshine parlours and barber shops gave other cheap services while further food was given away at religious meetings.

> If I could tell my troubles, it would give my poor heart ease,
> But depression has got me, somebody help me please.
>
> *Depression Blues* – Tampa Red (1931)[7].

At first relief of distress was almost entirely provided by local authorities with very little help from the Federal Government, but with their own funds depleted by falling revenues, the States and cities were quite unable to cope. Some managed more than others – Toledo, Ohio, provided 50,000 meals a day at 6 cents each – but the scale of the national problem was too great. In Birmingham, Alabama, where in January 1932 only 8,000 out of 108,000 workers were receiving normal wages and 25,000 were completely out of work, the city set up a canal construction project providing 750 jobs – there were over 12,000 applications. In many areas, especially in the already poor South, it became impossible even to maintain existing expenditure; in Alabama 81 per cent of the children at school were on enforced vacation through cuts in education spending.

When it came to relief in the South, whites almost always got assistance more quickly and more fully than blacks. The work given to blacks was the toughest and lowest paid; in 1932 blacks working on State government camps in Mississippi were receiving a mere ten cents an hour, working twelve hours a day, seven days a week. Provision for blacks was rather better in the North and by 1933 fully 35 per cent of black families were on public relief in Ohio, Illinois and Pennsylvania.

Federal intervention was minimal in the early part of the Depression because the President, Herbert Hoover, continued to subscribe to the prevailing notions of the years of prosperity, which meant reliance on individual self-help. He believed that public relief would sap morale and resolve, leading to a degeneration of the individual's will. The measures Hoover did undertake proved wholly inadequate: they were too little and too late. It also appeared to many that his efforts at intervention were disproportionately directed towards helping business out of an almost mystical faith in a business-led recovery. He seemed blind to the contrast between the help in this direction and his apparently heartless refusal to provide more public relief. Gloomy, aloof and estranged from the public, he became the butt of a wry and bitter humour. Newspapers became 'Hoover blankets', and the names 'Hoovervilles' or 'Hoover Valley' were applied to the pathetic makeshift shanty towns constructed at the edge of cities or wherever the homeless or transients congregated.

> . . . And we have a little city that they call down in Hooverville,
> Times has got so hard, they ain't got no place to live.
>
> *It's Hard Time* – Joe Stone (1933)[8]

The gray despondency that emanated from Hoover's White House was promptly dispelled by his successor Franklin D. Roosevelt who won the election of 1932 and took office the following year. F.D.R. entered the Presidency promising a 'New Deal' to the American people, and his approach and demeanour was in marked contrast to his predecessor. He exuded radiance and confidence with an easy smile, a jaunty wave and a lively disdain for his crippled legs. His broad Harvard accent had a warmth of tone and friendliness of delivery that brought him popularity through his regular 'fireside chats' on the radio. While Hoover had seemed depressed and dispirited and his Administration dull and disconsolate, Roosevelt's entourage were bubbling with ideas and a dozen schemes.

> He woke up one morning he was feeling might bad,
> He woke up one morning he was feeling might bad,
> He began to think about the poor people and he began to feel sad.
>
> 'Fight on, boys, fight on, I'll make everything all right,
> Fight on, boys, fight on, I'll make everything all right,
> If I don't see you November, I'll see you Christmas night.'
>
> *President Blues* – Jack Kelly and His South Memphis Jug Band (1933)[9]

It seemed that at last the 'forgotten man' would be remembered and that the will existed to bring relief to the struggling masses of poor and unemployed. If he achieved nothing else Roosevelt transformed the atmosphere and emotional climate of the Depression. Where before all was despondency and a bitter but hopeless apathy, the New Deal raised spirits and re-awakened the hopes and energies of America.

In 1933 a bewildering patchwork of 'alphabetical' Federal agencies were set up to encourage economic recovery, provide relief and in some cases initiate reform. There was the Agricultural Adjustment Agency (AAA) to revive farm prices, the National Recovery Administration (NRA) to bring stimulation and regulation to commerce and industry through pricing codes, and by the end of 1934 over two thousand million dollars had been spent providing relief through the Federal Emergency Relief Administration (FERA), the Civil Works Administration (CWA) and the Public Works Administration (PWA). In a land which had had no provision for unemployment insurance and virtually no Federal relief, there was an amazing 11 million living on relief by January 1934, rising to 19 million by December. In some Northern cities 50 per cent of black families, and sometimes more, depended on relief. The most favoured and least demoralising kind was the work project, where relief was in the form of wages in return for working on schemes like building and repairing schools, laying playgrounds or digging drains. In the space of a month the CWA put more than 4,200,000 people to work on such projects.

> I hollered, 'Hey woman,
> Lawd, God, is you goin' my way?
> 'Cause I got a job workin' for the CWA.'
>
> *CWA Blues* – Walter Roland (1934)[10]

But while the early New Deal measures and the sense of dynamism they generated did much to lift the gloom of the Depression, they did not bring unalloyed benefits, especially to black people. The Agricultural Adjustment Administration brought further disaster to the already impoverished sharecroppers of the South. In order to raise farm prices the AAA paid subsidies to farmers to limit production by ploughing crops under and reducing planting, and while these subsidies were perhaps of some benefit to owners and planters, the effect was devastating for workers, tenants and sharecroppers. Cuts in production led to many being pushed off the land, with no jobs to go to. The National Recovery Administration led its drive towards regulating industry with a bonanza of propaganda cavalcades, posters and badges emblazoned with the NRA Blue Eagle. It introduced price codes and certain measures to protect workers, particularly enshrining the right to join a union. But as blacks were not involved in fixing the codes, and as discrimination kept them out of most unions, the result for many was higher prices and the loss of jobs. Many blacks came to feel that NRA stood for 'Negroes Ruined Again'.

> Now I'm gettin' tired of sittin' around,
> I ain't makin' a dime, just wearin' my shoe-soles down,
> Now everybody's cryin' 'Let's have a New Deal,
> 'Cause I've got to make a livin' if I have to rob and steal.'
>
> *Let's Have a New Deal* – Carl Martin (1935)[11]

While the New Deal did bring some benefits to black people and the provision of relief kept many from actual starvation, poverty and discrimination both in the cities and in the rural South remained fundamentally the same. Despite specific instructions against racial discrimination in providing Federal relief, for blacks in the South it was still harder to get onto relief rolls and grants were often lower.

Virtually the whole range of services provided by city and State governments was inferior to those provided for whites. They always had been. In education, for example, the difference was enormous: in 1935–36 Mississippi and Georgia spent an average of only 9 dollars per black child per day, compared with 45 dollars a day per white child. In ten Southern States the value of segregated black schools was worth only one fifth that of white schools. The difference in school expenditure was often greatest in those States where the proportion of blacks in the population was highest; having raised taxes equally from black and white alike, the higher amounts spent on white schools were being effectively paid for by blacks.

In the North there was less direct discrimination either in the provision of relief or in expenditure on public services. The cities were anyway richer than the South, and while Alabama, Arkansas, and Mississippi had an overall average expenditure of 30 dollars a day per pupil, in New York it was 115 dollars. But even in the North education for blacks and poor whites was hindered by overcrowding in schools in the densely populated poor areas.

> Lord, Mister President, listen to what I'm going to say,
> Lord, Mister President, listen to what I'm going to say,
> You can take away all of the alphabet but please leave the PWA.
>
> *Don't Take Away My PWA* – Jimmy Gordon (1936)[12]

Unemployment remained the most persistent problem of the Depression, not only for blacks but for whites too. It was the visible reminder that the economy remained unbalanced and inequitable. Throughout the 1930's there were never less than 7 million people out of work and unemployment on this scale was only ended by the Second World War when war industries and military expenditure soaked up the vast pool of excess labour. Roosevelt's lack of overall strategy led to a shift from one scheme to another, some designed purely to relieve distress, others to increase purchasing power by 'priming the pump', and some aimed at making worthwhile public works and conservation schemes, like the programme Sam Chatmon worked on in Mississippi in 1934, cutting the ditches down through the East Delta. 'I worked on that for 6 bits a day, cuttin' ditches and the snow was so deep that we have to wade through to get a chance to cut the trees, and walk across to a little bridge on ice.'[13]

In 1935 a combination of Federal State and local funds were supporting over 6,400,000 households involving more than 22,470,000 people. In other words 17 per cent of the American population were relying on relief. In that year one of the most important agencies of the Depression years was started, the Works Progress Administration, or WPA; by the next year it was giving work to more than 3 million people on projects involving parks, zoos, playgrounds, sewerage, airports, public buildings, slum clearance, rural housing, rural electrification, land reclamation, soil erosion prevention, reafforestation, roads, schools and hospitals. While 80 per cent of the projects involved labouring or construction work, the WPA also financed a variety of arts schemes for actors, musicians and painters. There were also literacy classes run by the WPA which brought benefits especially to black children and even adults.

Despite the vast amount of public work taken on by the WPA, there were many criticisms, particularly that the jobs being created were pointless and unnecessary and to which were applied the term 'boondoggle'. Another complaint was that WPA workers were idle layabouts – 'Don't shoot our still-life – it may be a WPA worker at work.'[14] Boondoggling or not, WPA workers hardly had an easy time and wages were deliberately kept low to avoid competition with private industry. Nor was there much security on the project, for at any time a worker faced the threat of receiving a 304 slip with his pay, meaning his job had been terminated.

> Working on the project, what a scared man, you know,
> Working on the project, what a scared man, you know,
> Because everytime I look around, oooh, well, well, somebody's
>   getting their 304.
>
> *New Working on the Project* – Peetie Wheatstraw (1937)[15]

Despite the insecurities of the Federal Relief schemes, and the difficulties many rural blacks in the South faced in getting enrolled, their mere existence was an improvement on the meagre provision of local relief. In 1935 the WPA wage, low as it was in the South, was still as much as eight times better than, for example local relief in Georgia. Public relief became such an important black occupation in the 1930's that it was surpassed only by domestic service and agricultural work.

> I went to the poll and voted, an' I know I voted the right way,
> I went to the poll and voted, an' I know I voted the right way,
> Now I'm praying to you Mister President, please keep the PWA.
>
> *Don't Take Away My PWA* – Jimmy Gordon (1936)[16]

Apart from the provision of work and cash relief, there was also relief in kind; by 1940, 8 per cent of the total population was receiving assistance in this way, especially in the South. With far fewer work projects particularly for blacks, relief in kind was almost the mainstay of the South as if in continuation of the old paternalism. When it was federally financed, the black had more chance of receiving it.

> Now the gov'ment took it in charge,
> Said they're gonna treat ev'body right.
> Give you some peas, beans n' meals,
> And then four or five cans of tripe.
>
> *Welfare Blues* – Speckled Red (1938)[17]

The New Deal as a whole saw more social provision by the Federal Government than ever before in America's history. There was greater recognition that in the complexity of a mass society, when economic disruption could lead to millions losing their livelihoods, it became nonsensical to believe that self-help alone could secure a person's destiny. With people tossed by social forces wider than were comprehensible to the individual, the organisation of society had to include systematic provision of the means for support and assistance.

While conservative critics attacked Roosevelt for 'socialism', many of his measures still provided less than had been long available in parts of industrial Western Europe. It was only in 1935, with the New Deal Social Security programme, that federally administered old-age pensions were established. There was no health service at all, and security coverage was severely limited. While blacks were as entitled to benefits as anyone, the exclusion of agricultural and domestic workers from the terms of the legislation left many blacks uncatered for. Nonetheless, with work relief, relief in kind, and the beneficial effects of many of the projects – for example the WPA taught 400,000 blacks to read and write, and the PWA paid up to 55 per cent of the cost of building new schools – the New Deal's social intervention was a radical departure from the past.

There were even benefits not immediately recognised by blacks that developed out of the New Deal's economic interventionism. A major element of the National Recovery Administration's industrial code system had been to secure the rights of workers to join the union of their choice, which brought the hatred of industrialists, employers and financiers down on Roosevelt's head. When in 1935 the NRA was declared unconstitutional by the Supreme Court, many of these codes were enshrined in subsequent legislation, and union rights were secured in law by the establishment of the National Labor Relations Board. The persistent attempt of the employers to have that too declared unconstitutional led to a long and bitter struggle with organised labour, involving strikes, sit-ins, spies, police and private armies, and vicious fights on the picket lines. In the short term, widespread union discrimination meant that blacks had less immediate benefit from the improved legal status which the unions had acquired, but increasingly the logic of worker solidarity demanded that black and white work together, and so in the late 1930's black participation in the labour movement began to grow.

While the New Deal, with its lack of overall philosophy or consistent strategy failed to make the radical changes in American society that some measures seemed to be pointing to, the 1930's nonetheless witnessed a shift in black America's relationship with white. There was a greater sense of involvement in the mainstream of society; more blacks began to look to the government in expectation that something *might* be done. This is traceable even in the blues of the 1930's, where far more make reference to wider social and political events. As far as the blues of the 1920's were concerned politics might as well not have existed; enthusiastic references to Presidents like Harding,

Coolidge or Hoover were unthinkable, whereas Roosevelt crops up, if not many times, on enough occasions to suggest he had permeated the thinking of even the humblest of blacks. The era of the New Deal brought a greater sense that black people were involved in a shared national problem. There had been something of the same feeling during the First World War when blacks enthusiastically joined in America's war to 'Make the World Safe for Democracy'; but at that time white discrimination and the policies of segregation of the military authorities introduced a bitterness to the experience.

The New Deal gave partial recognition to the distinctive problems of the black community by banning discrimination in Federal Relief projects. But more importantly it tacitly acknowledged that the solution of America's problems as a whole must include black people. Roosevelt himself appointed an unprecedented number of blacks to positions of authority in the Government, forming a so-called 'Black Cabinet', while his wife Eleanor worked closely with black leaders, visited black schools, invited blacks to the White House, spoke at black meetings and in general was a strong advocate of civil rights. While no measure was passed securing blacks' constitutional rights as equal citizens, and Roosevelt gave only lukewarm support to anti-lynching measures, the Federal Government did more – not enough, but more – than at any time since the failure of Reconstruction, to accept responsibility for protecting the black community against discrimination.

Although Roosevelt was frequently attacked by black leaders for not doing more, a fundamental and important shift of political alignment took place as blacks deserted the party of Lincoln and supported the Democrats. F.D.R. had begun the process of forging a new coalition, a new and uneasy alliance between the labour unions and the working class vote, the blacks and the conservative Democrats of the 'Solid South'. By adopting the cause of the 'forgotten man', the poor and the dispossessed, and applying measures which challenged the assumptions of the old order, Roosevelt symbolised the aspirations and aroused the hopes of millions. As Big Joe Williams said, 'Well, I liked everything, most he did. I think he one of the greatest Presidents we had. President Roosevelt, he brought the dead to life, it's worth saying, a way of speaking. Because when he taken over there, the country was in a bad shape. Hoover left it tied all up, you know what I mean? People were starving, he come and helped the jobless: that's the man you want.'[18]

When the President died in office in 1945 the blues pianist Champion Jack Dupree composed his *F.D.R. Blues*.

I sure feel bad with tears runnin' down my face,
I sure feel bad with tears runnin' down my face,
I lost a good friend, was a credit to our race . . .[19]

City blues

Slowly but remorselessly the Depression changed the public face of the blues. The 'Classic' blues were rapidly becoming an anachronism and the new era demanded new heroes and new heroines. With rising competition from 'talkies' in the cinema, the old T.O.B.A. circuit was on its last legs, with falling audiences and a declining quality of show. The vaudeville singers and 'classier' performers turned away from the blues, some to find work in the movies, others hoping to work in cabarets. Times were so hard for the travelling minstrel and tent shows that many were disbanded on the road, leaving performers completely stranded.

The recording industry in general was in a state of collapse, with record sales in 1932 a mere 6 million (compared with 104 million in 1927) and the Race market in particular shrinking almost by the week. Field recording trips were reduced to a handful, with Memphis ignored from 1931 to 1939 and only a few in Dallas, Atlanta and elsewhere. This meant that the thriving diversity of 1920's country blues on record was over. No longer were obscure and virtually unknown performers given their chance of a session or two; from now on the blues was dominated by regular almost 'star' performers, most of whom were in the cities and close to the recording studios.

One element in the new urban blues had developed slightly before the Depression, in the thriving sub-culture of the House Rent Party circuit. Along with food and drink, the main feature of the rent parties was dancing to music provided by pianists like Speckled Red.

'That was the life of the party – dance! Oh yeah. You know, wasn't too much of a dance but just walkin' around anyhow. They done nearly all kind a' dances. One step, two step, an' all waltzes an', what you call it – Chatterin', Black Bottom an' all them. Every kind a' dance that come out, well they done it. They all get out there and do rubs. They got to feelin' good an' all they'd need was a rug or a towel on the floor.'[1]

'Clap hands here comes Nelson!' cried pianist Romeo Nelson

on his 1929 record *Gettin' Dirty Just Shakin' That Thing*, and in 1964 he described to Pete Welding and Erwin Helfer what it was like to play the parties in Chicago.

'You could get away with anything – just hit the keyboard with your elbows and fists, it didn't make no difference to them, they were so drunk by then. But me, I wasn't a drinker – didn't smoke neither – so I used to play all the time I was working at one of the parties. In fact, that's where you get your ideas for new things. You try something out, and if you like it then you just work with it, until you have it all shaped up.'[2]

There was a lot of experimenting among pianists in the late 20's and on into the 30's as many moved up from the Southern barrelhouse circuit and mixed with the city musicians. Some were regular professionals, getting work in vaudeville theatres, accompanying singers, or throwing in comedy routines, tap dancing and doing a 'buck and wing', while others were almost exclusively party pianists. But whatever their background, they would pick up themes wherever they heard them and hand them on, moving from Chicago to Detroit or to St Louis or anywhere blacks were living.

Some pianists spent the whole time in one place, but endless others were on the move, some as hobos, some finding work on honky-tonk trains – excursions run by the railroads with pianos provided by the company to entertain the passengers. Just as the country guitarist would sing of movin' on, or the harp-player would blow his train imitation, the stock in trade of the blues pianist was the sound of the railroad. Blues piano is mainly based on bass patterns in the left hand, sometimes but not always walking basses, set against endless rhythmic variations and improvisions in the right.

Little Brother Montgomery explains:

'That's the way the bass part is, that's the way a train goes, you know, cha-cha, cha-cha, cha-cha. My great grandmother, her name was Olivia Montgomery, she put me on her knee: the train was right in front of our house, the Illinois Central, train go on saying cha cha, cha cha, cha cha, cha cha, so she said, "Brother, you know what that train saying?" I said no. She said. "That train is telling you *Pay me cash I carry you faster, pay me cash I carry you faster . . .*"'[3]

Played fast, the rolling, on-rushing impetus of the piano gives the sound of a train rattling on the lines, clicking over switches, or thundering over bridges and plunging through tunnels. One blues singer Cow Cow Davenport got his name from one of his train pieces; originally called *Railroad Blues* it became *Cow Cow Blues* when he put in a part where the switchman boards the cow-catcher on the front of the train. He once ended the song in a theatre singing: 'Nobody here can do me like Papa Cow Cow can do,'[4] and the name caught on.

Cow Cow Blues was one of the most influential of all piano pieces, but Davenport himself, with his lilting and bluesy mixture of barrelhouse, ragtime and walking-bass, was only one of dozens of city pianists creating the sounds to get on record in the late 20's. Some were never recorded till later, like the extravagant, entertaining, hoarse-voiced, piano-stomping, finger-snapping Cripple Clarence Lofton, or the quieter, more introverted-sounding Jimmy Yancey. Yancey was slightly older than some of the pianists he guided and taught in Chicago, and after a career as a comedian and tap dancer he worked at a baseball park. He could play a fast-rocking boogie with the best of them, but he most often played with a poetic simplicity and a gentle tranquillity. Others, like Montana Taylor, who was also a superbly sensitive pianist, were briefly recorded only to sink into oblivion, till rediscovery by jazz and blues enthusiasts brought them back to the studio.

Recorded or unrecorded, the musical ideas of pianists from every part of Black America mingled together, drifted apart and formed anew, giving a creative vitality to the piano blues in the late 20's. These were a second generation of pianists following the older piano songsters of the barrelhouse circuit, and they gave a new name to one of the many piano styles. There had always been names and techniques before, 'black buff', 'overhand', 'rolling bass', 'dudlow Joe', 'catch up bass', or 'the rocks', 'the chimes', 'the fives' and a dozen others; but one style in particular caught on – boogie-woogie. Both the music and the word boogie had been around for years; brothels were called boogie houses, and to 'pitch a boogie' could mean to throw a party, or something more sexual, but it was the 1928 recording of *Pinetop's Boogie-Woogie* by Pinetop Smith which pinned the name to this rough, driving piano style. Talking over the walking bass and stop-time rhythms, Pinetop gave a spoken commentary:

'Now listen here all of you! This is my Pinetop Strut. I want everybody to dance just like I tell you!'

He instructed the dancers: 'Hold y'self!' . . . 'Git it!' 'Mess around.'[5]

Cow Cow Davenport claims to have given Pinetop Smith the name boogie-woogie when they met in a honky-tonk in Pittsburgh. Pinetop was playing away, and Cow Cow told him:

' "Boy, look here, you sure have got a mean boogie-woogie."
Pinetop didn't know what he was playin' nohow. I began to tell
him what it was, then he tried to sing it. He never could rhyme it
together, just said "Come up here gal, to this piano . . . playin'
my boogie-woogie".[6]

But the story of Pinetop's boogie-woogie doesn't stop there.
At around the same time in 1928, when his record was making a
big splash in Chicago, he was living in the same rooming house
as two other pianists, the famous Albert Ammons and Meade
Lux Lewis, both old friends of Jimmy Yancey. The three of them
were playing together, swapping ideas and jamming, when at one
point Pinetop took Ammons to one side and told him, 'Albert, I
want you to learn my *Boogie-Woogie*.'[7] In the late 1930's, partly
sparked off by the 'rediscovery' of Meade Lux Lewis who had
made a single, classic record in 1927 called *Honky Tonk Train
Blues*, there was a brief period of glory for boogie-woogie.
Ammons and Lewis, and a Kansas City pianist called Pete
Johnson – they were known as the Boogie-Woogie Trio –
appeared in society cafés, on the radio and at the prestigious
Carnegie Hall, and the old tune of *Pinetop's Boogie-Woogie* was
recreated by Ammons in memory of his old friend. Sadly,
Pinetop himself never got the benefit of the boogie craze,
because shortly after getting Ammons to learn his piece he was
shot to death in a Chicago West Side dance hall, as Little
Brother Montgomery remembers: 'it was a stray bullet. The
bartender and a customer shooting at each other and he got hit
with a stray bullet.'[8]

The aggression and tension of ghetto life could sometimes be
briefly sublimated by boogie-woogie into the joy of physical
release through the pounding excitement of the piano. The
ritualistic insistence of the dance could affirm a sense of sharing
and participation in a community which sanctioned expressive
needs. If there is a 'message' in boogie it is an old one, that there
is nothing wrong or sinful about having a good time and that
there is human warmth in coming together.

Alongside the outgoing and rocking energy of boogie
there was also the quieter side of piano blues, the slow
blues of intricate rhythmic subtleties and drifting improvis-
ation.

In 1928 a pianist who performed with these qualities, and who
was to become a dominating influence on the urban blues of the
1930's, Leroy Carr, made his first record, *How Long – How Long
Blues*.

1 *Minstrels in Knoxville, Tennessee, in 1897. Having originated in the last century, shows like this were still popular well into this century.*

2 *Mamie Smith with her band in 1920. She made a major breakthrough for black artists when she became the first singer to make a blues record.*

3 *Blues country: cotton pickers in Pulaski County, Arkansas, 1935.*

4 *A cotton waggon near Milestone in the Mississippi Delta, 1939.*

5 *The fiery cross of the Ku Klux Klan, persistent reminder of white racism and bigotry.*

6 *A chain gang in Georgia in the 1930's. Black people could have little faith in the justice of Southern courts.*

7 *Above left: The only known photo of Charley Patton, one of the greatest of the early Mississippi blues singers.*

8 *Above right: Leadbelly, a 12-string guitar player and songster from Louisiana.*

9 & 10 *Below: 1920's Press adverts for records by Henry Thomas, 'Ragtime Texas'. Born in 1875, he was one of the earliest blues singers to be recorded.*

11 *Sam Chatmon, half-brother of Charley Patton, at his home in Hollandale, Mississippi, in 1976, aged 77. He died in 1983.*

12 *Gus Cannon, banjo-playing jug band leader at home in Memphis, Tennessee, in 1976, when he was 93.*

13 *Above left:Clara Smith – 'The World's Champion Moaner' – one of the great women stars of the 1920's.*

14 *Above right: Bessie Smith – 'The Empress of the Blues' – in 1923.*

15 *The 'Mother of the Blues', Ma Rainey with her Georgia Band, including the famous Georgia Tom Dorsey (standing to her right).*

16 *'The Black Queen', Victoria Spivey at home in Brooklyn, New York, a few months before her death in 1976.*

17 *Below: Ida Cox advert: 'Race' records were widely advertised in the black press in the 1920's.*

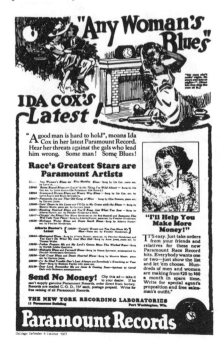

Blind Blake

18 *Above left: Advert for Blind Lemon Jefferson records, including the only known photo of the Texas singer.*

19 *Above right: Blind Blake, a popular ragtime guitar player in the 1920's.*

20 *Above left: Blind Willie McTell, a much-travelled, much-recorded 12-string guitarist from Georgia.*

21 *Above right: Blind Boy Fuller, a 1930's recording star who played for tobacco workers in North Carolina.*

22 *Rural poverty: ten people lived in this shack in Caroline County, Virginia, in 1941.*

23 *Henry Townsend at home in St Louis in 1976. He played and recorded with many of the finest artists of the 1930's and 1940's.*

24 *Little Brother Montgomery in Chicago in 1976. He played piano in Southern honky tonks and sportin' houses, and later in Chicago house-rent parties.*

25 *Chicago's South Side, target for the waves of black migration from the Deep South in the 1940's and 1950's.*

26 *Sonny Boy Williamson (No. 2), harmonica-playing star of Radio KFFA's* King Biscuit Time *in Helena, Arkansas. He was broadcasting on and off from 1941 till his death in 1965.*

27 *Joe Willie Wilkins and Houston Stackhouse, two of Sonny Boy's original King Biscuit Boys, playing in Memphis, Tennessee, in 1976.*

28 *One of the greatest blues singers ever, Muddy Waters, one-time King of Chicago's South Side. Note the slide on his left hand.*

29 *Above left: Sam 'Lightnin'' Hopkins, a tradition-based musician from Houston, Texas, who was still selling plenty of records in the 1950's.*

30 *Above right: T-Bone Walker, also from Texas, has had enormous influence on modern electric guitarists, despite his death in 1975.*

31 *Above left: One of the finest exponents of the old Delta blues, Booker White, at home in Memphis, Tennessee, in 1976, shortly before his death.*

32 *Above right: B. B. King, cousin and boyhood admirer of Booker White. He is probably the most popular and commercially successful living blues artist.*

33 *Above left: Little Walter Jacobs, a master of the amplified harmonica, whose records helped shape Chicago blues in the 1950's.*

34 *Above right: Howling Wolf (Chester Burnett) was a dominating presence both in person and on record till his death in 1976.*

35 *The Aces in 1976; left to right Freddie Below (drums), Louis Myers (guitar) and David Myers (electric bass). They still play regularly in Chicago having worked with Little Walter in the 1950's.*

36 *Albert King, a modern bluesman who has remained popular with black audiences through the Soul era.*

How long, how long, has that evening train been gone?
How long, how long, baby, how long?

Standing at the station, watch my baby leave town,
Feeling disgusted, nowhere could she be found,
How long, how long, baby, how long.

I can hear the whistle blowing, but I cannot see no train,
For it's deep down in my heart, baby, that I have an aching pain,
For how long, how long, baby, how long . . .[9]

The record was an immediate commercial success, selling
hundreds of thousands of copies, and as with Jim Jackson's
Kansas City Blues, it led to new versions. Leroy Carr went on to
make *How Long How Long Blues No. 2*, *How Long How Long Blues
Part 3* in 1928, and a *New How Long How Long Blues* in 1931.

The song has a haunting sadness, carried by an evocatively
persistent melody and Leroy's expressive, wistful voice; and
there was warmth too, in his gently rolling piano accompaniment, which betrayed no bitterness, and no anger. Leroy Carr's
blues were those of resigned regret; simple statements of
sadness. But what made his records outstanding was the stinging
guitar-playing of his partner Scrapper Blackwell. Individually
both were fine musicians, but it was the combination of the two
which was so influential; Blackwell's strong, cutting incisiveness
on guitar contrasted with the softness of Carr's restrained mood,
bringing tension to the sound. At their best they showed an
almost telepathic sympathy in their duets, with Scrapper chiming
electrifying treble notes against the easy-rolling bass of Leroy's
piano followed by perfectly pitched bass note boogie runs.
Sometimes Leroy would call out appreciative comments:

'Knock it on out, boy. I know what you're talking about. Lord
. . . it's a killer.'[10]

They generated a romping momentum in their faster tunes
with the infectious drive of barrelhouse boogie; but it was in the
slower pieces that they were at their best. Tuneful and rich
instrumentally, the songs were often finely constructed with a
poetic simplicity.

I had the blues before sunrise, with tears standing in my eyes,
I had the blues before sunrise, with tears standing in my eyes,
It's such a miserable feeling, a feeling I do despise . . .

My mind was running back to days of long ago,
My mind was running back to days of long ago,
And the one I love, I don't see her anymore.

Blues Before Sunrise (1934)[11]

As if loath to burden people only with his sadness, Leroy would
sing the occasional pop-inflected ballad or break the mood with a
bouncing stomp; sometimes with the feeling of a wistful smile in
his voice he would sing of cheerful boyhood days when he
Carried Water For The Elephant in a circus. But the image he
conveyed, and his success shows it was an attractive one, was that
of a person saddened by failed relationships, and his blues were
pervaded by a feeling of friendly openness and a willingness to
communicate and share himself.

One quality of blues during the Depression was this directness, a drawing away from the allusiveness and ambiguity of the
20's country blues, where the rougher intensity of performance
and 'illogical' incoherence of lyrics sometimes conveyed a more
isolated and personal emotion. It was as if the shared social
disaster demanded a coming together, and a recognition of one
another's problems.

Another piano and guitar combination of those early Depression days were the highly popular Georgia Tom and Tampa
Red. From one of their first recording sessions they created one
of the biggest ever Race hits, the good-time, double-entendre
It's Tight Like That.

> Now the girl I love is long and slim,
> When she gets it it's too bad, Jim.
> It's tight like that, beedle um bum,
> It's tight like that, beedle um bum,
> Hear me talkin' to you, it's tight like that.[12]

The first of many royalty cheques received by Georgia Tom was
for $2400.19, and more was to come. These two, with Tom
playing an easy-going piano and Tampa a clear and resonant
guitar, created a brief vogue for 'Hokum' blues – light, jolly
innuendo pieces like *Selling That Stuff*, *Beedle Um Bum* or *No
Matter How She Done It*, with harmony singing and catchy tunes.

Georgia Tom now remembers his Hokum-playing days with
great pride and affection. 'Blues, Hokum; now they had such a
thing they call Hokum. It had live beats to it. We didn't want to
call ourselves blues singers, and we didn't want to call ourselves
popular singers. I don't know what the word Hokum means
myself right now, I got to look in the dictionary now, if there is
such a word in the dictionary. But it was a good word to carry, for
nobody knew what it meant and they say "Hokum, Hokum Boys,
we going to see something." And they did see something.'[14]

Hokum blues were perhaps the swansong of the old era, the

last fling of urban optimism of the 1920's. Many copied the big hit *It's Tight Like That*, but the good old days were numbered. In 1932 as the Depression worsened, Georgia Tom decided to leave the blues and turn to his real love, religious music, becoming a leading figure in gospel music with compositions like *Precious Lord*. But before he left the blues he had already done much to lay the foundations of a new era. Although Hokum blues almost died with the early Depression, there still remained that strain of outgoing, good-time bawdy group blues for the rest of the decade. While other blues dealt with the grimmer side of life in the Depression, effervescent and raucous little groups still kept up the old spirit of Hokum – *Let's Get Drunk and Truck* or *Let Me Feel It* – as if in a desperate attempt to swing away from those Depression blues. Georgia Tom's old partner Tampa Red was one of the many who played this kind of small-band jive music in the later 30's with his Chicago Five, and the old feeling was still there in 1942 in songs like *Let Me Play With Your Poodle*.

One of the many 'cover' versions of *It's Tight Like That* was recorded in 1929 by Lonnie Johnson; duetting with Spencer Williams they gave it the title *It Feels So Good*.

> Said the chicken when she ate the worm,
> It makes me wiggle when you start to squirm,
> Cause it feels so good,
> Oh, it feels so good,
> I like good bait, because it feels so good.[14]

Johnson's recording career lasted longer than almost anyone's in blues history, off and on from 1925 till the mid-1960's, during which time he achieved a different kind of popularity with different audiences. His musical diversity was amazing – he recorded solo, he played piano, guitar, violin and mandolin, he accompanied the roughest of country singers like Texas Alexander whose singing was like a free-form field holler, he contributed some of the finest ever jazz guitar solos to Louis Armstrong's Hot Five recordings, he duetted with Victoria Spivey, he recorded with Duke Ellington ... the list of his achievements in the blues and jazz field is almost endless. In the middle years of the 1930's the Depression forced him out of business for a while, although his influence continued to be felt not only in urban blues, but also in the Deep South where his superlative musicianship as a guitarist was avidly studied and admired.

Lonnie Johnson recorded material ranging from the bawdy to

the sweetly sentimental, but he was one of many to give a new articulation to urban black culture as a highly serious blues singer.

'I sing city blues,' he told Valerie Wilmer in an interview in 1963. 'My blues is built on human beings on land, see how they live, see their heartaches and the shifts they go through with love affairs and things like that – that's what I write about and that's the way I make my living. It's understanding others, and that's the best way I can tell you. My style of singing has nothing to do with the part of the country I come from. It comes from my soul within. The heartaches and the things that have happened to me in my life – that's what makes a good blues singer.'[15]

Johnson was always a city man, spending his childhood in New Orleans and living for long periods in St Louis, Chicago and New York. His whole musical style and manner spoke of urbane sophistication, from the clarity of his bitter-sweet voice to the clean-cut precision of his highly original guitar-playing. Yet when he accompanied the hollering Texas Alexander, while never abandoning his technical proficiency, he showed a sensitive empathy for the rough, emotional directness of the country blues. And when singing himself there was an involvement in the material which always stopped his urbanity becoming merely slickness. He was a serious man, much concerned with the complexity of human relationships and the stresses put upon them, and over the years of his recording career he continually returned to the subject, worrying away at it, sometimes with a melting sentimentality, sometimes with anger and bitterness and sometimes facing the anguish of failure with attempts to understand.

Lonnie was himself a married man; in 1925 he married Mary Williams, a St Louis woman who had come up from Mississippi with her widowed mother. Mary Johnson also became a blues singer, much to the sorrow of her devoutly religious mother who warned her that she was 'pavin'' her way to hell'.[16]

In the early years of their marriage, with Lonnie a big commercial success, Mary used to help with his compositions; after one such lyric-writing session he told her 'Sweetheart, why don't you compose yourself?'.

Mary was very popular in the St Louis clubs with her quiet moaning delivery, usually accompanied by one of the many pianists in the city like Roosevelt Sykes or Henry Brown. When she started recording, as she told Paul Oliver, 'my first number was a hit – the *Black Man Blues*. I don't know where I got the idea of "A man in Atlanta and one in St Louis too" – I didn't have all of them!"[17]

Whether or not they wrote from direct personal experience, both Mary and Lonnie Johnson sang blues of the ghetto. In her 1929 record *Barrelhouse Flat Blues* Mary took her theme from a section of St Louis where Italian bootleggers used to hang out.

> I'm gonna build me a little barrelhouse flat way out on Dago Hill,
> Where I can get my beer and whiskey when it's fresh from the
> still.
> (*Spoken*) Police Sergeant just won't let me be, he tried to find my
> whiskey everywhere I hide it.[18]

Lonnie sang about such things as jails, floods, cyclones or ghosts, but most often his blues were those of loneliness and the changeability of feelings and emotional insecurity in personal relationships. His *When I was Lovin' Changed My Mind Blues* (1926) turned on the persistent motif of kindness being repaid with indifference:

> You didn't want me baby when I was lovin' and kind,
> You didn't want me baby when I was lovin' and kind,
> Now you wants me but I have changed my mind.[19]

In *When You Fall For Someone That's Not Your Own* (1928) he cast an ironic eye on the painful side of adultery:

> A married woman is sweet, the sweetest woman ever was born,
> A married woman is sweet, the sweetest woman ever was born,
> Only thing wrong with her, every time she has to go back home.[20]

The pattern of his records shows the ambivalence of the feelings he sang about. From giving the advice *Let All Married Women Alone*, he adopted the boastfulness of being *Just a Roaming Man*. Then he turned to aggression and anger with *Sam You Can't Do That To Me*, or *Cat You Been Messin' Around* and *Sam, You're Just a Rat*. Sam seems to have survived, however, in *Jelly Killed Old Sam*, while Lonnie philosophically considered the *Faults Of All Women And Men*. Then feelings would swing back to the affection of *I'm Nuts About That Gal*.

With the Depression at its worst Lonnie Johnson's career took a downward turn. He was forced to take a series of manual jobs and as soon as he returned to recording in 1937 he expressed the feelings of a vast proportion of blacks in the Depression by declaring *Hard Times Ain't Gone Nowhere*.

> People ravin' 'bout hard times,
> I don't know why they should.
> If some people was like me they didn't have no money when times
>   was good.[21]

In the meantime, his marriage had ended in separation and acrimony when Mary moved back with her mother in 1932. In that year she recorded her *Rattlesnake Blues*.

> Ah that's all right, daddy, that's all right for you,
> Some day you'll want for Mary and she'll be so far from you.[22]

In the same session, her *Mary Johnson Blues* declared her real bitterness:

> I once was a married woman, sorry the day I ever was,
> I once was a married woman, sorry the day I ever was,
> I was a young girl at home and I did not know the world.

> I'd rather be an old maid than to be worried and blue each and
>   every day,
> I'd rather be an old maid than to be worried and blue each and
>   every day,
> 'Cause these worrysome old men will cause your head to turn
>   white and grey.[23]

It is of course impossible to say how far Mary and Lonnie Johnson's blues reflected the details of their marital problems, but in a 1939 recording session Lonnie turned again to the theme of marriage:

> The reason why so many good women's done gone wrong,
> Just trying to find the love and happiness
> That they don't get at home.
> *Why Women Go Wrong*[24]

Though some may have found the title irritating to say the least, he showed a similarly philosophical and conciliatory face in the next record, *She's Only A Woman*.

> Some men always saying that every woman is just the same,
> But don't say that because there is two sides to everything.[25]

At the same time he appealed: *Trust Your Husband*, and there can be no ambiguity about whom he was addressing in *She's My Mary*.

> My friends all scorn me, talk all over the town,
> They try to make trouble for me, the news is out all around,
> But after all she's still my Mary and will be until the deal goes down.

She was my Mary when this whole world turned me down,
She was my father, mother, sister, brother, she helped me to
    carry on,
And she will still be my Mary when everything goes wrong.[26]

In a sense it's not important how far the Johnsons' blues corresponded to their own lives, and some might feel it anyway an intrusion to make the connection; what is of more general significance is the tendency they illustrated for the urban blues to present themes with simple directness and coherence. The blues singer was holding a mirror to society and the audience could see images presented of a concrete and unadorned reality. With the mass impersonality of the city and its problems of acute economic distress and social instability, the language of communication needed a wider currency than the metaphorical allusiveness the country blues could provide. This is not to say that metaphor was gone from the ghetto blues. Another response to the new way of life and the new era was the presentation of the singer himself as an almost mythical figure. There is an element of this in the life of another St Louis singer who sometimes worked with both the Johnsons. This was Peetie Wheatstraw – The Devil's Son-in-Law, or the High Sheriff from Hell – one of the most successful and popular of a large group of blues singers working in St Louis.

Blues in St Louis

St Louis had a long blues heritage: when jazz musician Harry Dial moved there at the age of two in 1909, 'the first music I heard was the blues, which was being whistled, sung and shouted from every street corner and alleyway in St Louis. The blues was so much part of our lives that we never gave it a thought as being a special music.'[1]

The blues was the music of the poor and the down-and-outs, an embarrassment to the aspirations of the black middle class. It had low-life connotations going back long in St Louis' history, from the days when the wide open red-light district with gambling and bawdy houses had first become part of the world of civic corruption and racketeering. Long before the era of Lonnie Johnson and Peetie Wheatstraw, black music in general was a thriving part of St Louis life. In the 1880's and 1890's Mammy Lou, 'a gnarled, black African of the purest type', was singing *Frankie and Johnny* to whites at Babe Connors' night club in the heart of the red-light district as part of an entertainment featuring 'creoles' dancing in little more than stockings. Mammy

Lou was one of the first to sing 'spirituals and field songs to white men'.[2]

The famous murder saga of *Frankie and Johnny* is sometimes said to have come from the violence and lawlessness of St Louis, where brutality was an everyday fact of life; when W. C. Handy was there in 1892 it was a frequent sight to see policemen swinging their night sticks at vagrants and transients trying to sleep. Equally common was to see the stevedores singing on the Mississippi levees where a breezy packet trade flourished, and all night long as Handy slept rough on cobblestone streets he heard the music of the ragged guitarists.

If music had long associations with the sleazy night club world on the one hand and with the labouring poor on the other, the city's early musical reputation was made in the ragtime era; of all the Mid-Western cities, St Louis had the strongest claim to be the heart of the craze, when clubs and theatres pranced and cakewalked to the tinkle of ragtime pianos. For a generation afterwards the city had a continuing tradition of piano music and especially piano blues.

In the 1920's St Louis was one of a number of cities in the border States where blues were fed and replenished by blacks moving up from the South. Just as Chicago and Detroit saw the blues flourish, other cities in strategic positions on the migratory routes connected by roads and railroads became part of the circuit; blues musicians could easily move about and find work in Louisville, Indianapolis, Cleveland, Cincinatti, Kansas City or the smaller cities nearby like Cairo and Granite City, and as the focus of migration and the centre of an endless flow of move-ment St Louis was comparable to Memphis in the vitality of its blues. While some people came up river, like the hosts of New Orleans jazzmen, others rode the Illinois Central Railroad or came in on Highway 61 from the Delta.

The big blues stars like Mamie Smith, Bessie Smith and Ethel Waters would all perform at places like the Booker T. Washing-ton Theatre. Jazz musicians like Jelly Roll Morton would play on the excursion steamers on the river. But there was also the world of low-life blues, the kind disapproved of by the bourgeoisie, played in pool halls, sporting houses and gambling joints down near the levee or round Morgan Street, the infamous 'Deep Morgan'.

Like 'Deep Ellum' in Dallas, Beale in Memphis and Decatur in Atlanta, this was the bright-lights sporting centre of St Louis, the spawning ground of blues, where drifters, hustlers, stevedores, pimps and prostitutes mingled with bootleggers and crooks and with the poor of the city hoping to make a buck or just have a good time. In the joints, barrelhouse flats, night clubs and speakeasies, or in house parties, dozens of musicians found work in St Louis, with guitarists and pianists from the South mixing with the old regulars. Many guitarists from the city recorded in the late 20's and the early Depression, several of them coming from Mississippi like Hi Henry Brown, who sang about the Deep Morgan prostitutes,

> Some draw a check, oh babe, some draw nothin' at all,
> Well, they don't draw nothin' they husbands bust them on the jaw.[3]

or Jaydee 'Jelly Jaw' Short with his rough flailing and accelerating guitar style, or Henry Townsend who for many years worked with the sombre pianist Henry Brown. Townsend, a thoughtful and articulate man, much admired Lonnie Johnson and his brother Steady Roll, and spoke kindly of others of his old partners like the pianists Walter Davis, Roosevelt Sykes and Sylvester Palmer, or Little Alice Moore, 'a nicer mixer with the public and a fairly intelligent girl'.[4]

There was a richness of musical diversity in St Louis with guitarists playing singly or in pairs, and barrelhouse and boogie pianists often teaming up with guitar-players and even forming little bands, sometimes with 'gut bucket' trombonist Ike Rodgers. Styles ranged from the roughest country strumming to rhythmically subtle finger-picking, like the crisply firm guitar of Charley Jordan, who played a delightfully raggish *Keep It Clean*.

> If you want to hear that elephant laugh,
> Take him down to the river and wash his yas, yas, yas.
> Now roll him over,
> Give him Co-Coly,
> Lemon Sody,
> Quart of ice cream,
> For to keep it clean . . .[5]

If St Louis had an overall style it was a certain tautness and restraint, a betwixt and between feeling somewhere combining raw tension and musical control. There were good-time blues from St Louis, but compared with Memphis, the tone is more sombre, perhaps reflecting the more tense atmosphere of the city. Henry Townsend explained the significance of the blues:

'It really is this to me: it's a relief for pressure. In most cases now it can be a happy song, the story's being told through a song, it's a relieve of pressure. We all have had something in mind and we didn't want to talk about it to anybody, but the burden was real heavy until you could make some kinda sound about it, you could express yourself to somebody, sort of lighten the thing up.'[6]

And there were plenty of things wrong in the lives of people in St Louis. The downtown part of St Louis has been described as 'probably one of the ugliest spots in the world'. Orick Johns knew the city from his childhood and he described the place as he saw it in the Depression.

'With a magnificent river site the city has left its crumbling old warehouses, primitive granite-block levees and grimy streets exactly as they were fifty years ago.' He saw the mile-long Hooverville 'which hung over the river bank, south of the bridges, and was cut off from the city by a network of railroad tracks. I had seen many similar shanty towns in the West, stalked by hunger. In Oakland, California, I had inspected a "city" composed entirely of men living in big concrete pipes on the lot of a conduit company which had practically ceased doing business. But there had been something ship-shape and self-respecting about those pipe-dwellers. I had never seen such stark destitution as that on the river front of South St Louis. The people were practically imprisoned there, discouraged by police and watchmen from going into the city . . . Some got baskets of vegetables from the welfare bureau, which were divided with their neighbours. Most of them lived on Mississippi cat fish.'[7]

Big Joe Williams used to play in the Hooverville and paints a slightly different picture: 'They go down there and put up paper houses, set right by the river. The Government gave it to them during the Depression, and the next day you know they had a barrelhouse down there, and the next day they had a whiskey-still down there, and the next thing you know, building house, a brick house. You can't hardly keep 'em down . . .'[8]

Blues singers like Big Joe had a way of life hardly different from the mass of their working class audience. It was however an undoubted advantage to be a musician because of the extra opportunities to make money at the house parties or in the store front speakeasies that Henry Townsend used to play in. He used to make about a dollar and a half a night working on his own or about 7 dollars a week as a team with Roosevelt Sykes, and either way that was often better than what many people were living on. 'The people in St Louis was like everywhere else, they had pretty rough time,' Townsend recalled. 'Of course just like anything else the smoother people they lived the best. There was certain type of people had to go to the soup lines and what have you. These organisations like churches we had here, Father Dempsey, he had a feed line. But for *me* this wasn't so. I don't recall ever having to go anywhere to get a meal. 'Course it took some doing but I'd play with my guitar a while and even before I started playing the guitar I would shine shoes, I would do almost anything, you know, in the sense of making a nickel or a dime.'[9]

Inextricably tied to the blues culture of St Louis was the smaller city of East St Louis just across the river in Illinois, where musicians both lived and played in the notorious 'Valley' slum district, a hot-bed of crime, vice and political corruption. With landlords living outside the Valley, it was the home of poverty and social decay, where pimps, bootleggers, and racketeers found their living alongside blues singers. It was an ugly city, made almost unredeemedly so by the still lingering atmosphere of hatred and racism created by one of the most vicious anti-Negro riots in American history in July 1917.

'ANTI-NEGRO RIOTERS AGAIN PLY THE TORCH. Three more bodies found today at East St Louis, making total 27 – Additional troops may be sent there,' ran a newspaper report on July 3.[10]

During the riot at least 39 blacks and 9 whites were killed, many of the blacks being burned alive as 6,000 were driven from the city and over 400,000 dollars worth of damage done. Racist sentiment had been fired by the use of Southern black strike-breakers imported by employers involved in an acrimonious labour dispute with white unionists and the atmosphere of violence became explosive following reports and rumours of thousands of blacks pouring into the city. In the violence that followed the police and the National Guard were ignobly complicit with the terror tactics employed against blacks. It is said that the bitterness created by the riot has not been dissipated to this day.

It was in the slum district of East St Louis that Peetie Wheatstraw lived. Years later a black librarian told Peetie's biographer Paul Garon:

'Now I've heard of Peetie Wheatstraw; when I was a little girl, I heard talk of him; he was a piano player. But of course we had nothing to do with people like that. Peetie Wheatstraw, Lonnie Johnson and all of them – they were from the "Valley", you know, and they didn't mix with us. No, you won't find any picture of Peetie Wheatstraw, even in the colored newspapers, not unless he got into trouble. They were a different class; low-life is what they were. That's all ... But he was popular, all right. He was well known enough.'[11]

His real name was William Bunch, but as the East St Louis *Metro Journal* wrote when he was killed in a car crash in 1941, he was known to his 'jive' fans as 'Peetie Wheatstraw'. He created a potent mythical persona chrystallised in the manner, swagger and the lyrics of his *Peetie Wheatstraw Stomps*.

> Everybody hollering, 'Here comes that Peetie Wheatstraw',
> Everybody hollering, 'Here comes that Peetie Wheatstraw',
> Now, he's better known by the Devil's Son-in-Law.
>
> Everybody wondering what the Peetie Wheatstraw do,
> Everybody wondering what the Peetie Wheatstraw do,
> 'Cause every time you hear him, he's coming out with something new.
> (*Spoken*) Show 'em what Peetie do, boy.
>
> He makes some happy, some he make cry,
> He makes some happy, some he make cry,
> Well, now, he made one old lady go hang herself and die.
>
> This is Peetie Wheatstraw, I'm always on the line,
> This is Peetie Wheatstraw, I'm always on the line,
> Save up your nickels and dimes, you can come up and see me some time.
> (*Spoken*) Play it a little bit, boy.
>
> Now what I say ... Save up your nickels and dimes, you can come up and see me some time.
> *Peetie Wheatstraw Stomp No. 2* (1937)[12]

Peetie played and sang with a drawling ease, his words slurred and casual to the point of incoherence and his rolling piano giving out a stomping momentum. His manner was detached and throwaway, with hints of irony and laughter in the midst of his lazy boasting. He had an immediately identifiable piano sound and a slightly hoarse voice, his trademark cry of 'oooh, well, well' peppering his songs. He comes across as the man who has seen it all, knows what it's all about, has got it made; he has seen hard times, lived in a hobo jungle, worked on a WPA project, likes his whiskey, has plenty of girl friends, knows their double-crossing, deceiving ways, knows how to handle them. That is the image, the rounder who isn't going to marry and won't settle down, who drinks, fights and believes women are no-good, false-hearted, and exploit hard-working men. Yes, he's that too.

When a man is out working, working hard on the line,
Some low-down rascal, always trying to steal his wife.
But here I am, hard working man,
Doin' the best I can.

Doin' The Best I Can (1934)[13]

In his more than 160 recorded songs stretching from 1930 to the
end of 1941, Peetie Wheatstraw did more than give out a mythical
character. Everything comes back to the central idea of the man
who has survived every kind of set-back and pain in this world;
whether it is people treating him like a country clown, or 'these
men that always grinning in my face'.[14] or being betrayed by the
woman he loved, still he surfaces up with a careless jaunt to his
stride, snapping his fingers at the fates, showing humility to no
man.

The persona Wheatstraw created exerted a powerful impact
on other singers – Jimmy Gordon billed himself as 'Peetie
Wheatstraw's Brother'; Floyd 'Dipper Boy' Council called himself 'The Devil's Daddy-in-Law' on one record; Harmon Ray
was 'Peetie Wheatstraw's Buddy' on others, while Robert Lee
McCoy (Robert McCollum) was labelled as 'Peetie's Boy' on
one of his. But an even more intriguing appearance of the
character is in Ralph Ellison's novel *Invisible Man*, where the
narrator meets a blues-singing jive-talker pushing a cart in the
streets of Harlem who, in the midst of a high-speed slangy
patter, calls himself 'Peter Wheatstraw . . . the Devil's only
Son-in-Law . . . a piano player and a rounder, a whiskey drinker
and a pavement pounder'.[15] Ellison apparently based the
fictional character of the cart-pusher on the general personality
and speech of Peetie Wheatstraw whom he had not only known
but had played with in St Louis.

How far the myth is true to Peetie's own life is hard to say.
Henry Townsend told Paul Garon, 'I would say that Peetie's
personality was very similar to the one on the records (the
Stomps). He was that kind of person. You know, a jive-type
person.' The Tennessee singer Yank Rachel, who also knew
Peetie in St Louis said, 'Sure, I remember Peetie Wheatstraw –
the Devil's Son-in-Law – he had a long head. He liked his
liquor, but I never heard nothing bad about Peetie Wheatstraw.
He had what you call a nice personality, easy to get along with.'[16]

In the nightmarish context of *Invisible Man*, the bizarre and
allusive humour of the cart pusher seems a reassurance – a
figure of defiance, someone who has gone through to the other

side and come up with wit, warmth and an enigmatic strength –
'Damn if I'm-a let 'em run *me* into my grave . . . All it takes to get
along in this here man's town is a little shit, grit and mother wit.
And man, I was born with all three.'[17]

Blues in Chicago

Despite the activity of artists in St Louis, it was Chicago which
remained the centre of the urban blues both for record-making
and for the vitality of its local clubs and rent party life.

A man who played a vital role in shaping urban blues, and
indeed blues on record, was a white music publisher and record
company executive called Lester Melrose. In the 1920's he had
been involved in the world of jazz with such people as King
Oliver and Jelly Roll Morton, and had connections with the
Gennett record company. He then moved to the American
Record Corp. (later Vocalion) who, to beat the depressed state of
the market, had issued a number of cheap 'dime store' records.
But when the New Deal lifted the economy, and the end of
Prohibition lifted spirits, Melrose saw further possibilities.

'In February of 1934, taverns were opening up and nearly all of
them had juke-boxes for entertainment. I sent a letter, which was
just a feeler, to both RCA Victor and Columbia Records,
explaining that I had certain blues talent ready to record and that
I could locate any amount of rhythm-and-blues talent to meet
their demands. They responded at once with telegrams and
long-distance phone calls. From March 1934, to February 1951, I
recorded at least 90 per cent of all rhythm-and-blues talent for
RCA Victor and Columbia Records.'[1]

The roster of musicians that Melrose handled at one time or
another is staggering – the Famous Hokum Boys, Big Bill Broonzy,
Washboard Sam, the Yas Yas Girl, Tampa Red, Lil Green, Big Boy
Crudup, St Louis Jimmy, Roosevelt Sykes, Memphis Minnie,
Bumble Bee Slim, Big Joe Williams, Walter Davis, Sonny Boy
Williamson, Doctor Clayton, Lonnie Johnson, Tommy
McClennan, Big Maceo, Leroy Carr, Victoria Spivey, Jazz Gillum
and many others. Among these names were some of the biggest
stars of the era, the people who defined the urban blues.

'My record talent was obtained through just plain hard work. I
used to visit clubs, taverns and booze joints in and around
Chicago, also I used to travel all through the Southern States in
search of talent, and sometimes I had very good luck. As a rule I
had considerable trouble with plantation owners, as they were
afraid that I would be the cause of their help refusing to return.'[1]

On one such occasion, when he was looking for the gravel-voiced Tommy McClennan, a rough and intense singer from near Yazoo City in Mississippi, he was warned by Big Bill Broonzy of the dangers of entering a plantation.

'But no, he wouldn't do like I told him and he did get into trouble . . . and a lot of it too, because he had to run and leave his car and send back after it and leave money for Tommy to come to Chicago . . . "They don't call me a white man down there," Mr Melrose told me. "They call me a Yankee. What does that mean, Bill?" "I told you they don't like a white man from the North out on their farms or anywhere they have five or six hundred Negroes working. I told you that you might get hurt out on one of them farms, or camps." "Get hurt, get hurt, hell, they nearly killed me, and they would have done if I hadn't run like hell. I'll certainly never go down there again." '[2]

When he reached Chicago further aggravation surrounded McClennan. As Big Bill recalled in his entertaining auto-biography, McClennan would insist on using the word 'nigger' in his hit song *Bottle Up And Go*; at one house-party his exit was more abrupt than his entrance, through a window with a smashed guitar round his neck.

In his book Big Bill talks about many of his old friends in the blues world, about the parties they had, or blues singing competitions for prizes, or going fishing with Tampa Red, or falling asleep at a baseball game with Sonny Boy Williamson; the atmosphere he conveys is of a friendly neighbourhood community, where musicians and their wives and husbands knew each other and enjoyed a good laugh together. Bill himself was a kind man, well known for his generosity in helping newcomers to Chicago, letting them play in the clubs where he got his work, introducing them to other musicians and so on. He was a close friend of Tampa Red's and likely as not anyone coming up to Chicago to record would end up at Tampa's house.

'The house went all the way from the front to the alley,' recalled pianist Blind John Davis. 'He had a big rehearsal room and he had two rooms for the different artists that come in from out of town to record. Melrose'd pay for him the lodging, and Mrs Tampa would cook for 'em.'[3]

Tampa was quiet, friendly and helpful and when not himself rehearsing he would watch the others or go off with his wife Frances and write songs. From all accounts she was his 'back-bone', his organiser and psychological support, and when she died in the 1950's Tampa never really recovered from the loss.

But in the good days, when he and Big Bill were at their peak, they were the front-runners in developing modern blues. Rehearsing, song-writing, playing the small black clubs in Chicago, fixing up recording sessions, arguing about music, drinking together, the musicians came to know each other and gradually their blues came to move in the same direction.

Like Tampa, Big Bill had a range of musical abilities that spanned several styles. He had started playing easy-paced guitar duets and country reels when he began recording; he was one of the Hokum Boys with Georgia Tom in the *Tight Like That* era, and then he moved on to guitar and piano duets, all the time showing a facility for raggy, syncopated guitar-playing. His slower blues, with Black Bob on piano, were melodious and sad.

> Eeh, when my mother died, my dad give po' me away,
> When my mother died, my dad give po' me away,
> Lord, I'm just a bum baby, that's why I got no place to stay.
>
> Sometimes I wonder why my dad give po' me away,
> Sometimes I wonder why my dad give po' me away,
> Lord, because I was dark-complexioned, Lord they throwed me away.

I'm Just A Bum (1935)[4]

But gradually in the brash club world of Chicago, and on record especially, he started taking on more musicians and expanding his band. Following Tampa Red and his Chicago Five, Big Bill presented his Memphis Five, using trumpet, clarinet, second guitar, piano and bass. Sometimes he would use a drummer, and this became the trend in the later 30's.

The good-time feeling of Hokum was given a heavier beat and a more pronounced boogie piano. At the same time electric guitars were gradually taking their place in the line-up, not with the power and amplification of the modern era, but just enough to lift and sustain the sound over the other instruments. Just as greater regularity and organisation had been required of the jazz bands accompanying the classic singers, so the Chicago blues bands played to a pattern, with instrumental breaks for the pianist or the guitarist to take the lead, or the clarinet or trumpet to blow a solo. At their worst, the early Chicago blues bands were predictable and mechanical, using the same old solos over and over again; but at their best they generated a mighty swing in up-tempos and gave a push and emphasis to the slow numbers. Recordings were increasingly produced out of a pool of performers who swapped songs, played on each others sessions, used the same musicians. Jazz Gillum would play harmonica with Big Bill, Bill would play guitar with Washboard Sam, and so on, and all would draw on a succession of Chicago's many pianists, like Black Bob, Blind John Davis, Joshua Altheimer, Roosevelt Sykes, or Horace Malcolm, Simeon Henry and Memphis Slim.

Not everyone in Chicago was using large bands. Roosevelt Sykes would usually make his records with perhaps a bass or drums, and Big Bill and Tampa themselves didn't use them all the time. A general lightness of tone and an emotionally low-key mood still pervaded the urban blues.

There were however exceptions. One highly successful singer who remained immune to the new developments was the frenzied Georgia bottleneck guitarist Kokomo Arnold. In Chicago he was a steel worker, and in his spare time played the bars and taverns but more importantly he ran a booming 'moonshine' liquor trade from his bath-tub still, a business undiminished by the repeal of Prohibition. In 1930 he had already made one record in Memphis as Gitfiddle Jim, but though he played the clubs and bars of Chicago, he was not enthusiastic to record.

'I was doing well with my moonshine business, making it in the basement. I always had customers coming to buy it when I returned from the steel mill, and I didn't wish to leave it. You see I couldn't leave my basement, otherwise I would lose my customers.'

Finally, in September 1934, blues singer Kansas Joe McCoy and Decca Records executive Mayo Williams persuaded him.

'When they took me to the studio first – that was Joe McCoy and Mayo Williams – they let me wait about for hours because the studio wasn't free. So I said to myself, "What's the hell's the use of this; I better go home to see my customers and give them that moonshine." So I went out of the studio without recording and came straight back home; I asked the landlady to tell everybody I'm not at home. Yes, they came to look for me, but I was in the basement making my moonshine and I was hearing the landlady answering them and telling them I was outside. You know I never was interested in making records and I always preferred to live a quiet life; just unknown in my basement.'[5]

A few days later Joe met Kokomo in the street and took him to the studio again. 'You know, there were several people there that time, and they didn't let me go until I cut my record!'[5]

Kokomo Arnold had an entirely individual, high-speed and

frantic bottleneck style and he sang with a moaning hum. The blasting whine of the guitar and the mumbling, almost spoken singing with its sudden eruptions into assertive clarity, gave him an immediate double-sided hit, *Milk Cow Blues* and *Old Original Kokomo Blues*.

> . . . Now you can read out your hymn-book, preach out your bible,
> Fall down on your knees and pray the Good Lord will help you –
> 'Cause you gonna be, you gonna be – my help some day;
> Mammo if you can't quit your sinnin', please quit your low down ways.
>
> Says I woke up this mornin' and I looked out doors –
> Says I know my mammy's missin' pretty milk cow, Lord by the way she lows.
>
> Lord if you see my milk cow buddy, please drive her home,
> Says I ain't had no milkin' butter mamo, Lord since-a my cow been gone . . .
>
> *Milk Cow Blues* (1934)[6]

Arnold's idiosyncratic style was to be heard on more than a hundred records till either falling sales or a dispute with the company ended his recording in 1938. He finally quit music for good in 1941 to return to his quiet life, smoking his pipe in anonymity.

If the intensity and country-sounding irregularity of a Kokomo Arnold was a rarity in Chicago, the spiritual home of the blues remained the South. The audience for the records produced by the Chicago blues singers was no less in the South than in the city itself, and their music reflected rural as well as urban themes. The musicians in the Big Bill-Tampa Red circle were themselves all from the South. The harmonica-player Jazz Gillum had come up to Chicago in 1923.

'I'd been treated so bad I wanted to go somewhere if somebody hits you you can hit 'em back. In Mississippi, if somebody hits you, you got to run. You can't walk out of Mississippi, you got to run . . . walkin' is most too slow.'[7]

> I got the key to the highway,
> Yes, I'm billed out and bound to go,
> I'm gonna leave – leave here runnin'
> Because walking' is most too slow.
>
> *Key To The Highway* (1940)[8]

Despite the ease and low-key confidence of the blues that went before, by the late 1930's and early 1940's the emotional level of blues in Chicago was beginning to be cranked up. By now the migrants' ghetto had established its own cultural roots. There was a new feeling of assertion in the combination of attacking boogie piano, bass and solidly accented off-beat drumming, generating a sense of group solidarity and power; exultant cries of 'Look out!' as a band member rode in for a solo, or 'Beat it out, boy!' in encouragement, added to the sense of involvement and excitement.

Driving his bands on with the rapping impetus of his thimbled fingers on a metal washboard, Washboard Sam was one of those creating the new assertiveness, working with Big Bill or Jazz Gillum, composing and making records himself. He had a big, abrasive voice, which he used to power through up-tempo good-time songs, or sometimes he would deadpan jive-talk his way to the chorus:

> Now a nickel is a nickel, and a dime is a dime,
> You spend your money, and I'll spend mine,
> If you think you can boss me, and eat up my grub,
> You are a lyin' sweet woman, so get up outa that mud.
>
> (*Chorus*) Your game is too strong, mama,
> Yes, you're dice is too bad,
> So find you another chump, baby,
> Oooh well, because I'm not the lad.

I'm Not The Lad (1941)[9]

His tough manner gave his straight blues a warning note of direct complaint.

> I been treated like an orphan and worked just like a slave,
> If I never get my revenge evilness will carry me to my grave.

I've Been Treated Wrong (1941)[10]

Like the lesser classic blues singers, many of the 30's urban blues are now distinctly dated. When popular taste moved on they were left high and dry and there has been no particular attempt to revive them. On their own terms the best are still expressive and entertaining, but unlike the old country blues, and the later urban blues, they have not generated much interest or support. When Big Bill Broonzey caught the imagination of the folk music enthusiasts of the 1950's it was as a country bluesman, singing and playing his guitar: gone were the clarinet, trumpet, bass, piano and drums.

Of more lasting influence has been John Lee 'Sonny Boy' Williamson, sometimes known as Sonny Boy No. 1 to distinguish him from the second Sonny Boy (Rice Miller) Williamson who incidentally always claimed to be the first.

Sonny Boy created a bridge first between the country blues of the South and the Chicago blues of the 30's, and then with the modern Chicago blues. He was born in Jackson, Tennessee, in 1914, and in his teens he was playing harmonica, working a regular circuit with Sleepy John Estes, Yank Rachel and Home-sick James. He arrived in Chicago via St Louis in the mid-thirties and when he first started recording in 1937 he still had the strong flavour of the South; with his slightly mumbled singing and mournfully expressive harp he sounded much like a country-boy.

> I said, 'You know how times is nowadays;
> Can't no one man find no job.'
> I say, 'I can't even take care of my wife and baby,
> And I might' near to let my own family starve.'
>
> I said, 'Please give me two more weeks,
> Insurance man, please do that for me.'
> Well, I say, 'Don't live up North,
> My home is back down in Tennessee.'
>
> *Insurance Man Blues* (1938)[11]

He played with all the rhythmic subtlety of the best country blues, slurring and wailing the harp notes, making voice and harmonica almost a single entity. He often worked with guitarists such as Henry Townsend, Robert Lee McCoy or Big Joe Williams, and mandolin players Yank Rachel or Willie Hatcher, and they added to the rural feeling.

But gradually the rural sound changed, as if the country-boy was wising up to city ways.

> Santa Claus, Santa Claus, can I get you to understand,
> I want you to bring my baby one of those radios, and two or three of those electric fans.
>
> *Christmas Morning Blues* (1938)[12]

Sonny Boy was to revolutionise modern blues by creating a front-line instrument out of the harmonica. Harps had always played their part in the blues, especially in the jug bands, but Sonny Boy was identified as the lead man, completely tied to the sound of his instrument. The fast interplay between little instrumental riffs and voice, the up-front drive of his blowing and his vocal mannerisms were much admired, bringing him a rapid rise to pre-eminence in Chicago. Frequently working with

Big Bill both on record and in the clubs, he became a dominant figure, updating his sound with piano, bass and drums. His voice took on a peculiar expressiveness from a slight speech impediment which he overcame by fast gabbling, packing syllables into a line with a rhythmic flow and running on into the harp. His combination of rural intensity and modern backing was showing the early signs of how the blues were to develop. In May 1940, backed by the rocking piano of Joshua Altheimer and the thudding drums of Fred Williams, he cut the mighty *I Been Dealing With The Devil*.

> I got the meanest woman you most ever seen,
> She sleeps with an ice-pick in her hand, man,
>   and she fights all in her dreams.
> I been dealing with the devil,
> My woman don't love me no more.[13]

The next year he recorded the slow, poignant *My Black Name Blues*.

> Now I hear my black name ringin' all up and down the line,
> Now I hear my black name ringin' all up and down the line,
> Now I don't believe you love me, mama,
> I believe I'm just throwin' away my time.[14]

Fast and rocking or slow and intense, light-hearted and humorous or restrainedly sad, all Sonny Boy's records were distinctive reflections of his own personality. A heavy drinker, like many of the singers he could sometimes get into scrapes, but the almost universal consensus among his contemporaries seems to be of his good nature and generosity. As Billy Boy Arnold recalled:

'He was 'bout one of the finest fellers I know . . . He worked to help the people with somethin' to eat and somethin' to drink. When pay-day come he didn't have anything – he had *no* pay-day. He was just good – he bought everything they wanted to drink; everything they wanted to eat. He was good to the crowd around him. That's all he did, was work for them.'[15]

He and his wife Lacey Belle, whom he often referred to in his songs, were well known for their friendliness and hospitality, with Sonny Boy showing endless patience in demonstrating harp technique to up-and-coming youngsters like Billy Boy himself. His enormous popularity, his influence in shaping the modern Chicago blues, make all the more tragic the bitter and brutal end of his life, when in June 1948 he was stabbed in the head. Lacey

Belle found him lying on the doorstep where he gasped 'Lord have mercy . . .' He slipped into a coma and died.

> Honey, if I ever mistreat you, God knows I don't mean no harm,
> Honey, if I ever mistreat you, God knows I don't mean no harm,
> Because I ain't nothin' but a little country boy, an' I'm right down
> off the cotton farm.

Million Years Blues (1941)[16]

There was sadness too in the life of a pianist who often played with Sonny Boy Williamson, Big Maceo Merriweather who, at the height of his powers in 1946, was partially paralysed by a stroke at the age of 41. But from the time he started recording in 1941, Big Maceo was one of the major contributors in the resurgence of 'primitivism' in the Chicago blues. With all the weight of his 245 lbs he played a thunderous boogie, with relentlessly rolled bass figures and hammered trebles. Gone were the hints of ragtime of the early barrelhouse players; his was a style pared down to essentials, and he created a classic in the genre in his *Chicago Breakdown*, a rhythmically dense instrumental with an unflagging power.

Since Georgia Tom had quit the blues, Tampa Red had used a variety of piano-players, but the partnership he set up with Big Maceo seems to have given him renewed energy. The combination of earthy piano and Tampa's fat-toned electric guitar, with either Tampa or Maceo singing, gave their records a rough drive. On Maceo's *Tuff Luck Blues* there are calls between the two of 'Git it and git it good!', and an excited 'Yes, I know!'

> It's too bad, things are going so tough with me,
> You have heard my story, people won't you think of me.[17]

Maceo's husky voice had a smoky gentleness, and his slow blues were restrained and sad, drawing on a clearly rural feel and imagery as in his impressive *County Jail Blues*.

> These stripes don't hurt me, but these chains they kill me dead.[18]

Big Maceo was born in Georgia in 1905, and although living in Detroit and Chicago he never lost the rough down-home sound that was beginning to break the urbanity of the Chicago Blues of the 30's. Most copied and best remembered of all his songs (recorded by rhythm-and-blues singers as diverse as Ray Charles and Chuck Berry a decade and more later) was his quiet and touching *Worried Life Blues*; with elements drawn from the crying country singer Sleepy John Estes' *Someday, Baby*, he made this his own theme song.

Oh Lordy Lord, oh Lordy Lord,
It hurts me so bad for us to part,
But someday baby I ain't going to worry my life anymore.

So many nights since you been gone,
I been worried and grieving my life alone,
But someday baby, I ain't going to worry my life anymore.[19]

The way the urbanity and repetitiveness of the Chicago blues could give way to injections of rougher, more aggressive forms is seen in the career of Memphis Minnie, one of the greatest of all the women singers of the 30's, or of any other period. Born in Algiers, Louisiana, in 1897, she married a succession of blues singers, Casey Bill Weldon, Kansas Joe McCoy and Little Son Joe (Ernest Lawler). She started recording in 1929 and her guitar duets with Kansas Joe had a superbly emphatic swing. Her hard voice had authority and distinction, making her one of the big stars of the 30's. Then, like the rest, she started using larger groups, with extra guitar, or mandolin, bass and piano and even the occasional trumpet or clarinet. She continued recording right through to the 1950's but her peak of popularity was in her famous Blue Monday parties at Ruby Lee Gatewood's Tavern in Chicago, one of the most famous joints of the time with its large floor space and dining facilities.

She played in the smaller clubs too, and at midnight on New Year's Eve, 1942, she was seen at the 230 Club by the poet and writer Langston Hughes, who described the scene in his *Chicago Defender* column 'Here to Yonder'.

'The electric guitar is very loud, science having magnified all its softness away. Memphis Minnie sings through a microphone and her voice – hard and strong anyhow for a little woman's – is made harder and stronger by scientific sound.

'The singing, the electric guitar, and the drums are so hard and so loud, amplified as they are by General Electric on top of the icebox, that sometimes the voice, the words, and the melody get lost under their noise, leaving only the rhythm to come through clear. The rhythm fills the 230 Club with a deep and dusky heartbeat that overrides all modern amplification. The rhythm is as old as Memphis Minnie's most remote ancestor . . .

'Then through the smoke and racket of the noisy Chicago bar float Louisiana bayous, muddy old swamps, Mississippi dust and sun, cotton fields, lonesome roads, train whistles in the night, mosquitoes at dawn and the Rural Free Delivery that never brings the right letter. All these things cry through the strings on Memphis Minnie's electric guitar – amplified to machine proportions – a musical version of electric welders plus a rolling mill. Big rough old Delta cities float in the smoke too. Also border cities, Northern cities, Relief, WPA, Muscle Shoals, the jooks. *Has Anyone Seen My Pigmeat On The Line, See See Rider,* St Louis, Antoine Street, Willow Run, folks on the move who leave and don't care. The hand with the dice-ring picks out music like this. Music with so much in it folks remember that sometimes it makes them holler out loud . . .'[20]

The rural South

In March 1932 Congressman George Huddleston of Alabama described the conditions of sharecroppers to a committee of the U.S. Senate:

'Any thought that there has been no starvation, that no man has starved and no man will starve, is the rankest nonsense. Men are actually starving by their thousands today . . . I do not mean to say that they are sitting down and not getting a bite of food until they actually die, but they are living such a scrambling, precarious existence, with suffering from lack of clothing, fuel and nourishment, until they are subject to be swept away at any time, and many are being swept away.'[1]

Sharecropping had always been the lowest form of tenancy and existence had seldom been better than marginal. Tenancy itself, for blacks and whites, had become increasingly widespread so that whereas in the 1880's a third of the farms in the South were tenant-operated, by 1920 the proportion had increased to a half. Not all tenants were sharecroppers and there were many variations in the system, some being full croppers and other mixing cropping with wage-labour, but tenancy continued to increase. By the early 1930's there were over 8.5 million people embroiled in the system and a third of these were black. As Son House told Julius Lester in 1965, sharecropping was the way of life blacks accepted as normal in the 1920's.

'At that time, there was mostly farm work, and sometimes it got pretty critical. Low wages . . . well, people kind of suffered a little during some of those years. Suffered right smart. In some places they got along a little better than they did in others. But they stayed up against it mostly. Bad housing and all that kind of stuff. Of course, they'd get plenty of just old common food, but they didn't make enough money to do any good. Some of those that grew crops . . . if they paid their debts for the food they ate during the year, why, if they came out and cleared as much as forty or fifty dollars for a year they were satisfied. Out of a whole year's work! Of course, along then, they didn't worry over it because they always knew if they didn't have the money, they was still going to eat and have a place to stay such as it was. So they didn't complain and worry about it.'[2]

However, the Depression spread tenancy and at the same time worsened conditions of tenure, so that as many as one in three tenants changed farms each year. 'The agricultural ladder for these American citizens,' said Roosevelt, 'has become a treadmill.'[3] Half the black population of the South were tenant farmers in 1930, and of those 44 per cent were sharecroppers for whom conditions were desperate. Working from dawn till dusk, they lived in wretched wooden cabins without sanitation, eating sowbelly meal and molasses and drinking bad water. Disease was rampant, particularly pellagra, malaria and ague.

> I'm sinkin' down with the fever, and it won't let me sleep,
> I'm sinkin' down with the fever, and it won't let me sleep,
> It was about three o'clock before he would let me be.
>
> *High Fever Blues* – Bukka White (1940)[4]

There were few medical facilities and the landlords' attitude remained 'all that a sharecropper needs is a cotton patch and a corn cob'.[5]

Tragically for the sharecropper the New Deal was more concerned with restoring farm economy than with directly bringing help to the poor. The early policies actually made conditions of life worse for the sharecroppers. In 1933, with cotton prices so low they hardly covered production costs, the Agricultural Adjustment Administration (AAA) tried to push prices up by restricting the amount of cotton on the market. They paid subsidies to farmers to reduce acreage with the devastating result for sharecroppers of further reducing the need for plantation labour. In the best paternal traditions some planters kept on their croppers even when there was little work for them, and some croppers shrewdly ensured that they got enough 'furnish' from the boss to end the season in debt, assuming he would keep on those who owed him money. But many were simply pushed off their shares as crops were ploughed under, creating a large pool of homeless unemployed.

The New Deal had evoked new emotions both of hope and despair in the South, feelings reflected in the letters which poured into Washington. A Georgia farmer wrote:

'I have Bin farming all my life But the man I live with Has Turned me loose taking my mule and my feed . . . I have 7 in family. I ploud up cotton last yeare I can rent 9 acres and plant 14 in cotton But I haven't got a mule no feed ... I want to farm I have Bin on this farm 5 years. I can't get a job so Someone said Rite you.'[6]

Under the terms of the AAA 'Cotton Contract' between government and farmer, both landlord and tenant were theoretically eligible for financial assistance. But in practice the scheme became little more than a subsidy to the planters. While many retained workers they didn't need and gave their tenants their fair share of the AAA payments, even more did not. They dominated the Sheriffs at County courthouses and had the support of Congressmen in Washington. By shifting their workers from sharecropping to wage labour and by other legal manoeuvres, many planters kept the hand-outs for themselves. Government research in 1936 showed that while landlords had each received an average of 822 dollars per plantation, the amount received by *all* the tenants on a plantation put together averaged only 108 dollars.

By forsaking the old pattern of sharecropping and creating wage labourers who could be hired or fired at will, the landlords were inadvertently contributing to a breakdown in the old way of life. With migration reduced by unemployment in the North, the growing surplus of labour and the hazardous conditions of work for the remaining croppers and labourers, mistrust and resentment were building up among the already destitute black workers. No longer could the paternalism of the landowner be relied upon to provide for 'his niggers' even though it had by no means entirely disappeared. Talking about how hard life was for blacks, Sam Chatmon points out: 'There was plenty of white folks didn't have nothing just like we didn't have nothing, and they seen the same sort of time as we had. Or take white people, they don't like poor white folk, they'll do a whole lot more for a colored person than they will their own color.'[7]

With agitation in the air throughout America, the sharecroppers began to stir themselves into action. The first sharecroppers' union was organised in Tallapoosa County, Alabama, in 1931, and more importantly the Southern Tenant Farmers' Union was organised in Arkansas in 1934. The STFU challenged the traditions of Southern life not only by its mere existence but by its alliance between blacks and poor whites (many of whom were ex-Klansmen).

At first the landlords didn't take the STFU seriously, but as its leadership strengthened, the success of its meetings and the vigour of protest increased, they were forced to react. And their reaction was a wave of terror. The 'Riding Bosses' intimidated the sharecroppers and hunted down the union organisers as their predecessors had hunted runaway slaves. Norman Thomas, who had been Socialist Presidential Candidate in 1932 and was a popular leader in the union, received a characteristic letter from a cropper's wife:

'We Garded our house and been on the scout until we are Ware out. and Havent any Law to look to. Thay and the Land Lords hast all turned to nite Riding ... they shat up some Houses and have threten our Union and Wont Let us Meet at the Hall at all.'[8]

Another STFU organiser, Howard Kester, described the situation in his *Revolt Among The Sharecroppers*, published in 1936.

'While violence of one type or another has been continually poured upon the membership of the Union ... it was in March 1935 that a "reign of terror" ripped into the country like a hurricane. For two-and-a-half months, violence raged through northeastern Arkansas and in neighbouring states ... Meetings were banned and broken up; members were falsely accused, arrested and jailed, convicted on trumped up charges and thrown into prison; relief was shut off; union members were evicted from the land by the hundreds; homes were riddled with bullets from machine guns; churches were burned and school-houses stuffed with hay and floors removed; highways were patrolled night and day by armed vigilantes looking for the leaders; organisers were beaten, mobbed and murdered until the entire country was terrorized.'[9]

In Birdsong, Mississippi, Norman Thomas was attacked, knocked from his speaker's platform and having been told 'we don't need no Gawd-damn Yankee Bastard to tell us what to do with our niggers,' he was run out of town.[10]

The STFU eventually foundered but, in showing joint black and white political agitation for the first time in the South since the 1890's, it was to be a forerunner of the bitter struggle for civil rights in the 1960's. And the old pre-Civil War spiritual the union sang in the late 1930's was to be their anthem of freedom.

> We shall not be,
> We shall not be moved,
> We shall not be,
> We shall not be moved,
> Just like a tree that's planted by the water,
> We shall not be moved.[11]

But those involved in union activity were a minority, and there remained a dull, despair-ridden, haggard belt across the South populated by a worn-out, apathetic and hopeless class of rural workers, black and white. In the mid- and late 1930's the public became increasingly aware of the plight of the croppers through the writing of people like Erskine Caldwell and Margaret Bourke-White. In 1935 Caldwell described what he saw in a Georgia cropper's cabin:

'In one of the two rooms a six-year-old boy licked the paper bag the meat had been brought in. His legs were scarcely any longer than a medium-sized dog's leg, and his belly was as large as that of a 130 pound woman's . . . On the floor before an open fire lay two babies, neither a year old, sucking the dry teats of a mongrel bitch.'[12]

In 1935 Roosevelt established the Resettlement Administration (RA) to meet the problems of rural poverty by moving farmers from submarginal land to give them a fresh start. Having planned to resettle half a million families it only succeeded with 4,441 cases. Government will and cash were lacking. More successful, but still only barely touching the problem was the Farm Security Administration created in 1937. The FSA extended long-term, low interest rehabilitation loans to farmers to help them buy family-size farms and it was the first agency to do anything substantial for tenant farmers, sharecroppers and migrant workers turned off the land. By the end of 1941 the FSA had spent over one billion dollars in grants and loans, disbursed with scrupulous fairness to blacks and whites alike. But the FSA was hindered politically; croppers and migrants usually had no vote whereas the landlord class was well represented in Congress, and the desire of the farm corporations and planters for cheap labour made sure financial appropriations for the FSA were kept low.

The basic humanitarian concern of the FSA did bring benefits – the transient work camps, some sponsored co-operative ventures, the provision of a certain amount of rural dental and health care and so on. They also funded a large group of photographers to record the living conditions of the poor in the rural areas. The photography of Walker Evans in James Agee's *Let Us Now Praise Famous Men*[13] again helped focus attention on the poverty of the South, and they stand as testaments to the strength and human dignity of even the most impoverished. At the same time there was a growing interest in the folkways of the American poor, and people like John and Alan Lomax, working for the Library of Congress, recorded folk music of every kind, including the blues from Lead Belly to Son House and from Blind Willie McTell to Booker White.

There were other New Deal measures which helped improve the standard of living in the South; the Tennessee Valley Authority (TVA) with its radical concept of regional planning established a network of dams which helped both flood control and the prevention of soil erosion, and also did much to provide cheap electricity. In 1935 a Rural Electrical Administration was set up bringing almost unalloyed benefits to the poor rural areas. At that time only 10 per cent of farms had electricity but by 1952 the proportion had risen to 90 per cent. This was to be of great significance for the blues, as guitar-players began using amplifiers and radio stations started beaming programmes to black audiences.

Despite the planning and Government measures, the fundamental problems of the rural South remained the same – economic backwardness, poverty and overpopulation. To raise the standard of living meant modernisation, diversification and mechanization nearly all of which, as machines replaced men, was liable to lead to still further unemployment.

> Now you ought to cut off so many trucks and tractors,
> White folks, you ought to work more mules and men.
> Now you ought to cut off so many trucks and tractors,
> White folks, you ought to work more mules and men.
> Then you know that would make, ooh babe,
> Money get thick again.
>
> *Working Man Blues* – Sleepy John Estes (1940)[14]

The surge of migration out of the South resumed. In the early 40's the war industries in the North and on the West Coast went into top gear, drawing thousands of blacks into the factories. Between 1940 and 1950 over a million blacks abandoned the South.

A way of life was beginning to disappear. Sam Chatmon told the story of how he himself finally quit sharecropping in 1950:

'The man told me, say, "Sam, I'm writing down everything that peoples says about the First of the Year Resolution. Everybody else told me their Resolution, I want you to tell your own." I told him, "Why, you may not want to hear mine." He said, "Well, I'm going to write it down, you tell it." I said, "I'm going to put a prayer, New Year's Morning. I'm going to tell the Lord to search my heart, and if he finds anything been hanging round me like a double shovel, a gang plough, a mule, a cotton sack, I want him to move it, and cast it into the sea of forgiveness so it won't rise against me in this world either the world to come." He said, "Do you mean it?" I told him, "I sure do." And I ain't ploughed a mule since.'[15]

Blues in the South

> Blind Boy had a million friends, North, East, South and West,
> Blind Boy had a million friends, North, East, South and West,
> Yes, you know it's hard to tell which place he was loved the best.
>
> Well, all you women of Blind Boy, how you want your lovin'
>   done?
> Well, all you women of Blind Boy, how you want your lovin'
>   done?
> I'll do my best, I'll do my best to carry Blind Boy Fuller's business
>   on,
> Good-bye, Blind Boy.
>
> *The Death Of Blind Boy Fuller* – Brownie McGhee (Blind Boy
>   Fuller No. 2) (1941)[1]

In 1941 Brownie McGhee recorded *The Death Of Blind Boy Fuller* to commemorate one of the most popular of all the 1930's record stars. While the Race record market had been dominated by the urban singers of the North and Mid-West, there were still some stars from the South and Blind Boy Fuller was one of the biggest. From the time he started recording in 1935 till his death in 1940 he cut some 135 titles, and in most cases with considerable commercial success.

Neither the dominance of the Northern cities nor the ravages of the Depression stemmed the continuing and endless activities of blues singers in the South. In almost every community, large or small, there were musicians performing for dances or parties, in honky-tonks and bars or simply for the contentment of their own minds.

A small, quiet and polite man, Blind Boy Fuller made his living as a street musician around the tobacco towns of North Carolina. Smartly dressed in a sober suit and tie, he was probably never happier than when he was singing for street corner crowds and workers from the warehouses and tobacco factories.

'Blind Boy Fuller? 1934, Yeah. I played on a street with him, that's where I first met him,' recalled harp-player Blind Sonny Terry. 'He was in a place called Wadesboro, North Carolina. I was playin' on one side of the street and he was on the other side. So I heard that whinin' guitar over there wailin' y'know . . . I had some little boy with me . . . I said: "Go over there and tell him to come over here" . . . And by the time I found the one to tell him to bring him over, he had someone brought at me!"[2]

In the Depression the tobacco towns of the Piedmont were good places for street singers to work. Protected from the worst of the Depression by the continued sale of cigarettes, there was just that little bit of extra cash around. Brownie McGhee, who much to his irritation was called Blind Boy Fuller No. 2 on some of his early records, used to work in Winston-Salem. It was an important tobacco centre, making *Camel* cigarettes, where the factories employed plenty of women. Brownie would start playing outside as the workers came pouring out:

'Man it was pay-day every night, if you work it right! Mebbe a girl take you up, feed you a good meal too.'[3]

Blind Boy Fuller made his base in Durham, North Carolina, and it was here he made his break into records. His reputation had reached the ears of a white chain store manager, J. B. Long, who not only sold blues records but also fixed up sessions with record companies. Long became Fuller's manager, arranging recording dates and even helping to write his songs, and the partnership lasted until Fuller's death.

Fuller's great popularity must have been in the distinctiveness and variety of his performances. Sometimes he recorded with only his own guitar, and on the other occasions he was accompanied by Bull City Red's washboard or Sonny Terry's whooping and swooping harmonica. He played good-naturedly swinging country dance tunes like *Rag, Mama, Rag, Piccolo Rag,* or *Jitterbug Rag,* or sang highly entertaining double-meaning songs.

> Says, I stepped on your starter, Great God, and you know your
> motor turned over slow,
> Says, I stepped on your starter, Great God, and you know your
> motor turned over slow,
> If you ain't getting your night spark, little woman, Great God, call
> on Blind Boy Fuller for more.
>
> *Worn Out Engine Blues* (1940)[4]

He sang with a clear voice, and then his voice would thicken and drop into darker tones.

> And I feel like snappin' my pistol in your face,
> Let some brownskin woman be here to take your place.
> Now you know you didn't want me when you lay down across my bed,
> Drinkin' your moonshine whiskey and talking all out of your head.
>
> *Pistol Snapper Blues* (1938)[5]

Blind Boy Fuller was the most recorded and best remembered of the Piedmont singers, but he was essentially an eclectic musician, representing a high point in a tradition which had begun well before his success and continued after his death. He adapted music he had heard on records or learned directly from other musicians. In the Piedmont district there was an easy-going independence of spirit, with diverse kinds of farming and large numbers of black farmers who owned their own land. The blues of singers like Fuller reflected this way of life in their out-going dance rhythms and sense of stability.

The continuity of country blues traditions were to become important when the surge of migration in the 1940's took the country blues once again to the cities. From the South Eastern States the line of migration continued to be along the Atlantic Seaboard to the North East and particularly to New York and Newark. But in these places country blues never became more than a minority taste, lost in the high-speed cosmopolitan extravagances of the Harlem ghetto. The expressive needs of the new city dwellers were no longer served by simple country dance tunes and guitar rags.

There were exceptions to this. After Blind Boy Fuller died, Brownie McGhee and Sonny Terry formed a partnership which has lasted to this day. In keeping with the pattern, they moved to New York in the 1940's and were already finding the recognition that has given them their current world-wide popularity as 'folk artists'. But in the late 1940's and early 1950's they were highly successful in New York and Newark in adapting the older country blues to more modern styles. In clubs and on record Brownie used an electric guitar and employed larger bands such as the Mighty House Rockers or the Jook Block Busters, with saxophone, piano, bass and drums. With the band's pounding boogie piano and heavy beat, Brownie found no difficulty in making the adjustment.

'I could adjust to a band just as quick as I could do anything. I never was a lone cat . . . What we were doing in the blues field, I stuck with it. The change changed, but I didn't change. I been doing the same thing for thirty years . . . The content that goes into the form has to be real . . . I know what I am inside. I'm an honest-to-God story-teller, and I use my guitar to help me along my way.'[6]

While the 1930's blues of the East Coast transplanted uneasily to the Northern cities, those of Texas were more successful in the West. During the mass migration from the South it was to cities like Los Angeles and San Francisco that many Texans headed, carrying with them the blues they had grown up with.

In the 1930's blues were to be heard in Texas wherever there were congregations of black workers. There was the usual demand for musicians in the cotton areas, but the deadening effect of the Depression pushed many off the land into the cities like Dallas or Houston so although there was still employment for pianists on the old barrelhouse circuit in the lumber camps of the Piney Woods, increasingly they looked for work in the clubs and joints in the towns. Guitarists and pianists travelled on the network of railroads connecting cattle markets and oil towns, stopping off to play in the camps set up for cotton pickers and oil workers on the way, and then on to the honky-tonks in places like Richmond, Houston or Galveston. At the risk of over-simplifying the richness and diversity of the Texas blues it is perhaps safe to say that overall they share a feeling of relaxation. Compared with the brooding, threatening anxiety of life in Mississippi, Texas society was more varied and opportunities for status and independence were greater. Reflecting this difference there was less urgency and tension in their blues. There was a sense of ease in the singers' blurred smoky voices and in the guitarists' use of long melodic phrases and embellishments. The barrelhouse pianists knocked out fast boogies often enough, but their shuffle rhythms and slow blues had the same emotional containment and control. When wartime job opportunities in the West Coast defence factories sucked workers out of Texas these blues styles easily adapted to new city ways. They not only continued to thrive undiluted well beyond the war, they also contributed to the growth of the smoothly urbane and sophisticated West Coast blues which subsequently developed. The addition of saxophones and drums, and of amplifiers for the guitars, made for a mellow and melodic 'cool'. The 1940's blues of the West Coast were comfortable and classy, but with their origins in Texas they still had roots in the blues underworld.

While migrants from Texas went to the West Coast and those from the South East to the Eastern seaboard, the Deep South States like Mississippi, Arkansas and Tennessee once again saw their population heading North. The blues that emerged in Chicago in the later 1940's and early 1950's were the direct descendants of the country blues of the Mississippi Delta.

In the 1930's Mississippi remained much as it had been since the earliest days of the blues, with well over 70 per cent of the

black population tenants and sharecroppers on the cotton plantations, trapped in poverty, constrained by segregation,
patronised or brutalised by whites.

'Back in the 1930's and 1940's it was rough . . .' recalled
slide-guitarist Hound Dog Taylor, who later made his name in
Chicago's small clubs and taverns. 'Nobody'd back you up.
Everybody'd run like scared rabbits. At that time a white man
would go in your house, grab your woman, even if she was sick,
drag her out of bed and make her go out into the field, and you
better not say nothing to him.'[7]

Houston Stackhouse also remembers the ever-present threat
of violence. 'Well, they go round and beat on them (the blacks)
and knock on them and go round and force them to do different
things.' At that time Stackhouse was on a plantation. 'It was a big
plantation, a white man's farm; a lot of us working on it, you
know. He done very well himself, but the other folks around
wasn't too hot, you know. He was all right but other people, you
go on their plantation too much they'd be clowning with you
(*laughs*). They'd want to rap you upside the head with something,
you know, if you acted stubborn. If you didn't act right, didn't go
on like they say they wanted, they rap you, they rap on you and
get you and beat on you (*laughs*). Yeah, he done bruised my head
and I ain't done nothing but just go on playin'. You got a good
head-bruising and then had to go right on, you see. But if you act
nice and go on when they tell you, everything all right.'[8]

In the decade that followed, when over a million Negroes left
the South, Mississippi lost half its young adults.

Of all the different parts of the South there was probably more
support for blues in Mississippi and nearby than anywhere else.
There were blues played in just about every circumstance; on the
plantations, in shacks and house parties, in the streets, in the
taverns and joints, in the cotton centres like Greenville, Greenwood, Yazoo City or Clarksdale, up to Memphis, or across the
river into Arkansas and the cotton and timber towns of Hughes,
Helena, West Memphis, Blytheville and Forest City and even up
into Missouri heading for St Louis. The end of Prohibition in
1933 helped the blues singer as more taverns opened; Mississippi
itself remained 'dry', and hard liquor was illegal, but in Arkansas
there were plenty of places. Johnny Shines used to play in
Helena:

'The joints, the places that we would play at, naturally they
were in the colored section of town, which was pretty big because
there were quite a lot of colored people living there then. Lots of

music around too . . . The town was loaded with musicians. And lots of places to play there too. Juke joints, I'd guess you'd call them . . . Now, a juke joint is a place where people go to play cards, gamble, drink and so on. So far as serving drinks like you would in a bar or tavern no, it wasn't like that. Beer was served in cups; whiskey you had to drink out of the bottle . . . See, they couldn't use mugs in there because the people would commit mayhem, tear people's head up with those mugs. Rough places they were. When you were playing in a place like that, you just sit there on the floor on a cane-bottomed chair, just rear back and cut loose. There were no microphones or P.A. set-ups there; you just sing out as loud as you can.'[9]

The core of Mississippi blues, and especially in the Delta, re- mained the droning rhythmic tension, the constricted, almost speech-like voice, the dirtily blurred bottleneck guitar and an over- all feeling of anxiety. In the roughened moan and falsetto swoops of the voice, as if cut off from European concepts of musicality and tunefulness, the whole sound was 'African' and 'black'.

Not all Mississippi blues were like this. There had always been the ethereal delicacy of a Skip James, the haunting restraint of a Tommy Johnson, or the instrumental flexibility of bluesmen like the Chatmons; the Mississippi Sheiks were being recorded from 1930 to 1935 and Bo Carter kept piling up records till 1940. But the harsher tradition of the old Delta blues continued.

In 1940, despite the comparative neglect of the Southern singers, Lester Melrose brought to the recording studios one of the most primitive-sounding Delta singers, 'Bukka' White. At the peak of the jumping urban blues era, and at a time when breezy and optimistic up-to-the-minute swing band and jitter- bug music was sweeping the nation, White recorded a series of classically pure unadorned Delta blues, rich in themes of death and imprisonment.

> I'm lookin' far in mind,
>> I believe I'm fixin' to die,
>> I believe I'm fixin' to die;
> I'm lookin' far in mind,
>> I believe I'm fixin' to die;
> I know I was born to die, but I hate to
>> leave my children cryin'.
> *Fixin' To Die Blues*[10]

'Bukka' (his full name is Booker T. Washington White) had been recorded before in 1930 and had even had a small hit with *Shake*

'Em On Down in 1937. But for reasons that are obscure he had been sent to the notorious Parchman Farm, a prison farm in Mississippi. He seems to have had a relatively easy life there, playing his music and he even recorded a couple of numbers for John A. Lomax from the Library of Congress:

'I didn't do any more because I knew he wasn't going to give me any money. I didn't want to cut them two, but I just said, "He done made that long trip . . . Sometimes it's better to give than to receive," so I just gave him the records there for him to get out of my face.'[11]

But in his 1940 sessions he recorded twelve blues, some drawing on his experiences of prison (especially his hatred of the striped uniform in *Where Can I Change My Clothes*), and others inspired by the deaths of people close to him. Taken as a whole his 1940 records represent a high point in the old Delta blues, with Booker's half-talking, half-chanting voice and his ringing bottleneck guitar.

> When a man gets troubled in mind he wants to sleep all the time,
> When a man gets troubled in mind he wants to sleep all the time,
> He knows if he can sleep all the time his trouble won't worry his
> mind, won't worry his mind . . .
>
> *Sleepy Man Blues*[12]

By 1940 Booker's style was being slowly superseded. When Charley Patton died, his blues were already beginning to seem out of date. It was his friends Son House and Willie Brown who continued playing together well into the 1940's who kept the tradition going. Son House was especially influential. Muddy Waters who was later to become almost unrivalled among Chicago blues singers recalls:

'One night we went to one of these Saturday night fish frys, and Son House was there playing. I was using the bottleneck because most of the Delta people used this bottleneck-style thing. When I heard Son House, I should have broke my bottleneck . . . Son House played this place for about four weeks in a row, and I was there every night . . . You couldn't get me out that corner, listening to him, what he's doing.'[13] As Muddy told Tony Standish, 'That guy could preach the blues . . . sit down there and sing one thing after 'nother, like a preacher.'[14]

Son House had indeed been a preacher and his life as a blues singer has to this day been a source of unresolved conflict. For large portions of the community the blues was still the devil's music, the music of immorality, licentiousness, eroticism, whisky-drinking, juke-joints, low life, violence, a source of corruption and the harbinger of social disruption. And to many blacks salvation was to be found in ridding from the Race its stereotyped image of irresponsibility and unreliability.

Writing in 1941 the black sociologist Charles S. Johnson described what he called the 'underworld' of the rural South:

'It is composed of individuals who fall outside the recognised and socially sanctioned class categories, that is, those persons who are free from the demands of society – the "wide" people, the vagabonds, the "worthless" and "undeserving poor" who are satisfied with their status, the "outcasts", the "bad niggers", prostitutes, gamblers, outlaws, renegades, and "free" people. Life in this underworld is hard, but its irresponsible freedom seems to compensate for its disadvantages. These are the people who create the "blues" and secular songs of the demimonde. They are the ones who have in greatest measure a sense of irresponsibility. Persons in this category may be criminal or merely loose. Some of them are even protected and used by white persons for their own ends, and as compensation are licensed to be "hellions" in the Negro community.'[15]

It was a source of profound dismay to see the blues singer representing all the 'worst' elements of black life, not only in his own lifestyle but in the very words of his song. It was felt that only by becoming worthy of 'respect' would the Race achieve any improvement. Partly through education and especially by conducting oneself with extreme politeness and decorum, it was hoped that the world would take note that the 'Negro' had 'proved' his right to a better place in society.

Because education was recognised as a vital part of any social improvement for blacks, the enticements of the nether world of the blues could be a severe distraction. With many hours of a youth's day already taken up with farm working, dancing and entertainment presented a far more attractive proposition than the rigours of such education as was available. As Muddy Waters said:

'I wouldn't say I was supporting myself exactly, but I worked. I didn't get much in the way of schooling. The schools weren't too good, and No. 1 I didn't really have time, I thought, in those days to be bothered with it. I didn't know that you need schooling down through the years. It's one mistake I made.'[16]

Houston Stackhouse was another singer who didn't get much education. 'Oh, I got to the fifth grade and I, I gotten mannish you know, then I had to marry a girl – well, that's broke up my little schooling then'.[17]

But the blues were antithetical to the standards a preacher was expected to represent in a purely religious sense. The fire-and-brimstone emotionality of the preacher was rich in its own mythology of fate, death, hell and the Devil, and in a world as close to the arbitrariness of nature as Mississippi itself where boll-weavils, floods or simply a bad harvest could devastate a person's livelihood, such symbolism had enormous power. Many blues singers felt torn this way and that, enjoying the good times of the juke joint but still believing they would someday turn their backs on the blues. Belief in the power of faith and the possibility of redemption unto Heaven meant that however far a brother or sister might stray from the fold, there was always that possibility of a return to the paths of God.

So House made his choice, but inconsistently; he would sometimes resume his part-time preaching, only to return to the blues. His singing has always had the strong flavour of a back-country preacher in its declamatory fervour, and he sometimes puts aside his guitar to sing an unaccompanied gospel song. And even in his straight blues he turns to the subject.

> Oh I'm gon' get me religion, I'm gon' join the Baptist church,
> Oh I'm gon' get me religion, I'm gon' join the Baptist church,
> I'm gonna be a Baptist preacher, and I sure won't have to work.
>
> Oh I'm gonna preach these blues now, and I want everybody to shout,
> Mmmm, and I want everybody to shout,
> I'm gon' do like a prisoner, I'm gonna roll my time on out.
>
> Oh in my room I bowed down to pray,
> Oh I was in my room I bowed down to pray,
> Say the blues come 'long, and they drove my spirit away.
>
> Oh I had religion, Lord, this very day,
> Oh I had religion, Lord, this very day,
> But the womens and whiskey, well, they would not let me pray . . .
>
> *Preachin' The Blues Part I* (1930)[18]

One of the musicians who learned from Son House was the young Robert Johnson, who has become an almost legendary figure among white blues enthusiasts. One of the many verses of House's two-part *Preachin' The Blues* became the first verse of Johnson's own *Preachin' Blues*.

> Mmm I was up this morning, all my blues walking like a man,
> I was up this morning, my blues walking like a man,
> Worried blues, give me your right hand.

And the blues fell mama's child tore me all upside down,
Blues fell mama child and they've tore me all upside down,
Travel on poor Bob, just can't turn you round.

The blues is a low down shakin' chill,
(*Spoken*) Yes, listen now.
Mmmm . . . is a low down shakin' chill,
You ain't never had 'em, I hope you never will.

Well the blues is a achin' old heart disease,
(*Spoken*) Do it now – you gonna do it – tell me all about,
That the blues is a low down achin' heart disease,
Like consumption, killin' me by degrees . . .

Preachin' Blues (1936)[19]

The legend of Robert Johnson has been created from the combination of the tragic brevity of his life and the overwhelming sense of inner torment and foreboding in his blues. He only recorded some thirty odd songs but taken together they create visions of a restless, self-destructive interior world filled with secret fears and anxieties. At times he seems scarcely able to control the extremities of feeling which press in on him or the tensions and neuroses which drive, harry and confuse him. As if on the edge of an abyss of complete psychic disintegration his voice changes from high frenzy to little-boy vulnerability, while his slide guitar shifts from controlled affirmations to exaggerated effects. Even when his voice is quiet and softly lyrical and his guitar delicately deliberate, the haunted pain is always close to the surface.

I got to keep movin', I got to keep movin',
Blues falling down like hail, blues fallin' down like hail,
Mmmm blues falling down like hail, blues falling down like hail,
And the day keeps on worryin' me,
     there's a hellhound on my trail,
Hellhound on my trail, hellhound on my trail.

Hellhound On My Trail (1937)[20]

Robert Johnson stands at the crossroads of several musical traditions. Having learnt much of his music directly from Son House and Willie Brown – who were anxious for him with avuncular concern – he inherited strong elements of the Delta blues tradition. But at the same time, whether through personal contact or from records, he also shows traces of other musical influences as diverse as Leroy Carr and Scrapper Blackwell, Hambone Willie Newbern, Skip James, Kokomo Arnold, and his own great hero Lonnie Johnson. Having assimilated what he

GILES OAKLEY

wanted – and he would also pick up any hillbilly tune, popular
song, ballad, 'sweet music' from the radio – he transmuted it into
his purely personal expression.

'His guitar seemed to talk – repeat and say words with him like
no one else in the world could,' recalled Johnny Shines. 'I said
he had a talking guitar, and many a person agreed with me. This
sound affected most women in a way that I could never understand. One time in St Louis we were playing one of the songs
that Robert would like to play with someone once in a great
while, *Come On In My Kitchen*. He was playing very slow and
passionately, and when we had quit, I noticed no-one was saying
anything. Then I realised they were crying . . . both women and
men.'[21]

> Mmmmmm – mmmmm, mmmmm, mmmmmmm,
> Mmmmmm – mmmmm, mmmmm, mmmmmmm,
> You'd better come on in my kitchen, it's goin' to be rainin'
> outdoors.
> When a woman get in trouble, everybody throws her down,
> Looking for your good friend, none can be found,
> You'd better come on in my kitchen, it's goin' to be rainin'
> outdoors.

Come On In My Kitchen (1936)[22]

'Things like this often happened, and I think Robert would cry just
as hard as anyone. It was things like this, it seems to me, that made
Robert want to be by himself, and he would soon be by himself. The
thing that was different, I think, was that Robert would do his crying
on the inside. Yes, his crying was on the inside.'[23]

Robert Johnson's place in blues mythology was secured when
in 1938 he died in Greenwood, Mississippi, at the age of 26,
probably poisoned. There are many conflicting views of the kind
of person he was – drunk, sober, moody, considerate, a
womaniser or a lover – but whatever impression his brief life left
on those who knew him, his music remained to inspire others,
including those who had no knowledge of him. Versions of songs
he recorded or which were associated with him have been made
by such singers as Muddy Waters, Elmore James, Johnny
Shines, Robert Jnr. Lockwood, Howling Wolf, Homesick James,
J. B. Hutto, Maxwell Street Jimmy Davis, Jimmy De Berry, Boyd
Gilmore, Baby Face Leroy Foster, Sonny Boy Williamson,
Eddie Boyd, Roosevelt Sykes, Junior Parker, Bobo Jenkins, Big
Joe Williams, Baby Boy Warren, Joe Carter, James DeShay, plus
innumerable rock musicians including the Rolling Stones.

Robert helped prepare what had been a music purely of the country community for transmission into the urban ghetto. It was not only the personal anguish he expressed, the sense of isolation, alienation and yearning, but the musical expression he gave it. He would contrast a heavy bass boogie riff with delicately sinuous treble slides, or use heavily strummed chords, or feathery, spaced out comments to give texture and atmosphere to his songs. He could make his guitar sound like three, and when holding the rhythm steady in the instrument he would ride across it with his voice, or when singing strictly on the beat would let his guitar range freely, creating its own rhythm and setting up another dimension. The effect was an expression not just of hurt and sadness but a sensual and joyful release. His multi-layered style was easily adaptable to a band setting and amplified instruments; the bass line could be carried by piano, bass and drums, while the electric guitar or harmonica took up the treble. So when Mississippians poured into Chicago, the blues of the 1940's and 1950's carried echoes of Robert Johnson.

But there were other developments in the Delta in the decade following his death which were modernising the old blues: the growth of local blues radio broadcasting in Arkansas and Mississippi.

The life of the average musician had always been hard scuffling, trying to find work, make a name. To have a record cut undoubtedly helped, it put the artist's reputation on the map, gave him some status, got him the better jobs. But when businessmen saw opportunities of advertising to the black market through radio broadcasts, it opened up new possibilities. A musician could not only reach a far wider audience and build up a reputation as a top man, he could even advertise where he was going to play.

In the mid-thirties Radio KLCN in Blytheville, Arkansas, started employing a friend of Robert Johnson's, the guitarist Calvin Frazier, and other musicians. There could be problems, as Houston Stackhouse heard from Peck Curtis who had asked the station boss if he could sing.

'Peck say he asked him to let him sing this song where it was about Good Gulf gasoline, you know.

"The monkey and the baboon playin' in the grass,"
so instead of he sayin',
"And stickin' his finger in the Good Gulf gas,"
he made a mistake and said,

"The monkey stuck his finger –, " you know,
and he said "Uh oh!" It was too late then, so the red light come
on. There was polices, there, all the polices . . .'[24]

The real breakthrough in blues radio was in 1941 when the
white-owned Radio KFFA was established in Helena, Arkansas.
Max S. Moore's Interstate Grocer Company were producing
King Biscuit Flour, and to advertise it to the large black
population in Helena they signed on two blues singers, Rice
Miller, a hardened harp-player in his forties, and guitarist
Robert Jnr. Lockwood, whose mother had been one of Robert
Johnson's 'girl friends'. To cash in on the popularity of the
Chicago singer, Miller was called Sonny Boy Williamson, a
name he ever after claimed as his own. Broadcasting live five
days a week at mid-day, 'King Biscuit Time' was an absolute
sensation. Sales of King Biscuit Flour zoomed and soon 'Sonny
Boy White Corn Meal' was on the market as well. King Biscuit
Time became an institution and the band expanded, taking in at
various times drummer Peck Curtis, pianists Willie Love,
Pinetop Perkins, Dudlow Taylor and guitarists Houston Stackhouse and Joe Willie Wilkins.

> Well evenin' everybody,
> People tell me how do you do?
> We're the King Biscuit Boys,
> We came out to welcome you . . .[25]

The King Biscuit Boys became so popular in the 1940's they
went out on the road, playing out in the country or in front of
grocer's shops as Stackhouse recalls:

'There'd be so many people around there, they'd drive up
there, they'd say, "Good gracious alive!" We'd get out there and
hook up our stuff right quick. Pinetop'd sit up in the truck and
play the piano 'cause it was too heavy to be takin' down and
settin' on the ground. We'd be just sittin' around on the ground
right at the back of the truck. Sonny Boy'd he blowin' the harp.
Boy, that sound good to the people. They was applauding and
goin' on. All of us'd line up. Some had on the same shirts and
same color and all. Had Sonny Boy Meal on the back of 'em,
King Biscuit Flour . . . They were a kind of yellow shirt. They
was full shirts, kinda silk-like. It's good cloth; had our names
knitted on the back of 'em. Old man Moore'd say, "Boys, that's
hot stuff now".'[26]

The success of the King Biscuit Show encouraged more
stations to get in on the act and opportunities for blues singers

sprang up all over. The radio stations gave exposure to a whole crop of musicians who had been seeking work since the 30's. Some went on to make very big names for themselves in the blues field while others merely sank back into their juke joint obscurity or gave up altogether.

In 1942 the success of King Biscuit Flour spurred the 'Bright Star' and 'Mother's Pride' Flour companies to compete. Using the melancholic slide guitarist Robert 'Nighthawk', (Robert McCollum) they had their own spot on KFFA. He had already made some records under various names, including 'Robert Lee McCoy' but his radio broadcasts made Nighthawk one of the big names in the Delta.

In the later 40's more and more stations entered the fray – Sonny Boy himself frequently deserted the King Biscuit Boys and worked such stations as KNOE in Monroe, Louisiana, and KGHI in Little Rock, Arkansas, before moving on to team up with Elmore James. In the 30's they had worked with Robert Johnson and now they advertised 'Talaho' tonic in Mississippi over Yazoo City's WAZF and Greenville's WJPJ. KWEM in West Memphis, Arkansas, joined the game when the success of 'Talaho' persuaded 'Hadacol' tonic to compete. West Memphis developed into a jumping blues centre, as Sonny Boy settled in town and got on the air. Just twenty minutes across the river from Memphis it was a 'wide open' town, with vice and gambling, night spots and joints where the blues singers hung out. Forest City Joe, Willie Love and his 3 Aces, B. B. King, one-man-band Joe Hill Louis (the Be-Bop Boy), Howling Wolf, Elmore James, and many others either came into town or performed over KWEM.

Once the rise of King Biscuit Time had opened up the market, the most significant development was when WDIA in Memphis entered the field. In October 1948, risking the threats of white business sponsors they put on their first black programme, a thirty-minute disc-jockey show. Such was its success that WDIA turned its entire air-time to its potential audience of 1¼ million blacks. Styling itself 'Mother Station of the Negroes' (avoiding echoes of paternalism), WDIA helped put the South back on the blues map. The era of field recordings returned, new studios were established in Memphis and elsewhere, and the South reasserted itself as the home of the blues.

This swing of the pendulum created huge opportunities for those with entrepreneurial energy like the young Ike Turner from Clarksdale, Mississippi whose knocked-out piano or wild electric guitar enlivened many a clattering boogie recorded by the 'Kings of Rhythm' or other bands. Some years before the Ike and Tina Turner Revue carried him to rock and soul stardom in the 1970's he was a beady-eyed talent scout and record company fixit man. Simultaneously dealing with Modern of Los Angeles, Chess from Chicago and Sun in Memphis (Sam C. Phillips' company which first recorded Elvis Presley) Ike Turner gave numerous musicians from the small-town outlands of Arkansas and Mississippi their first break. More importantly those changes in musical style and taste which he and others shaped both signalled and reflected the coming convulsions of post-war black society.

In the late 1940's and early 1950's there was a sudden vogue in the black ghettoes for the updated and amplified blues that had been spawned in the South. Some Delta men, like Muddy Waters, had reached Chicago in the mid-40's and the Southside was already rocking to the electric sound of down-home blues. But the recording industry was caught by surprise and it was to the South they looked for the talent. They sought out singers like Sonny Boy Williamson, Howling Wolf and Elmore James, who had already established themselves as local stars on the smaller radio stations.

For some the adaptation to wider fame was difficult. The man who had done so much to bring the rural blues forward, Sonny Boy Williamson No. 2, was already nearly sixty when he had his few hits in the 1950's. He had behind him a lifetime of roughing it in juke joints and country roadhouses, and was out of joint with the times. He failed to adapt to the increasing demands of rock 'n' roll, and while working in Chicago and Detroit he still intermittently returned to the King Biscuit Boys. Yet when he toured Europe in the early 1960's he felt completely at home with the British rhythm-and-blues bands he played with.

He was a strange man. Sometimes remembered as a tough, mean, embittered, temperamental and difficult loner, he still had many friends and an almost unrivalled influence as a harmonica-player. With stooping shoulders, a gleam of guarded irony in his eyes, a magnetically slow poise in his movements, his performances often began with an almost mocking simplicity. He would sing with an almost conversational intimacy, a hushed meandering gentleness, drifting into his imagination, and slowly building momentum, his harp played sparingly; little touches, working his cupped hands, beginning to sway, snapping his fingers, sucking and blowing harder, his voice stronger, his

hooded eyes more distant, his harp swooping, wailing and
distorting through the microphone, his words harsher, tougher
and rocking with power. Then the quietness returning, he would
subside, gently easing back down.

From the moment of the first King Biscuit Show there must
have been an enormous sense of racial pride in hearing black
performers on the air in the South. King Biscuit Time continued
long after Sonny Boy's death in 1965, and his records continue to
be played on the show by popular demand. His first record in
1951 was called *Eyesight To The Blind*. In the late 1960's a rural
black from the Delta quoted the lyrics to folklorist William Ferris
Jr.

'Just tell the whole world how the whole state doing us and
even how Sonny Boy, Sonny Boy Williams' back in his time, he
say, "Now look, I declare you pretty and the whole state know
you fine . . ." You know what comes up again? Black. White.
When you say "I declare you pretty and the whole state know you
fine", that go for you and me. And you know what that do when
he say that? That brings eyesight back to the blind.'[27]

Part Six

Post-war blues

'Saturday night, the Paradise ... A big name band and a crowded club. The sweltering air of people. Revolving lights swinging from the ceiling, splashing the club with waves of red, yellow and deep blue. Now purple, now a fuschia undertone. The lights give the club the type of fuzzy atmosphere that the world appears to have after you open your eyes from unrestful sleep. It leads you into intoxication without the help of alcohol. The crowd watches in noisy anticipation. The crowd is in the mood – the band gives them what they are looking for. The sexy wail of the sax screams triumphant notes above the boisterous audience. Trumpets brace the voice of the sax, riff loud and clear over the dissonant wail. Brassy, ragged runs sail smoothly into quiet undertones. The drums and bass accentuate the rhythm. The crowd is with the band, sways with the music, makes the air static with gyrating fingers and pounding hands.

"Blow that thing."

'The dance, a whirling parody of jitterbugging, applejack, the bop – "Baby, you know how to hucklebuck?" Champagne bubbles, the warm glow of scotch manifests a new world. Weird, crazy sounds of bop, the frantic beat of jazz, the good ole lowdown blues.

... "Some people like to do it in the Winter!"

... "*Yeh!*"

... "Some like it in the Spring – "

... "*That's me!*"

... "But, they call me daddy rolling stone – oh, my – when it's pouring down rai-ii-nnn-nn-"

'... The band got carried away and gave an impromptu floor show. They jammed for twenty minutes, hot wild notes of screaming dissonance, slow, sweet, tricky counterpoint following a basic pattern of rhythm and melody. The band loved itself. The crowd loved the band. They got what they had come to see – the night wore on, the band screamed the night away.'[1]

The blues at the Paradise described by Herbert Simmons in his novel *Corner Boy* could have been heard at any time around 1950, in almost any city. It would have been the same earlier or a little later, but wherever there was a dance hall or club, bright lights, glittering saxophones and snappily-dressed musicians created a world of excitement. The music was glamorous, assertive, rippling with muscle-flexing power, it was the blues of the city.

As the rural South lost its population to the cities in the 1940's and 50's, there were new moods in the black community. In some respects blacks had become more American than ever before. The Second World War had seen the involvement of blacks in a national effort on an unprecedented scale, in the army, the air force, the navy, the arms factories, turning out bombs, tanks, planes and ships. The rapid succession of events, the war, the new jobs, experiences abroad, were all energising and invigorating. Eyes were opened to new possibilities in life. Better money and opportunities created a greater sense of involvement and the feeling that the past was falling away.

But at the same time it was all too clear that many things remained the same. The slum ghettoes in the cities were already established and were known about even to those fresh migrants from the South. There were serious riots in the war years and after, in Harlem, in Detroit, Chicago and elsewhere. Some were widespread, explosive outbursts of black frustration and anger while others were little more than street-block rock fights as whites tried to keep blacks from moving into new neighbourhoods. For many the war-time rhetoric of struggling for democracy seemed an ironic commentary on the plight of those scrambling on the edge of the democratic process in America itself. While black living-standards improved and more entered the ranks of the bourgeoisie, there remained the large gulf between black and white in wages and opportunities. The problems facing ghetto-dwellers continued, the overcrowding and the lack of facilities, the poorer educational provision, and a growing dependence on welfare and relief whenever the economy took a down-turn.

But where there was change there was hope. The movement of enormous numbers of people from the country to the cities altered their sense of time itself. In a field or isolated cabin, change seems slow and hard to chart in anything other than seasons or weather. But in a city, however squalid the conditions, the sheer mass of new people seen every day and the very speed of events brought an ever-changing face to the world. Once this sense of time was changed it could seem as though the fundamentals of life were also different.

In visions of the Promised Land and the glories of freedom in the hereafter, religion had always provided notions of time, change and history. But city life made for something qualitatively different and more specific. Every day a new product was advertised on a hoarding or promoted on the radio and all the time newspapers and magazines pushed out new images of how to dress, do your hair or what shoes to wear. Change was in the air, literally.

The assertiveness and frenetic excitement of the saxophone-riffing dance-hall blues was not something that suddenly sprang fully clad and gleamingly new in the late 1940's. The jazzy rhythms, the glow of soloists letting rip with honking and shrieking notes, the singer shouting the lyrics over the blast of the band, or mellowing down for a 'mood' piece all had their origins in the big band jazz and swing era which had started before the war. There were innumerable black and white swing bands, playing to arrangements, with set pieces for solos, large brass sections, strong dance rhythms. Many featured vocalists, some almost for novelty effect, while others – the crooners especially – became almost the star attraction.

The post-war big-band blues style emerged particularly from the more bluesy end of the swing spectrum. In the South Western States and especially in Kansas City a series of magnificent jazz bands like Count Basie's or Jay McShann's developed, featuring blues singers like the 'shouter' Jimmy 'Mr Five-by-Five' Rushing, or Walter Brown. In fact, there is a connecting line extending either side of the blues of the late 40's back to swing and forward to rock 'n' roll, which was itself strongly rooted in the blues.

One of the Kansas City blues shouters who made the transition in person was Joe Turner – 'Boss of the Blues'. In the 30's Turner used to jam with musicians from the Basie band, and in the 40's he regularly worked and recorded with boogie-woogie pianist Pete Johnson.

'You didn't have microphones or nothing in those days, and you got so that you could sing and fill one of them big dance halls with one of them little paper horns. And that was something to do then, even if you could get the hang of it – singing to all those hundreds of people. I used to have a powerful voice before the mikes came in. But they were a fascinating thing. I figured it would give me a nice little riff and save me a while so's I could last out longer. But then I found out that it really made me sing harder. I'd get to singing, and it'd sound so good that I'd just keep on ... And I'd get the people all stirred up, just like a preacher. Stir 'em up!'[2]

Turner's birthplace, Kansas City, was 'wide open' for good times, and his blues were likewise big, expansive and warmly optimistic, bringing him regular work in California in the dance halls and clubs in the 40's. But surprisingly, his period of greatest commercial success was in the 1950's when he was in his forties. He got in on the beginning of the rock 'n' roll era, just when his career seemed to be tailing off. While other blues shouters, like Wynonie Harris, Bull Moose Jackson, Eddie 'Cleanhead' Vinson or Jimmy Witherspoon were left high and dry, Joe Turner started turning out rock hits for Atlantic records. One of the biggest was *Shake, Rattle And Roll*, a version of which Bill Haley adapted and bowdlerized to make an even bigger hit. His rock hits were still the blues and they saw no diminution of power, conviction or authority. For him music had always meant enjoyment.

'Blues I did mainly for the fun of it. I didn't really give much thought to what was behind the songs. Most of the time I feel that I can get the most emotion out of the people. I kind of work at the people in the audience, and once I get them on my side, I let 'em have it!'[3]

Even though he never had success as a rock 'n' roller, Louis Jordan was another musician from the swing era whose success carried him beyond the confines of the purely black audience. As the leader of a 'jump' band his popularity was with whites and blacks alike and it even spread across the Atlantic. Fronting his famous Tympany Five (which wasn't always a strictly accurate count) with his full-toned and gutty alto sax, Jordan was one of the most popular artists of the 40's. He had a stream of hits, including *Cho Choo ch'Boogie* which is said to have sold a million in 1946.

His appeal lay in fun lyrics and in his light, unaggressive voice with its sparkle of humour providing all-round infectious entertainment.

'What I really tried to do, when I first got into music, I used to go into clubs and see guys come in and sit there. The first thing they're into is what happened that day. I wanted to play music on stage that made people *forget* about what they did today. I always try to say something funny to corral their thoughts. That's my whole life. The blues live on'.[4]

The new blues of the city were directed towards performance, the public celebration of shared joys or the ritual expression of inward griefs.

> I've got so much, so much trouble,
> Sometimes I sit and cry,
> I'm gonna find my mother's grave,
> Fall on the tombstone and die.

Hard Luck Blues – Roy Brown[5]

Roy Brown was not a shouter nor a humorist but he was a performer of consummate skill. Bill 'Hoss' Allen, a disc-jockey with WLAC Radio, presented Brown in concert in Nashville in 1948.

'I remember it so well, Roy strolls into the spotlight so casually that he might have been just passing through. He moans . . . the band answers, he moans again, again, the band answers. So easily he pulls the audience all the way into himself as the initial number begins . . . it builds . . . some urge him on "Yeah, Roy" . . . "Come on, Roy" . . . and then seeming to sense that they are truly with him, he leans back, closes his eyes and moves into *Trouble At Midnight*, and he is instantly transformed from a performer on stage into a downhearted pouring out of his pain to a woman who has walked all over his heart.'[6]

With boogie piano and saxes well to the fore, Roy Brown mixed impassioned slow blues with infectiously rocking dance numbers like the many times recorded *Good Rockin' Tonight*,

> I heard the news, there's good rockin' tonight![7]

which shouter Wynonie Harris also recorded, as did Elvis Presley.

His voice was clear, rich and adult, and he contorted it into pleading, almost crying vulnerability. He pioneered a style which inspired straight blues singers like B. B. King, Junior Parker and gospel-style blues singers like Bobby 'Blue' Bland, rock 'n' rollers like Little Richard and soul singers like James Brown. But like most of the blues singers of the late 40's and early 50's, while the soul lingered on, Roy Brown's career dried up on him.

Showmanship was a large part of the new city blues. Saxophone players would often roll on the floor kicking their legs in the air while playing long screeching solos, or stand swinging the sax up and down between their legs honking all the while. The build-up of excitement was evocative of the showy stage tricks of the Classic blues of the 20's, and many theatres were again featuring blues acts. But not all the flashy stars were big sax players, or blues shouters. One of the most exciting acts was guitarist T-Bone Walker, who had a mild voice with a predilection for smoothness in his singing:

'More of a ballad,' he told Jim and Amy O'Neal of *Living Blues*. 'That's the kind of blues I like to play. And it's more smoother and more softer, more of a up-to-date thing. It's not a way down home blues.'[8]

With his neat short hair, carefully trimmed little moustache and quiet manner, T-Bone had a wild stage act. Dressed in lamé clothes or a long white jacket and bow tie, he would do the splits, swing the guitar round his back, hold the guitar by the neck away from his body and still manage to squeeze out notes with just the one hand; he would kneel down, standing the guitar on the ground, still playing one-handed on the neck while waving the other to the crowd; he would gyrate his hips and build momentum with long-held and sustained notes on his electric guitar and then catch up with the rhythm of his band with a flurry of chords. Like so many others, T-Bone also passed into eclipse when blues-based rock 'n' roll caught on and tastes in the black community rapidly turned away from the blues. But again, just as Roy Brown's vocal mannerisms have affected so many singers, T-Bone Walker's sophisticated, jazz-tinged electric guitar-playing has been a direct or indirect inspiration to virtually all the blues guitarists who remain popular today while all around them the blues are fading.

B. B. King: 'It was just before I went into the army about 40, 42 I think, I heard of a guy called T-Bone Walker and that was the first electric guitar I'd ever heard . . . and I went crazy, I went completely nutty . . . I think that he had the clearest touch of anybody I'd ever heard on guitar then.'[9]

Little Milton: 'T-Bone, now there's a cat. T-Bone Walker inspired me and a lot more guitar-players and singers because that cat always played clean. He would pick one string at a time and most of the other guitar-players in those days man, would frail it and make chords. He played one string at a time, no sweats. Then B. B. King came along. I'm sure he got a lot of pointers from T-Bone Walker.'[10]

T-Bone was endlessly on tour, sometimes with a nine-piece band, sometimes with a smaller combo. This kind of touring usually meant long and exhausting hours on the road to play one night in one State and then move on to another. The life was harsh and gruelling and T-Bone himself was often in acute, incapacitating pain from stomach ulcers. All too often musicians on the road were tricked and cheated out of their money by theatre or club owners.

'They'd tell you their wife had died,' says B. B. King. 'Their children had pneumonia. I once had a dude come say to me he couldn't make it 'cause he had four flat tyres!'[11]

Despite his nationwide touring and wide popularity T-Bone was mainly based in California. He had moved there from his native Texas in the 30's, and was one of many who contributed to the urbanity of the post-war West Coast blues.

In the ten years following 1940 the black population of California increased by nearly a third of a million to 462,000, and the growth continued in the years to follow. The migrants came from Oklahoma, Kansas, Louisiana and especially from Texas, looking for work in the fields of the San Joaquin and Imperial Valleys, or in the defence projects of Oakland and Los Angeles. There was a large black community in Oakland on the Eastern side of San Francisco Bay and some streets would be populated entirely by black Texans.

When jobs were available, they worked in light and heavy industry, in shipping and on the railroads. In the early 1950's singers found employment in the Oakland clubs like Rumboogie, the Three Sisters, Slim Jenkins', or Esther's Orbit Room, in nearby Richmond in Tommy's 250 Club and the Club Savoy, or in San Francisco itself in Shelton's Blue-Mirror or the Club Long Island.

Even more important as a blues centre was Los Angeles, in the swelling ghetto on the South East side, in Watts and along the side streets off Central Avenue and Broadway. Outwardly the Watts ghetto is deceptively unlike the dark, rat-infested tenements of Detroit, Chicago or Harlem; streets are lined with palms and shade trees and the climate is at least sunny. But houses which may look adequate from the outside are in fact so cheaply and skimpily built they rapidly deteriorate and fall apart. Most are frame houses built as single family homes but absentee landlords subdivide them and rent them out to several families. Just before the explosion of black frustration and fury in 1965 known as the 'Watts Riots', over 80 per cent of the ghetto homes were rented, while in Los Angeles County as a whole well over half the population owned their own houses.

In the late 40's and early 50's anger and frustration had not reached explosion point. Though post-war prosperity on the West Coast was not spread equally between blacks and whites, jobs, money and conditions were at least better than in the

South. There was a spirit of released energies and hope on the West Coast which found expression in the loose, swinging boogie and jump dance bands like those of Amos Milburn, Roy Milton and his Solid Senders, Joe Liggins and his Honey-drippers and Jimmy Liggins and his Drops of Joy. Record companies and labels were sprouting up to cater for the new black audience. Modern, RPM, Specialty, Imperial, Swingtime, Hollywood and Aladdin, or the smaller Big Town and Art-Tone. From Watts, Johnny Otis – sometimes known as the 'Godfather of Rhythm-and-Blues' – toured nationally with his 'Rhythm-and-Blues Caravan' in the early 1950's. It featured many fine singers like the ballad-blues singer Little Esther Phillips, Marie Adams and Willie Mae 'Big Mama' Thornton, who was more of a down-home singer at a time when few women were singing blues. It was a glamour-package show, and as Otis recalls, 'I billed my various singers and instrumentalists individually as separate features and this appeared on our placards and brochures making it seem like a conglomerate carnival was coming to town – and in a sense it was!'[12]

In the 1970's Johnny revived the idea in the shape of the Johnny Otis Show, bringing back to public attention artists neglected in some cases for almost 20 years. With differing line-ups the Show played in America and Europe and featured people like Esther Phillips, Roy Brown, Ivory Joe Hunter, Cleanhead Vinson, Pee Wee Crayton, Joe Turner and Margie Evans. Otis himself had started in big bands but the cost of keeping together large groups of musicians was prohibitive:

'We were forced into a small band situation but through my years with the big bands I'd realized that the thing that people really loved was what we loved too, the blues. We didn't need to get fancy just to do what comes naturally and effortlessly. It was the folk music with the driving beat and it differed from the old country thing because I just had to have some horns . . . I suddenly realized I didn't want four trumpets and five saxes, absolutely not. I wanted four horns with the baritone sticking out, that bluesy sound.'[13]

Otis formed the Barrelhouse Club on Central Avenue 'in that part of the L.A. ghetto known as the East Side. The police department would not issue me a dance or entertainment licence and I went under.' With some friends he started a new Barrel-house Club in Watts.

'We put up 100 bucks apiece and on opening night still had 20 dollars left over! Couldn't do that today with ten times as much. Inflation is alive and well in L.A.!'[14]

While the Barrelhouse featured the new raucous, jumping rhythm-and-blues, many other clubs wanted something more restrained and quieter. Many blues singers would try to straddle several styles to cater for all tastes. This has continued to be the case for Lowell Fulson, one of the finest of the West Coast guitarists. In his long career he has played with large saxophone-heavy arrangements, quiet country guitar duets with his brother Martin Fulson, small group jump blues, and more recently with white rock musicians, but always showing his own dextrously 'loping' and controlled guitar-playing, and smooth and richly expressive voice.

'See, some houses you go in, they don't want no blues, less'n it's a blues ballad. Kind of soft blues, they don't want the hard blues in there. And so you try to get somethin' a little polished up, where if they settin' around there with their evenin' stuff on and sippin' tea or somethin', you can drop in a bass or baritone and sing sweet songs to 'em, you know. Which is rough, 'cause I like to shout sometimes . . .'[15]

Many blues singers kept away from what Fulson calls 'them old cigarette-smokin' barrelhouse blues' by choice. On the West Coast in particular, the smoothness often amounted to blandness. There was a whole group of musicians who owed something of their style to the pop balladeer Nat 'King' Cole, who used to play in clubs in California in the 1940's. By no stretch of the imagination was Cole a blues singer, but his quiet restraint, the style of his own piano accompaniment and the lightly brushed drums set the cocktail-lounge mood for Johnny Moore's Three Blazers, featuring Charles Brown on piano and vocals. The sound was relaxed and sophisticated, with the blues feeling conveyed with an intimate sadness.

Charles Brown also recorded under his own name and became one of the most successful singers across the nation. Between 1949 and 1952 he had seven top ten hits in the rhythm-and-blues charts and other performers of a similar vein had big sellers too, like fellow Texan Floyd Dixon, or Lloyd Glenn. In fact, the bluesy ballad style was to have an effect on many musicians, like Ivory Joe Hunter, Percy Mayfield, Johnny Ace and even the young Ray Charles.

If the brash combo sounds of the jump bands were confident and assertive, Charles Brown's tinkling piano backed by sympathetically mellow saxophone and lightly amplified guitar conveyed a feeling of dependence and even helplessness.

Well, I'm driftin' and driftin' like a ship out on the sea
Well, I'm driftin' and driftin' like a ship out on the sea
Well I ain't got nobody in this world to care for me.
Drifting Blues – Charles Brown[16]

The end of an era

'Among the important developments that have been taking place in the rhythm and blues field over the past year, one of the most prominent is the increasing importance of the country or southern style blues and country style singer in this market.'[1]

This was how the entertainment trade paper *Billboard* in March 1952 reported a development which heralded the last flowering of support within the black community for a rich diversity of blues. From the mid-1950's onwards the blues has become rapidly less and less supported, more and more rejected. The 1952 report continued:

'At one time there was a wide gulf between the sophisticated big city styles and rocking novelties waxed for the northern market, and the country or delta blues that were popular in the southern regions. Gradually, the two forms intermingled and the country blues tune, now dressed up in arrangements palatable to both northern and southern tastes, have been appearing on all r & b labels.'[1]

'R & B', or 'Rhythm-and-Blues', was an all-embracing expression which replaced 'race' music. There had been attempts to use 'sepia' or 'ebony' to describe black music for a black audience, but by 1949 most people used 'r & b'. It covered an enormous variety of styles, including some that were not blues at all: blues shouting, jump blues, blues ballads, country blues, harmony vocal groups and modern jazz. The old race market had been dominated by the major record companies like Columbia, Victor and Decca, but wartime rationing of shellac for record-making and a musicians' union ban on recording saw their interest in black music decline. When the majors returned, they stuck to old performers at a time when the mood was for change. Gradually at first, but in an ever increasing torrent, small 'independent' companies sprang up all over black America. Some were white-owned and white-operated, some white-owned and black-operated, and some entirely black. Many were tiny companies set up in back rooms, recording in garages or basements, distributing records by hand out of the back of trucks. Many had distinctly unorthodox production techniques.

'I built my own press,' recalled J. R. Fullbright who was based in Los Angeles, 'then I made my own dyes and fixed me a cooling system out of a frigidaire. I used to be able to run off 60 (records) an hour and I could make a living out of it. That's why some of my records break so. I used to make my own plastic and sometimes it wasn't nothing but charcoal.'²

Fullbright preferred to hold sessions in L.A. because of problems in the South, as when he wanted to record the Louisiana accordionist Clifton Chenier.

'When I was recording Clifton in Lake Charles (this was at a radio station), the white boy wouldn't do nothing to help. He wouldn't do no engineering work or test the machine. He got his cigar in his mouth and his newspaper and put his feet up on the desk. So I asked him, "Ain't you doing no engineer work?" And he jumped up like I hit him and said, "What the hell you talking about? You know where you at? You in Lake Charles!"'²

But even the South saw hundreds of sessions, some in proper studios, especially in Memphis, New Orleans and Houston, and others in clubs, ballrooms, auditoriums or anywhere microphones and tape recorders could be set up. North, South, East and West – literally hundreds of companies were established, many issuing records on several labels. Some would issue a single or two and quietly disappear, while others developed into multi-million dollar corporations, especially when rock 'n' roll helped black and white popular music share the same market. Some companies were directed at a purely local and regional market while others fought for national distribution and as much disc-jockey promotion on the hundreds of radio stations as personal contact, badgering and bribery could secure. Not all companies were devoted to rhythm-and-blues; they also covered white hillbilly and country-and-western music and any kind of popular music.

But some were, and are, entirely devoted to the blues, sometimes purely out of love for the music. Even now while the blues has become only a small part of black culture in terms of popular support, there are countless black- and white-operated blues labels recording new blues and reissuing 'oldies'. In the spring of 1973 *Living Blues* listed well over fifty companies in Chicago alone who had recently issued blues records, in some cases using several labels. There are singers themselves who have formed their own record companies, like Bobo Jenkins in Detroit who has issued a couple of albums of his own recordings made at home. With little finance, distribution difficulties, scant air time for the blues on black radio stations, most small companies are doomed to failure, or at least small commercial success. But there are still almost incredible numbers of blues singers devoted to their art, hoping for regular work at least and especially for a hit.

Commercially, the boom time for the blues was in the early 1950's. Almost all those singers who have remained stars within the black community started their recording career at about that time. Because there were so many record companies serving so many communities, an astonishing range of styles found commercial outlets, from the swinging jump bands to singers deeply rooted in country folk traditions.

One such location was New Orleans where piano music had its own distinctive rhythmic colouration traceable through several performers. Most featured in bands with full toned saxes and 'second line' drumming (derived from New Orleans funeral parades where the 'second line' of mourners dance and strut behind the musicians up front). The most popular and accessible was Antoine 'Fats' Domino, 'The Fat Man', who had a succession of rock 'n' roll million sellers, all variants of the blues and all showing a delightfully open-hearted warmth and danceability. Fats' band sometimes recorded with Smiley Lewis, born Overton Amos Lemons, a glorious shouter who also captured the characteristic bayou city charm.

There were other pianists too in New Orleans like Huey 'Piano' Smith and Professor Longhair (Roy Byrd), one of whose bands rejoiced in the name the Shufflin' Hungarians. 'Fess' seldom left the city and never had more than minor hits but until his death in 1980 he was one of the most extravagantly idiosyncratic pianists in America. His style was infused with the city's famous 'Spanish tinge' and he showed virtuoso control in his cascading use of cross rhythms.

At the same time as sophisticated New Orleans R & B was popular there still remained a market for rural-based blues. One of the greatest country blues singers who found consistent if not massive sales was Sam Lightnin' Hopkins who was born in Centreville, a small farming community near Houston, Texas. As he sang in *Goin' Back And Talk To Mama*,

> I was born March the 15th – man, the year was 19 and 12.
> Yes, you know, ever since that day poor Lightning ain't been doin' so well.[3]

Lightnin's lined face, usually hidden behind dark glasses and shaded by a cowboy hat, and his chain-gang ankle scars testified to the hardness of his life. His blues were intense but relaxed and effortlessly so, almost spontaneous conversational revelations of his own feelings and reaction to the world he had known. He played for country parties as he always had, sitting back with an air of casual detachment, acutely aware of his own mastery and artistry. His musicianship owed something to the childhood encouragement of his idol Blind Lemon in the irregular guitar patterns, the suspending of the rhythm to sing and answer the words with extended runs, and in an uncluttered directness of expression.

In the 1940's his reputation in Houston was colossal as he worked the streets with friends like Texas Alexander and Smokey Hogg and, starting in 1946, his record releases were prolific on labels such as Aladdin, Imperial, Gold Star, Modern, RPM, Sittin'-in-With. He could walk into a studio virtually any time, dash off a session and pick up a hundred dollars or so. He never liked travelling far from his Houston base, even though his popularity had taken him to record in New York. His stream of releases dried up in 1954 as the blues began to slump, and it was mainly the interest of enthusiasts like Mack McCormick and Samuel Charters bringing him to the attention of the folk world which revived his career. Now he still made the occasional juke-box single, some selling fairly well, and with regular college and club performances he had a certain status and a fairly prosperous standard of living. But he remained firmly part of the Houston ghetto, revered by those who knew him, with his gold-capped teeth, straightened hair and the unforced aura of being his own man. Sadly, he died in 1982.

Plenty of other Texas singers like Smokey Hogg, Li'l Son Jackson and Frankie Lee Sims were recorded at about the same time but, as *Billboard* had noted, the Southern styles were hitting the Northern cities. There were several blues singers in Detroit who had come up from the South, people like Baby Boy Warren, Eddie Burns, Calvin Frazier, Bobo Jenkins, but most successful of them all was John Lee Hooker who, as he told Pete Welding, arrived during the war.

'At that time, jobs wasn't hard to get . . . Good money too. You could go anywhere, any day and get a job; nothing to worry about too much.'[4]

The centre of blues activity was in the clubs and joints around Hastings Street, where Joe Van Battle ran his JVB record company at the back of Joe's Record Shop. French blue researchers Jacques Demetre and Marcel Chauvard described the area after their visit in 1959.

'Hastings Street is relatively narrow and only a couple of hundred yards long. Brick and wooden houses, in a sad state of collapse, stretch along both sides. We noticed a number of primitive shops – hairdressers, grocers and fishmongers – where customers looked so poor it was almost heartbreaking. Between some of the houses, dingy, narrow pebbled alleyways led through to allotments and wasteland.'[5]

John Lee Hooker came from Clarksdale, Mississippi, where he learned guitar from his step-father who was a friend of Charley Patton, Blind Blake and Blind Lemon. Having lived in Memphis, his move to Detroit saw him update the country blues to a tough amplified ghetto sound, using a four-piece band in the clubs. But when he was recorded it was usually just with his own electric guitar and the strongly emphasised stomp of his foot, producing a completely individual rhythmic drone, twisting and turning the sound through unpredictable and irregular bar lengths around his voice. He started recording in 1948 and produced a string of hits – *Boogie Chillen*, *In The Mood*, *Hobo Blues*, *Sally Mae*, in the rhythm-and-blues market – and there was strong competition among companies to get his sound on record. He was contracted to Modern records but he appeared as Texas Slim for King, Delta John for Regent, Birmingham Sam and His Magic Guitar for Savoy, Johnny Williams for Staff, The Boogie Man for Acorn, John L. Booker for Chance, Johnny Lee for De Luxe and in 1960 he rose to Sir John Lee Hooker for Fortune. As he explained, 'money's pretty exciting, you know'.[6]

By the time he was Sir John he was already moving into the folk world, the world of coffee houses and college performances. He now plays almost entirely for white audiences, either sitting quietly moaning slow country blues or swinging through dramatic and exciting boogies with his booming guitar slung low on his body, swivelling his legs and stirring crowds to their feet just as he used to in the Hastings Street joints.

While in the late 40's and early 50's Detroit only produced the one major commercial success, Chicago produced several. With the second largest city black population by 1950, Chicago became and remained the major centre of the blues outside the South, especially as the wave of migration had drawn so heavily from strong blues territories like Mississippi, Arkansas, Tennessee and Louisiana. Through birth rate and migration, the number of blacks in Chicago between 1940 and 1960 increased by over 200 per cent to become nearly a quarter of the city's population. Many of the thousands of migrants arriving in the late 40's came directly from isolated rural areas and they were soon cramming into the already overcrowded and increasingly subdivided slum houses. Some blocks almost developed into little Mississippi villages, where country manners and behaviour was the norm, to be scorned and looked upon with embarrassment and distaste by older or more sophisticated residents. For these unprepared newcomers the older Southern blues gave a reassuring continuity to their lives and provided an exciting and dramatic release from the growing tensions and anxieties of the swelling ghettoes.

In Mike Rowe's excellent study of blues in the city, *Chicago Breakdown*, he cites the unexpected success of Muddy Waters' record *I Can't Be Satisfied* released in April 1948 as the beginning of the era of greatest creativity and richness in the Chicago blues.

> Well I'm going away to leave, won't be back no more,
> Goin' back down South, child, don't you want to go?
> Lord I'm troubled, I be all worried mind,
> Babe, I just can't be satisfied,
> And I just can't keep from cryin'.[7]

With the directness of his singing, the tough urgency of his amplified slide guitar, backed by Big Crawford's rocking bass, Muddy cut right through the fashion for sophisticated and city-smooth blues of the day – just as in the 1960's the Rolling Stones, who took their name from a Muddy blues and used *I Can't Be Satisfied* on their second album, cut through pop music fashions. Muddy Waters (his real name is McKinley Morganfield) was a proud and ambitious man, convinced of the importance of his powerful and heavy blues, with their deep-down country conviction and authority. He had hated his native Mississippi, but was not a man to make apologies for his background; he took command of his feelings and put them out as magnificent studies in joy and anguish, filled with brooding pain, exuberant and defiant in pleasure.

Muddy now has a worldwide reputation as one of the greatest ever blues singers, even though his music has long since waned in popularity within the black community. His brand of modernized Delta blues has now become a distinctly anachronistic and minority taste, tainted with the flavour of conditions most blacks seek to escape and forget. Muddy was the direct inheritor of the 30's blues of Son House and Robert Johnson. As he told Peter Guralnick:

'I consider myself to be, what you might call a mixture of all three. I had part of my own, part of Son House, and a little part of Robert Johnson.'[8]

It is typical of the generous side of the man that he should give credit to his mentors, but as he knows full well, every time he has recorded – Alan Lomax recorded him first for the Library of Congress in the early 40's – he has been entirely his own man. He has even been recorded with white 'psychedelic' rock musicians and has still found his own voice. He rehearses and strictly controls his own band to get exactly the right framework, wanting 'a full bed of music there for you, waiting on you.'[9]

Though dictating to his own band, he does so with a quiet and gentlemanly firmness, for he has always allowed his sidemen to blossom in their own right. He has never feared competition and, being eternally grateful for the assistance of figures like Big Bill Broonzy when he reached Chicago, he has helped dozens of other musicians, including whites like the blues harmonica-player Paul Butterfield, or Paul Oscher who was for a long time his own regular harp-blower. Yet behind his high-cheek-boned and inscrutably quiet exterior lies a strongly combative and competitive pride. In the years around 1948 he and two of his band members, Little Walter Jacobs and Jimmy Rogers, used to call themselves the Headhunters and they would turn up at clubs where lesser groups were playing in amateur blues contests and blow them off-stage, out of sheer relish for being the tops.

When his style of blues rapidly fell from favour after the mid-50's Muddy and those in a similar position were hurt by the continuing assumptions among blacks that the blues were 'low-class', whiskey-sodden and from the gutter. It was partly through recognition of the blues by jazz and folk enthusiasts and partly through the influence of the Beatles and the Rolling Stones who deliberately drew attention to Muddy Waters, that he gained his international reknown. His reputation was solidly based on the classic records he made, and the exhilarating strength of his 'live' performances. Probably his greatest band, the one he remembers with most pride and affection, was the one which included Little Walter on harmonica and Jimmy Rogers on guitar. With the intensity of Muddy's slide guitar and his declamatory voice, Jimmy Rogers' guitar feeling round the beat and filling out the sound with bass runs, drummers Elgar Evans or Freddie Below socking behind them all, the band in full cry was gloriously powerful and given an added breadth of subtlety by Little Walter's perfectly controlled amplified harp, mournfully wailing behind Muddy's vocal, or driving ahead with intuitive sensitivity. Muddy's bands are so well co-ordinated they can continue the use of country-style unpredictability in bar lengths, giving free range to the blues feeling surging through the whole band as if it were one man.

Muddy's success helped push his record company Chess (formerly Aristocrat) into becoming a major independent. It was to become even bigger with the bluesy rock 'n' rollers Bo Diddley and Chuck Berry. Marshall Chess, son of one of the founders, explained Muddy's popularity:

'It was sex. If you had ever seen Muddy then, the effect he had on women. Because blues, you know, has always been a woman's market. On Saturday night they'd be lined up ten deep.'[10]

As important has been his ability to attract and mould the best available talent to his band. On record Muddy was often joined by Willie Dixon, one of the few blues or pop musicians who still use a full stand-up bass instead of a solid-bodied electric bass-guitar; he has been a prolific composer, writing several of Muddy's hits, and his influence on the Chicago blues scene as record producer and band-leader continued to be considerable. More important for Muddy's band was when he was joined full-time by his 'half-brother' Otis Spann, a subtle and unobtrusive pianist, but one also capable of a thunderous boogie reminiscent of Big Maceo. Long after Walter and Jimmy Rogers left Muddy, Otis remained a mainstay of the band, almost till his death. He was himself only recorded extensively after the decline of the blues but he proved to be an intimately expressive singer, with a smokey-voiced 'after hours' feel.

A large number of fine singers have been part of Muddy's band either regularly or on record, including harp-blowers Big Walter Shakey Horton, Junior Wells, James Cotton, guitarists Earl Hooker and Buddy Guy and of course Paul Butterfield, Jimmy Rogers himself, while still with Muddy, had a number of hits under his own name; with his 'cleaner' voice and lightly-swinging guitar technique, he made an excellent contrast to Muddy's dirty, down-home sound.

But the greatest of them all was Little Walter. When his record *Juke* was a huge hit on the Chess subsidiary label Checker in 1952, Walter quit Muddy's band, took over Junior Wells' Aces and for a time became a very big recording star. In 1954 he was never out of the *Cashbox* rhythm-and-blues charts, with his virtuoso harmonica backed by the light ensemble work of guitarists Louis and David Myers and the supple, jazzy drumming of Freddie Below. Influenced by the harp-playing of the two

Sonny Boy Williamsons and Big Walter Horton and the saxophone of Louis Jordan, Little Walter developed a superbly disciplined and echoingly imaginative amplified style. His sense of dynamics and tonal variety gave him an unrivalled flowing inventiveness, swooping and diving on rockers and dance boogies, or soft and melancholy on slow numbers. The harp would seem to be drifting away, when suddenly he would crash back up front with fierce stabbing notes only to turn back to a floating dreaminess. His quiet and sad voice made him John Lee Hooker's favourite singer, but he is best remembered for his eerily mournful harp, which has remained unsurpassedly influential in popular music as a whole.

Having started performing as a child in Louisiana where he was born in 1930, he was already hustling for work as a teenager in New Orleans, Arkansas and St Louis before struggling to Chicago. There he played for tips in the famous open-air Maxwell Street Market, where musicians still play today, hiring power lines for their amplifiers. Prematurely aged and hardened, he took his fall from stardom badly, becoming bitter and angry, drinking heavily and brawling repeatedly. His aggressive and moody behaviour made him increasingly hard to handle but he never lost the friendship of Muddy Waters, with whom he often stayed until his death from a coronary after a fight in 1968.

While Little Walter's toughness was belied by the often gentle warmth of his music, a Delta contemporary of Muddy's who came to Chicago in the 50's performed with an almost manic aggression: Howling Wolf. With his massive frame lurching round the bandstand, crawling and rolling on the floor, blasting out searing bursts on his harp and moaning and shouting his blues till the veins stood out in his neck and the sweat poured off him, he was one of the most menacingly forceful singers of his time, and one of Muddy's biggest rivals in the Chicago clubs. Once he had established his reputation in the South there was bitter competition to get him on record between Modern from California and Chess from Chicago – and both recorded him – but he was to remain with Chess, putting down his magnificently controlled dynamism backed with rolling piano and groaning saxophones.

In the eyes of blues promoter and disc jockey Pervis Spann Howling Wolf never lost his sense of identification and connection with his roots 'down home', as Spann explained shortly after the Wolf's death in 1976.

'Down-home blues is the blues that most of us used to sing

down home. For an example, we would take the Howling Wolf and as you know Howling Wolf, in my opinion, was a creative genius, were none better than the Howling Wolf as far as creating his music from nothing, and building it into a beat. He would walk out on stage, as I said the last time we had him in Memphis, and sing a song called "When I get up in the morning, I'm going to hit Highway 49". Now Highway 49 runs right into Memphis, Tennessee, out of Mississippi. Now anybody from Mississippi, Arkansas, or Tennessee would know about Highway 49, then he was going home to see his baby, and his baby was in Jackson, Mississippi, that's where Highway 49 run. He's singing about things that those people can relate to; that is "down-home blues".[11]

At about the same time as the Wolf, Elmore James came to Chicago, though like Sonny Boy No. 2 he often returned to the South. With his theme song of *Dust My Broom* adapted from a Robert Johnson number, Elmore was also recorded by more than one company, having discs issued by Trumpet of Jackson, Mississippi, Meteor, Flair, Chess and their subsidiary Checker, Fire and Enjoy and through all of these recordings his widening scope as a performer showed a thrilling development of the old Delta blues. On his first record he was backed by Sonny Boy Williamson No. 2, but he went on to use bands including sax-players like J. T. Brown and Boyd Atkins, the Big Maceo-style pianist Little Johnny Jones, and his cousin Homesick James on guitar. It was in Homesick's house that Elmore died in 1963 at the age of 45.

'Elmore James will always remain the most exciting and dramatic blues singer and guitarist that I've ever had the chance to see perform in the flesh,' recalled the Belgian researcher Georges Adins who was taken to see him at the Thelma Lounge by Muddy Waters in 1959. 'Before we even pushed open the door of the club, we could hear Elmore's violent guitar sound. Although the place was overcrowded, we managed to find a seat close to the bandstand and the blues came falling down on me as it had never done before ... Wearing thick glasses, Elmore's face always had an expressive and dramatic look, especially when he was real gone on the slow blues. Singing with a strong and rough voice, he really didn't need a mike. On such slow blues as *I'm Worried, Make My Dreams Come True, It Hurts Me*, his voice reached a climax and created a tension that was unmistakably the down and out blues. Notwithstanding that raw voice, Elmore sang his blues with a particular feeling, an emotion and depth that showed his country background. His singing was, I should say, fed, reinforced by his own guitar accompaniment which was as rough, violent and expressive as was his voice. Using the bottleneck technique most of the time, Elmore really let his guitar sound as I had never heard a guitar sound before . . . and when he gave free rein to his guitar, the people in the joint went crazy and some people ran to the bandstand throwing bills of 1 and 5 dollars at Elmore's feet.'[12]

While the Chicago blues have been characterised by the raw ghetto toughness of a Howling Wolf or an Elmore James, the most commercially successful performer was Jimmy Reed, a singer with an easy-going looseness. In the late 50's and early 60's Reed's appeal crossed over into the pop market and he racked up hit after hit for the Vee-Jay label while Muddy and the others had none. He played guitar and harmonica simultaneously, the harp in a rack in front of his face, and his style was based on slack but infectious boogie rhythms, strengthened by the insistent and resonant sound of his friend Eddie Taylor playing the bass strings of his back-up guitar. Reed sang lazily, casually slurring the words out of his lop-sided mouth, with his harp meandering shrilly over the heavy beat. Born on a Mississippi plantation in 1925, his style was popular in the South, especially in Louisiana, where the 'swamp' blues of Lightnin' Slim, Lonesome Sundown, Slim Harpo and Lazy Lester ('they call me lazy but God knows I'm only tired'[13]) showed traces of the sound.

Despite his wide appeal and impact on pop music in general with many people recording his songs, including the Stones, his own career was hindered by ill-health, alcoholism and personal problems, though an album of Reed's 'oldies' still managed to get in the soul charts as recently as 1974, an almost unheard-of-thing among straight blues singers.

Throughout the 1950's Chicago had continued to sustain an astonishingly rich vein of blues talent, people such as Snooky Pryor, Floyd Jones, J. B. Hutto, Billy Boy Arnold, J. B. Lenoir and Sunnyland Slim. All were fine expressive artists who cut excellently tight recordings for various companies but who never quite managed enough hits to push them into stardom. Even pianists Eddie Boyd and Willie Mabon who did have a brief surge of chart success soon slipped back to relative obscurity.

The audience for blues, especially down-home blues, remained working class at a time when greater degrees of complexity and stratification were being created in the black social structure. Bourgeois aspirations increased as employment diversified; patterns of identification were changing because more people worked not only in heavy industry but also in service industries, transport and municipal employment. It was inevitable that these developments should be reflected in changing musical tastes and although blues as an idiom remained a sensitive barometer of social moods its hold as the main secular music of the black community was weakening. Indeed for many it was beginning to seem old fashioned, even outdated. For the first time on any substantial scale people started to predict the imminent death of the blues.

While rock 'n' roll, vocal groups and gospel-sounding rhythm-and-blues rapidly overtook the older blues in the mid-50's, and Soul music swept the board in the 60's, the bar and club blues singers found it harder and harder to get jobs and even more difficult to get a hit. In a sense the blues was going back underground, the music of small localities supported mainly by poorer blacks, and those older than the teenagers whose taste dictated the trend of popular music. But within the ghetto clubs the blues continued to progress and develop, and an even more urgent and anguished style emerged in the late 50's and early 60's.

As the Chicago black population grew, it gradually spread into new areas, as whites moved out to the suburbs. On the West Side, amid decaying and dilapidated tenements, a number of younger singers were playing the clubs and taverns, men like Otis Rush, Buddy Guy, Magic Sam, Jimmy 'Fast Fingers' Dawkins and the Texan Freddie King. Theirs was not Delta music, but ghetto blues with strong emphasis on their guitar virtuosity. Where Muddy, Walter and Wolf relied on the percussive ensemble sound, with the younger singers the guitar stood out in front, with shimmering arpeggio runs and burning solos. Freddie King was the most successful in terms of sales, having four pop hits on the King label. He had a slightly different technique, alternating between heavy bass runs and sustained treble notes in rocking instrumentals like *Hideaway* or *Driving Sideways*. His peak year was 1960, but later he often worked with white rock musicians, like Leon Russell, blending his old blues with new textures. Magic Sam died young, on the verge of gaining wider recognition among white audiences; Otis Rush now avoids the tough ghetto bars, while Buddy Guy, who teams up with harp-player Junior Wells, gets only occasional wider exposure with rock groups like the Stones. Jimmy

Dawkins, with his restrained voice and unflamboyant manner, is a performer of subtlety and craftsmanship as yet largely ignored. But while as individuals their success has been small, their influence on rock music has been huge.

Many of today's rock guitarists draw on the musical ideas of Buddy Guy and Otis Rush, and occasionally they try to draw peoples' attention to them, and especially to the man who influenced them all: B. B. King.

Say it loud

'I've seen B. B. King deliver many tunes any number of times, and *he* has done it thousands of times; yet each time what he sings and plays is a true experience. I've seen women faint when he climaxes a solo or hits his wailing falsetto. In one instance, in Louisiana, a woman was dancing deliriously, and when he hit his falsetto and held it – I believe it was on *Worry, Worry* – she went limp, falling back into a chair. The proprietor arrived, and, slapping her cheeks gently, asked if she was alright. She only replied, "I'm fine, baby, I just dig his singing, is all". And she smiled, gloriously.'[1]

Inevitably called 'King of the Blues', B. B. King is today probably the most commercially successful blues singer with black audiences. With the grace and precision of his electric guitar-playing, the long swooping and winging notes seem like a congregation answering the soaring voice of a preacher. He himself has been moved to tears by his own music: 'Its kinda like the note that breaks the glass.'[2] His guitar style has now crossed many boundaries to influence blues and rock musicians, white and black alike.

But with dwindling black support for the blues, it has been a struggle. In the 1950's and 60's, before he reached his wider audience, it meant performing in probably more than three hundred different places a year, criss-crossing America through an endless stream of clubs, dance-halls and theatres, and on each occasion being expected to deliver the goods, to appear suave, in control and exciting.

'I really began to fight for the blues,' B. B. King told Stanley Dance. 'The things people used to say about those I thought of as the greats in the business, the blues singers, used to hurt me. They spoke of them as though they were all illiterate and dirty . . . To be honest, I believe they felt they were trying to lift the standards of the Negro, and that they just didn't want to be associated with the blues, because it was something still back *there*.'[3]

B.B. is proud to identify himself completely with the blues, and consciously works as a gentleman ambassador for the music. He graciously lists all those who have influenced him, from blues singers Blind Lemon, Lonnie Johnson and T-Bone Walker to jazz guitarists Django Reinhardt and Charlie Christian – and not forgetting his cousin Booker White. As a blues singer he is the complete antithesis of the illiterate shambling drunk of popular image, and feeling as he does the music as a personal commitment, he has been hurt, like others of his generation, by black rejection of the blues.

'The blues are almost sacred to some people,' he says, 'but others don't understand, and when I can't make them understand, it makes me feel bad, because they mean so much to me . . . I remember my childhood, the race problems, and how bad it was in the 30's. I remember how it hit us . . . Maybe some people don't want to be reminded that it happened to them too.'³

Unless a blues singer can break into the wider pop market with lucrative white college dates and foreign tours as B.B. now has, and the unrelated Albert and Freddie King have, the blues is consigned to the fringe of black popular music, pushed out by the ever widening variety of soul, funk and disco music.

The declining support for the blues and the emergence of soul as the voice of black America coincided with the enormous shifts of mood within the black community itself. While conditions of acute poverty, discrimination and social instability have remained, there had been a growing sense of resistance, strength and pride. Stoical resignation had been replaced by the feeling that change must be made possible, that things once accepted as inevitable were now thought of as unacceptable.

Helped by the Supreme Court order of 1954 which called for the ending of segregation in public schools, the rising tide of anti-discrimination boycotts, lunch-counter sit-ins, Freedom bus rides and Civil Rights demonstrations led eventually to the massive and spontaneous outbursts of ghetto anger and resentment in the 60's – Watts, Newark, Detroit, Chicago and elsewhere. The defiance, the spirit of assertion, the seemingly irreversible and almost revolutionary transformation of social, economic and political consciousness culminated in Black Power. More than a movement, it was an attitude of mind, a determination to end black dependance on the all-embracing white power structure. No one could ignore the new development; it affected the whole of the black community. In the ghettoes it found expression in the fierce drive of the heavily amplified blues bands in the clubs and bars, but the blues singer played little part in the wider development. The blues epitomised the past people wanted to get away from, and the anguish and alienation of the music spoke more of isolation than of communal strength. No blues singer became a symbol of Black Power in the way soul singer and Soul Brother No. 1 James Brown did – 'Say it Loud – I'm Black and I'm Proud'. Blues singer Willie Cobbs' reaction to that was 'It's easy for James Brown to say that; he's a millionaire. I say, "Sing it low – I'm black and I'm poor".'[4]

Soul music was closer to the new mood than the blues, with its roots not only in the blues themselves but especially in church and gospel music.

In the 1970's Pervis Spann of Radio WVON was one of the few disc jockeys still playing blues records in Chicago. Talking in 1976 he saw soul as very much the natural development of both blues and gospel music.

'Well, you can call it a copy of both. There's a good deal of gospel being transpired into the soul music, the gospel music itself is the backbone, I think, of all black-orientated music. Most of our singers come out of the church. For an example if you want to really hear some real good soul-type singing, you should attend some Baptist churches, and if you attend the Baptist church in the black community, you are going to hear the cream of the crop, as far as black singing is concerned. For example Aretha Franklin, she came directly from the church; you probably know Aretha Franklin, we call her the Queen, here, in the States, she's our Queen, as far as soul singing is concerned. You take for an example the Staple Singers, which is by far the number one family group in America. The group started from the church and they stayed in church until about 8 or 10 years ago, they just came out of church. The late Sam Cooke, passed away, Sam came from the church. Most of the soul singers either started or came out of church, sometime they get out and don't do so well, they go back to the church. So most of their singing blues or soul starts with the church. Black people basically are religious people, and church is where most of it starts.'[5]

The church had always given a sense of community and participation where even the humblest member in the tiniest storefront church could feel they had a place, and were important. The feeling of togetherness and of communal strength is intensified by the call and response of preacher and congregation – 'Say it brother', 'Yes Lord, that's the truth' – creating a world where burdens are shared, and problems are faced together. The gospel music technique, which has spilled over into some forms of blues and particularly into soul music, relies strongly on the repetition of phrases, simple at first but rising in emotionalism, arousing the congregation, becoming carried away with feeling, extending words, 'Lord . . . Lo-oorrd', becoming more fervent, the crowd shouting encouragement, joining in with sighs, claps, groans and 'Amens'.

One of the younger and more successful soul-blues singers, Little Johnny Taylor, actually started out as a gospel singer. Asked to describe his blues he said, 'I can't describe that, because you got too much in here . . . it's something I cannot describe. It's what I'm talkin' about, soul. Oh God . . . yes. I read the Bible every day. I came from church. Most people say I shoulda been a preacher, but . . . I have to hold on my way for a little while.'[6]

Most of the currently popular blues singers draw heavily on gospel and soul, just as Roy Brown had evoked gospel techniques in the 1940's. Bobby Bland, Junior Parker and Little Milton often recorded pure soul numbers and they all began their music careers at the same time in the 1950's, and all in Memphis with B. B. King.

The city itself was a hive of radio and recording activities and a melting pot of musical styles; it was there that Elvis Presley fused white country music with the old black blues to create his own lip-curling, hip-swinging rock 'n' roll, along with other white country boys like Jerry Lee Lewis and Carl Perkins. Meanwhile the blues singers were creating their own new styles, mixing older blues with the sophisticated smoothness of the West Coast, jump blues and gospel music. Bobby Bland, who is probably B. B. King's closest rival for blues popularity, says: 'It started more or less like a church thing. This is my background, all the way up to the blues that I'm doing today. It's a spiritual background, because I started in a choir.'[7]

With his richly-textured mellow voice, Bland is equally at home with blues, soft and sweet ballads, soul or gospel blues. His voice is warm and enveloping, and he appeals by keeping an intimate contact with his audience. 'He remind me of a Cadillac automobile on a highway,' says Pervis Spann. 'He takes it with so much ease, no strain to sing.'[8]

'A joy to watch Bobby's way with women,' wrote J. B. Figi describing a Bland club performance. 'He is equally popular with both sexes, a Clark Gable thing, but men are more cool about showing it and the women more fun to watch . . . Women work with Bobby, urge him on, encourage his innuendos, call out requests – not all of them for songs. *Stormy Monday.* Bobby drops on one knee before a full-blown gal at a front table. ("Sunday I go to church, and I kneel down . . .") The woman at the next table scolds, "You better be praying, down on your knees like that!"[9]

With the most popular blues being those closest to soul music, the older styles are dying away; Bland no longer calls himself Bobby 'Blue' Bland as he did in the 50's. In general those blues singers who have remained successful are those furthest removed from 'down-home' and 'in the alley' associations. There is more support for 'clean' rather than 'dirty' tones; the shimmering clarity of B. B. King's or Little Milton's guitar, the ballad smoothness of Bobby Bland or Junior Parker (till his death in 1971) are better liked than the moaning toughness of a Muddy Waters. The black teenage record buying market virtually ignores the blues, but for older people liking to 'go back' and reminisce about their youth, sleekness, sophistication and glamour helps remove the worst associations of the music and its past. As Pervis Spann remarks, talking about the importance of the blues today; 'With the older people it is *very* important.' From his knowledge of his radio audience in Chicago he adds, 'As people begin to grow old in this area, they become more 'customed to blues, they can relate to it better. When someone is telling you it's hard to make a living and you grow older and you find out it's hard to try to make a living, you begin to listen to that. That's the blues. When someone tell you that "my baby left me, she took all I had", that's the blues. When they're looking for some hope and they just can't find it, that's the blues. Things of this nature will start you to be more 'customed to listen, to listening to the blues.'[10]

But stars like B.B., Bland and Little Johnny Taylor are a tiny minority in the ever-changing world of soul. With little radio time for the blues on the soul stations, and with people looking down on it as 'slave time' music, the blues is dying out as black popular music. Some performers only turn to the blues for white audiences, while sticking to soul in their local bars; some use their vacations from assembly lines or steel mills to tour Europe performing the music that has little market at home. Nonetheless, all over the States there are still neighbourhood clubs which rock to the old blues, and the music is not yet dead. Folklorists, jazz fans and researchers from journals like the British *Blues*

Unlimited and the American *Living Blues* have helped remind people of the richness of the music which has contributed so much to jazz, rock and soul music, and countless obscure musicians find exposure in student campuses and special blues festivals.

The roots of the blues remain in black America, and while many singers are resentful of the black rejection of the blues as a denial of their heritage, soul is in fact a continuity with that heritage. Soul is not simply a rejection of the past that the blues are felt to represent: like blues it is the music of feeling, and the feeling is of togetherness. As the Chicago disc-jockey Butterball of WVON told Michael Haralambos:

'The old blues singer's sayin' no matter what the world is makin' out of you, how you allowing the world to twist your mind and break your spirits down, I'm gonna keep on pushin', I'm gonna get by somehow. A blues singer always sings about himself most of the time. The new breed now, or the soulful people instead of the blues people, which are still soulful, but I'm saying the new breed, they're talkin' about this togetherness because it's more united now. Years ago they were individuals and they had individualistic attitudes. Now they say we're rolling on, we're gonna keep on pushin', we're gonna make it. It's the togetherness. I guess it's a movement.'[11]

Afterword

Dealing with the Devil—Into the Nineties

Over twenty years have now passed since this book was first published, and only slightly fewer since a revised and expanded second edition was issued in Britain in 1983. In the course of those two decades there have been immense changes within the African-American communities which nurtured the blues and saw this elemental artform spread around the world. A central thread running through *The Devil's Music* has been the placement of the creative accomplishments of the most significant blues singers in the context of the turbulent times in which they lived, and as we approach the end of the century this is a good moment to pick up the story.

The book was originally written in 1976 in connection with a BBC-TV documentary series of the same name. The aim had been to capture on film as wide a range as possible of different styles of blues from various parts of the United States. We filmed in Chicago, St. Louis, New York City, down south in Memphis, and in numerous key historical locations throughout Mississippi and Arkansas. We were determined to let the men and women who created some of the most expressive music in western culture speak in their own terms about their lives as black people in the United States. And speak out they did. Gus Cannon, aged 93 and deaf, once leader of Cannon's Jug Stompers, one of the finest blues-playing Jug bands of the 1920s, and a delightful and entertaining old man, turned momentarily serious to say, on film: "Oh my folk tell me I talk too much but you all white folk can do any God darn thing you wanna do."

All of the contributors to the films, who have been quoted extensively in this book, took the project seriously. They had tremendous pride in the blues, and many were already seeing the music in terms of "Heritage," a concept which was to become key to the survival of the blues in the 1980s and beyond. Pervis Spann, for example, a disc jockey at the time with Radio WVON in Chicago, stressed how important blues was to his mainly black audience: "Blues is very important, very important, due to the fact that most of the black people in this area were from rural areas, for example Mississippi— I'm from Mississippi myself—Arkansas, Alabama, Louisiana, Tennessee, those places. And when you're from down there you just have blues embedded in you—it's a part of your heritage."

There are many people who are distrustful of notions of "heritage," and are legitimately suspicious of the packaging and marketing of what used to be a self-sustaining form of popular culture, created in the back-country lanes and city streets of poor black neighborhoods. But the growth of the blues heritage industry has been an authentic response both to the hopes of countless blues performers themselves and their own communal audiences. The common factor has been a real desire for a respect for blues culture and what is has represented historically. In the words of B.B. King, who has become without any doubt the biggest star in the international blues firmament during the last two decades, "more than anything else it is important to study history ... To be a black person and sing the blues, you are black twice" (*Ebony*, February 1992).

Speaking in 1976, when he was 67, Henry Townsend, a singer from St. Louis who first made blues records in the 1920s, was particularly upset by the lack of respect for blues, and its near rejection among young blacks at that time. He explained why it had become unfashionable: "Well bluntly speaking I will tell you, because it was told and has been used and abused as such as it was *nothing*. And the young blacks of course down through time they got away from it because, let's say we are enslaved to one another in a lot of ways, and if one guy criticizes, 'Ah man, you like that junk?'

then this is where a lot don't want him saying that so they pull away from it . . . Blues has been kind of down for that reason, you know, and let's be a little blunt, a little, little honest about it—the blues more or less came from uncultured people. And if you're not a cultured person, why you know at one time that was just that, that's all: you didn't have anything to offer society."

The rise of the blues heritage industry has been a fascinating story in its own right. Its roots lie partly in the efforts of folklorists, black and white, to study and record all kinds of black folk music, culminating in the magnificent recordings for the archive of the Library of Congress in the 1930s and '40s. Then in the '50s and '60s, partly inspired by the moral fervor and righteousness of the Civil Rights Movement, which seemed to confer a kind of spiritual purity upon black poor people in the Deep South, a new generation of enthusiasts sought out often long-forgotten blues singers to get them on record again. Soon, growing numbers of books and reissued long-playing records were coming out, supported by reviewers in jazz and folk music magazines and specialist journals like *Blues Unlimited*. The stimulus provided by this newfound attention to the roots of the music coincided with a sudden lionization of more contemporary urban blues singers such as Muddy Waters, Howlin' Wolf, and Sonny Boy Williamson. British bands like the Rolling Stones, Animals, Yardbirds, and Fleetwood Mac adopted the raw, tough, and amplified blues styles of the city ghettos of the North.

Singers who were being superseded by the more fashionable sounds of soul music within the black communities were given a new lease of life. International festivals and concert halls beckoned as white audiences at home and abroad responded with a warmth and respect which sometimes took the black performers by surprise. Ignored or taken for granted by their own communities, they found benefits both emotional and financial in the blues boom that followed. As young, white college kids and even "good ole boys" from the South took up the music, older black musicians began to look upon their own past achievements with renewed pride. There were of course victims in all this—the blues singers whose songs were lifted wholesale without recognition or royalties and the grandstanding by white bands on the make, hogging the limelight—but overall the benefits hugely outweighed the disadvantages.

The extent to which blues had fallen out of favor and become unfashionable by the 1970s should not be exaggerated. There were major stars still playing to predominantly black audiences, especially Little Milton, Bobby Bland, and, towering above them all, B.B. King, but these were the exceptions. Where once blues had been central to secular black music, now it was getting shunted to the margins by soul, then disco, then funk.

In the following two decades there was to be an even more dramatic diversification of musical styles in black entertainment. Rap and hip hop, an explosively percussive and urgent range of sounds fed by new electronic technologies and the urban rage of the ghetto, erupted from the youth of the Bronx and Harlem in the late 1970s. Digital recordings, synthesizers, drum machines, samples, and fast, rat-a-tat vocal deliveries over swishing, surging rhythms came to define the new era.

There are arguments about whether rap and hip hop are lineal descendants of the blues or symptoms merely of the disordered pathology of the angry underclass. But it is interesting to note that one of the first record producers in Harlem to pick up on the new energy was the blues veteran Bobby Robinson. He had cut some of the last glorious recordings of the emotive slide guitarist Elmore James, including genre-defining classics like "The Sky Is Crying," "Shake Your Moneymaker," and "Done Somebody Wrong." Elmore died in 1963, but Robinson remained continually aware of changing trends in the music industry and never lost his ear for the sounds of the streets. After rap, another product of the '80s, house music, came pumping out of Chicago, still the blues capital of the U.S.A. This was a pulsating, dance-beat-driven music, with wailing vocals and staccatto rhythms, in many respects far removed from the blues. Exciting new genres and subgenres of African-American music continued to proliferate, still deriving core values from the older forms—gospel, blues, and jazz. On top of soul and hip hop there was swing beat ("New Jack Swing") and hard-edged hybrids of rhythm-and-blues. The speed of change was often breathtaking and some of the more aggressive manifestations of black culture saw outsiders recoil in fear or distaste.

For some, what was most disturbing was that many of the markers of the new urban toughness were being all too eagerly adopted not only by young African-Americans but also whites, Asians, and Hispanics. The deeper black styles penetrated into the mainstream of popular culture, the more threatening it all became. The macho posturing and open espousal of violence in gangsta rap, with its to-be-expected anti-police message, sent shock waves of alarm through the think-piece opinion-formers of the establishment media. Nor was all the angst and dismay to be found among fearful whites. The gently soulful and kindly middle-class world of *The Cosby Show*, a hugely popular showpiece TV entertainment from an earlier generation, was a million miles away from the bombastic aggression of the "b-boys" and heavy-duty rappers coming from ethnic-faultline cities like Los Angeles.

The serious L.A. rioting and looting of 1992 showed just how accurately the slamming menace of West Coast rap mirrored the anti-cop attitudes of inner-city youths. This was urban crisis with a soundtrack.

Blues as Heritage

It is against this convulsive background that the emergence of the new heritage industry has to be understood.

It might be thought that the espousal of blues by white society would damage its credibility within the black community. Perhaps for some it did, but only for a minority. Despite the extreme vulnerability many African Americans feel in the face of charges of "inauthenticity," "selling out," or "disloyalty to the race," the growing respect accorded to the blues by the establishment has seldom led to those accusations.

However much the blues has become a minority taste, just one form of music to be selected or rejected from the immense supermarket variety on offer, it still remains an enduring marker of black identity. Legitimate pride is taken in its own now astonishing diversity even among those people who don't actually like the blues as music or don't themselves want to listen to it. How has the blues heritage industry manifested itself? How has it been structured and what has it achieved?

It has been most successful through the nationwide spread of blues festivals, building on the earlier popularity of jazz and folk festivals. (*Muddy Waters at Newport 1960* had been a classic breakthrough album for electric band blues.) The San Francisco Blues Festival was launched in 1973 and has some claims to be the longest surviving pure blues fixture. Not surprisingly the biggest is now the Chicago Blues Festival, established in 1984, which regularly attracts over half a million customers.

All over the United States, coast to coast, north to south, blues fans of every kind can now usually find one of these package shows, often organized by one of the many local blues societies and held in picturesque open-air settings. Some are set up by city or county authorities, sponsored by small businesses or large corporations, while others are purely commercial events. Many are held in heartland blues territories, like the riverfront St. Louis Blues and Heritage Festival, which in 1993 featured local artists including James DeShay and the 84-year-old Henry Townsend, both of whom had been filmed for *The Devil's Music*. Two years later Henry was given a place on the prestigious St. Louis "Walk of Fame," commemorating the city's "cultural heritage." The metal marker on the sidewalk mentions that he had been "featured in a BBC documentary."

One of the most popular events is the New Orleans Jazz and Heritage Festival, which now showcases as many as 3000 musicians on ten different stages, playing every kind of music from around the world. It has helped promote interest in white, French-speaking fiddle-and-accordian cajun music and its black blues-based equivalent, Zydeco, the swinging, droning, swaying dance music played by the late Clifton Chenier, Rockin' Dopsie, and growing numbers of younger musicians.

Some of the most interesting festivals are in the Deep South in areas once noted for meting out some of the most barbaric treatment of black people in the old days of Jim Crow. Happily there are now numerous friendly and racially mixed events such as the Sunflower Blues Festival near Clarksdale, Mississippi, birthplace of John Lee Hooker. Nearby in Helena, Arkansas the King Biscuit Blues Festival now draws 50,000 people annually.

Politicians at all levels have not been slow to spot the advantages to be gained from wrapping themselves in the blues. The U.S. State Department was already funding international tours for performers like Howlin' Wolf and Buddy Guy as a way of promoting American culture in the 1960s.

By August 1977 President Jimmy Carter, a former Georgia peanut farmer, had invited Muddy Waters to perform at the annual White House staff picnic. "As you know," he said, introducing him to the crowd, "Muddy Waters is one of the greatest performers of all time. He's won more awards than I can name. His music is well known around the world, comes from a good part of the country, and represents accurately the background of the American people."

In President Reagan's era, Etta James, a roaring R&B vocalist and convincing soul balladeer who'd overcome drug problems in the '70s, was invited to sing at the opening ceremonies of the 1984 Olympic Games in Los Angeles. Reagan's successor George Bush invited another big-voiced vocalist, Koko Taylor, to his Inaugural Party, and then got B.B. King to play before eight hundred of his most wealthy Republican supporters in celebration of his first year in office. Meanwhile back down South, the ambitious, sax-playing Bill Clinton, as Governor of Arkansas in the mid '80s, established the Delta Cultural Center in Helena, the rivertown base of Sonny Boy Williamson and the King Biscuit Boys in Clinton's youth. State representative Ernest Cunningham told Martin Walker of the London *Guardian* how it happened: "Bill was always a jazz man, liked his blues, came to the festivals. He called me into the Governor's office one day and said he wanted to make something of Helena, a tourist center, a cultural and heritage place. Told me to dream big and he'd back me all he could." Now the old delta blues are part of that dream in the Center's museum.

Elsewhere in the South there are similar institutions, including the Delta Blues Museum in Clarksdale which displays memorabilia, artifacts, posters, instruments, books, records, tapes, and over 500 videos of Delta performers. Among the exhibits is a "didley-bow," a primitive one-string slide instrument of the type B.B. King, Muddy Waters, and Elmore James first learned to play music. There is also a modern guitar donated by Z.Z. Top made with a piece of cypress wood from Muddy's nearby childhood cabin. The cabin itself was bought in 1996 by the "House of Blues" organization to be shipped out of state and re-erected in New Orleans. One of B.B.'s guitars is also on show along with the battered amplified nine-string used for years by Big Joe Williams. He performed some of his classic pieces on it when he was filmed for *The Devil's Music* in 1976, including "Providence Help the Poor People" and "Highway 49." (He died aged 79 in 1982.)

Further north in Memphis, the Beale Street Blues Museum has been opened in the Old Daisy Theater as part of a largely successful attempt to revitalize the area, helped by B.B. King opening the first of his chain of blues clubs there in 1991. Beale Street is now almost always associated with the so-called "Father of the Blues," bandleader W.C. Handy, who died in 1958.

"I played with Handy," recalled Gus Cannon in 1976. "You heard tell of P'fessor Handy? I used to play with him. You know, complement. He put the banjo in the band. I played with Jim Turner. You heard tell of him? All them gone. I know a gang of them, I used to play with them, they gone. I'm here, but I'm just thinkin' about quit playin'." Gus died in 1979, but today Handy's name has been brought back to life through the Blues Foundation's annual W.C. Handy Awards. This event is highly valued by performers and record companies alike for the prestige and publicity afforded by winning any one of the coveted prizes. Since the scheme became established in the 1980s, the selection processes have sometimes been dogged by controversy, but there is no doubt the awards have injected a competitive edge to the heritage movement, avoiding a purely nostalgic and backward-looking approach to the music. Newcomers to the blues have often got their first national exposure through winning a Handy Award.

Underpinning this growing heritage industry remains a bedrock of serious scholarship and academic research. An astonishing number of books have been published on all aspects of the blues in the last twenty years. The story of just one of them illustrates how the status of the blues has changed during that time. Between 1970 and 1980, when he finally got his "Authorized Biography" of B.B. King published, Charles Sawyer had his book rejected by over fifty publishers. Since it came out, aptly titled *The Arrival of B.B. King*, it has hardly been out of print.

Alongside the books there are also the specialist research magazines which provide invaluable reviews of new record releases, including *Juke Blues* and *Blues and Rhythm* in Britain and *Living Blues* in America. (The latter has moved from its original home in Chicago to Oxford, Mississippi, and is now connected to the University of Mississippi and the Center for the Study of Southern Culture.) Also at "Ole Miss" is a major Blues Archive, itself a significant manifestation of the increased value placed on the blues in the New South. At a more popular level is another magazine promoting the blues, the glossy, well-produced *Blues Revue*.

Most but not all of these heritage institutions have been controlled by whites or the middle-class establishment. One of the most valuable of the *black* organizations, and in some ways the most poignant, has been the Blues Heaven Foundation in Chicago, established in 1982 by Willie Dixon, the veteran singer, bass player, bandleader, composer, producer, and behind-the-scenes luminary. He is said to have composed over 500 songs and the list of his hit compositions for other singers like Muddy Waters, Howlin' Wolf, Little Walter, and Bo Diddley is phenomenal. Many are titles which are likely to live on for as long as the blues is listened to: "I Just Want to Make Love to You," "I'm Your Hoochie-

Coochie Man," "Little Red Rooster," "My Babe," "Spoonful," and "You Can't Judge a Book by its Cover."

The foundation was named after yet another of his compositions, "Blues Heaven," recorded in 1965 by Koko Taylor,
then at the beginning of a marvellous career that saw her
roll-and-tumble blues-belting style win her ten W.C. Handy
Awards in the 1980s, more than any other artist. Dixon had
discovered her and signed her to the Chess label in keeping
with his desire to nurture the blues as an idiom and help
individual artists. In his excellent autobiography, *I Am the
Blues: The Willie Dixon Story* (Da Capo, 1989), jointly written
with Don Snowden, he explained what he was trying to
achieve with the Foundation, a non-profit organization which
keeps the blues alive through school programs and scholar-
ships and also provides financial support to destitute artists:
"The reason for doing Blues Heaven is when something is
rightfully owed to somebody, they deserve to have it. I want
it to be in a position where it can help the underprivileged
people, especially underprivileged musicians that don't have
any way of assistance. The average musician doesn't have
any income and no social security so when he becomes old,
he's got nothing and nobody to be leaning on. These people
need protection and if you can start an organization or foundation, everything starts from a little. On top of that, Blues
Heaven is a historical thing. The blues are a part of the history and heritage of our people and these things are supposed to be known through the rest of history" (pages 225–
6).

In his book Willie revealed that of all the countless songs
he'd written the one which meant most to him was not one
of the big hits or money-makers. It was a little-known blues
written in 1984, "It Don't Make Sense (You Can't Make
Peace)." As he observed, "The wisdom of the blues can be
used all through life and that's why most blues are written
as a statement of wisdom. I'd say that from 95% up to 99%
of the world believes that it don't make sense you can't
make peace . . . That's the real meaning and the real good
of the blues, a better education and understanding among all

people" (page 229). Willie Dixon died in January 1992, his dream of peace among people as far away as ever.

The blues-as-national-heritage probably reached its symbolic peak in 1994. In that year the United States Post Office issued a set of stamps commemorating six of the greatest-ever blues singers: Bessie Smith, Ma Rainey, Muddy Waters, Howlin' Wolf, Jimmy Rushing, and Robert Johnson (the latter with cigarette air-brushed out of the original photograph).

Blues Down Home—The New South

The new environment for the blues created new opportunities and new audiences, particularly white ones. But what was happening to the performers themselves in the '80s and '90s? And how was the music adapting to the changes enveloping the black communities? Given the perception shared by many singers that the blues reflects and is shaped by the reality of black people's lives, how have the blues maintained those crucial links with the black experience?

The answer is to be found in changing demographics, as has been the case so often in blues history.

In the 1940s and '50s, during the period of the great mass migration from the rural south to the "Promised Land" of the North, it was the familiarity of the deep, earthy "down-home" blues which the migrants carried with them. In updated, modernized, and electrified forms the music helped them settle in. By the 1980s a curious reversal was beginning. Just when even the more progressive soul-blues styles were becoming stale and outmoded, a strange, totally unexpected renaissance took place in the still mainly rural South. Reversing the trend of virtually the whole century, over half a million black people have moved back, away from the disintegrating communities of the northern inner cities. Parents in despair at the nihilism, violence, and drug-related crime of the ghettos have been sending their children to the calmer, quieter South to be raised by relations. Adults, desperate for work as unemployment rates escalate in the North, have gone to the South, despite the knowledge that compared to whites, dollar for dollar, blacks still earn less in Mississippi than in Illinois.

Dramatic changes in the South were already apparent in the 1970s. Jimmy Carter, elected President in 1976 from the "Cracker" redneck state of Georgia, symbolized the emergence of the New South.

Around that time Henry Townsend was acknowledging the changes. "The South was the South and that don't mean good," he said. "But now it *has* changed extremely. People is being considered people, I'll just put it that way, in a little better way than they used to. You know people was called something else, maybe 'animals' or 'coons,' which is a mighty tight way of something outside of people! So now they're considered people, in most cases. I guess there always will be a little of everything that ever was will still remain, but I would say the South is extreme changed."

Henry's wife Vernell agreed: "It *has* changed today because I would like to go back as it is right now. I could go back to live you know." (In fact the Townsends never did return, and, sad to report, Vernell died in 1995.)

In many respects the South that drew people back still manifested the old problems that had driven families away in the first place—the poverty, the lower standards of living compared to their white counterparts, and a more subtle de facto segregation which had replaced the overt, institutionalized racism of the pre-Civil Rights era. But what did remain attractive was the sense of community, the sharing, supportive set of relationships involving friends, family, and neighborhood. To go back felt like going home, and not necessarily in defeat or with a sense of failure. They returned with a certain optimism, knowing that others had been through the same things and there was something positive awaiting them.

The Malaco Story

One of the singers who first benefited from this mood of positive optimism and gave voice to it was the Texas-born Arzel "Z.Z." Hill. Sometimes rather harshly dismissed as a "journeyman" soul-blues singer, he had a succession of minor hits in the early 1970s. In 1980 he signed to the fledgling company Malaco Records from Jackson, Mississippi, and his first album, *Z.Z. Hill*, was well received by black fans.

But it was his second release in 1982, entitled, appropriately enough, *Down Home*, that really hit the mark. Featuring a song that has now become virtually a blues-anthem for the new era, "Down Home Blues," the album stayed in the black album charts for nearly two whole years, selling over half a million copies in the process, which was virtually unheard of among blues artists not reaching the white market. Z.Z. had further successes with his next two albums, *The Rhythm and the Blues* and *I'm a Blues Man*. His appeal was based on well-crafted songs, good musicianship, strong horn-based arrangements, and the production skills of Tommy Couch and Wolf Stephenson. They created a highly effective soul-blues sound sometimes drawing on a country and western ballad sensibility in songs about the everyday frailties of personal relationships, as in his biggest hit single of the period, "Cheating in the Next Room" (1982). Sadly, at the peak of his success Z.Z. died of a heart attack in 1984, aged 49.

By the time of Hill's death Malaco was firmly established as the predominant Southern label for black blues fans. It had been demonstrated that there was still a substantial audience among older black people in the South, and there was a market for albums. Other big names in the soul-blues field, like Bobby Bland, Latimore, and Little Milton, were snapped up by the label. Some of the song titles recorded by Malaco themselves brandished a kind of pleasurable pride in the blues: for Johnnie Taylor, who had been a major soul star for Stax Records in the '60s, it was "Still Called the Blues," while Little Milton declared, "The Blues Is Alright," soon to become another singalong classic for black audiences. It is striking how many of these songs had been composed self-consciously directing attention to their status as blues, the singer's role as a blues singer, or straightforwardly asserting the value of the blues. This was a continuation of a trend which had begun around the time that blues had first started losing support in the black communities. Willie

Dixon recorded "I Am the Blues" (later the title of his auto-biography) in 1969, the same year that B.B. King scored a substantial hit with "Why I Sing the Blues."

It was as if the blues community was fighting back, con-ducting a cultural argument through song in defence of it-self. In 1977 Muddy Waters recorded "The Blues Had a Baby and They Named It Rock and Roll" at a session pro-duced by the albino-white rock-blues guitarist Johnny Winter, himself eager to promote blues in its most direct, undiluted forms. The Malaco revolution helped win the argument: without their high-quality hits, their success and the glamor that followed the blues as a popular artform still genuinely rooted in working-class black culture might have faced ter-minal decline.

New South—New Blues

The blues resurgence spearheaded by Malaco had its most significant impact in the South. Performers whose careers had been flagging began to find things picking up again.

One singer who had begun his career in Chicago was the Louisiana-born Bobby Rush, who headed back to Jackson, Mississippi, from where he became "King of the Chitlin Cir-cuit" in the '80s. He is immensely popular with black audi-ences in live performances in clubs, show lounges, and road-houses across the small-town South. His act is full of energy as he parades and preaches around the stage, doing quick costume changes from shiny gold jumpsuit to two-toned pur-ple as his band grooves away. Rush has had the wit to re-spond to nearly every new development in black music and has even absorbed elements of rap and hip hop into his per-formances. He describes himself as a "lyric doctor" and, as reported by Jim O'Neal in *Blues and Rhythm*, he regards his music as "folk-funk." He has been criticized for the alleged sexism and macho posing of his act, but he has a huge fol-lowing among women, who respond with whoops and laugh-ter. One of his most successful albums has been the charac-teristic *I Ain't Studdin' You,* for Urgent! Records in 1991. What makes his work so fascinating is his ability to rework classic old-style blues into something utterly contemporary.

And it's clearly done with real gusto and affection for older traditions.

Another singer in the modern soul-blues idiom to benefit from the revived popularity of blues with the Southern black audience has been Artie "Blues Boy" White, Mississippi-born guitarist and owner of Bootsy's Lounge in Chicago until the mid-1980s, when he too returned to the South. In 1987 he was signed to Ichiban Records, a company in Atlanta, Georgia owned by John Abbey, formerly a journalist with the British magazine *Blues and Soul. Tired of Sneaking Around* got into the R&B album charts and helped consolidate the record company's reputation as one seriously committed to keeping modern blues in the forefront of black popular culture. One of the label's house producers was the multi-skilled Gary "B.B." Coleman, who died tragically young in 1994. Apart from making his own records he also attracted to Ichiban other artists such as the big-voiced Texan, Trudy Lynn, Blues Boy Willie, Buster Benton, Chick "Stoop Down" Willis, Little Johnny Taylor, and a group of former Muddy Waters sidemen, The Legendary Blues Band.

A significant feature of the Southern blues revival has been the dramatic impact made by a succession of supremely confident tell-it-as-it-is women singers. One has been Lynn White, a tough gospel-tinged soul-blues singer who dishes out typical Southern wisdom to other women in smoke-filled clubs. Even more popular as a purveyor of savvy bedroom blues has been Denise La Salle, a gutsy-voiced chanteuse from the Malaco stable, whose performance style is full of humor and straight-ahead sass. She's had considerable success as a songwriter, penning country singer Barbara Mandrell's hit "Married, But Not to Each Other," and her records have ranged from soul to funk to R&B. If anything, her commitment to blues has deepened, and she has even formed her own National Association for the Preservation of the Blues, which gives support to artists at the soul-blues end of the spectrum.

It may well be that this female assertiveness in the commercial blues market reflects a wider phenomenon within African-American society. We have already seen how the

confident and extroverted performances of Etta James and
Koko Taylor brought them unprecedented status and success
in the 1980s. Etta actually had more hits in the 1970s but
her prestige has grown steadily right through to the 1990s,
while Koko Taylor has now become the biggest female blues
star of them all. The common factor has undoubtedly been
the full-blooded nature of their performances: a determination to take control on their own terms and bring out their
emotional life with unabashed artistic relish.

This has its cultural roots in the lives and music of the
great women blues singers of the '20s, who were equally insistent upon taking regal if not imperial command. Singers
like Bessie Smith and Ma Rainey have remained iconic figures long after their deaths, names to be invoked with awe
by successive generations. Other, later jazz-based female
singers like Billie Holliday and Dinah Washington also exerted considerable influence, heightened by their own con-
fused and messy personal lives. Koko Taylor, Etta James,
and Denise La Salle were the most prominent of the women
artists in the new era, but there were plenty of others.
Among them were Big Time Sarah, herself a young women
who worked the clubs in Chicago, and the "Two Fisted
Mama," Katie Webster, who pounded out the old barrelhouse piano and hollered the blues in fine Louisiana fashion
as the "Swamp Boogie Queen."

Gonna Be Some Changes Made

The success of the big-personality women singers was not
only rooted in musical history, but also in deep changes
within contemporary black culture. Across the whole waterfront of black entertainment, from soul, rap, and hip hop
through to Oprah Winfrey, women have been presenting
themselves as strong, powerful, and unashamedly prepared
to make demands.

Over the last two decades black women have been greatly
affected by the general "feminization" of American life,
which has seen more women than ever going to work, going
to college, and becoming economically independent. Even
among those dependent on welfare it is often women who

are the prime recipients of relief because they take care of the children. More black women were in work than black men by the mid-1990s; of black people in employment, 53% were women.

These profound social changes in the recent past have not only been reflected throughout black popular music, including contemporary blues, but they have also reinforced deeply embedded social patterns that go way back. Ever since slavery, when black families were so ruthlessly broken up, black society has been largely matriarchal. Women have had to be the source of strength, often being forced to raise their children alone, given the chronic instability of life in low-income families. Today inner-city divorce rates are high while births outside of marriage have become commonplace. Meanwhile the economic pressures have become even more fierce. Between 1970 and 1990 Chicago's South Side, archetypal blues territory, saw the proportion of families in poverty rise from 30% to 50%. Whole communities are now experiencing for the first time a life in which a majority of adults will not be working in a typical week. In the postwar years, when black workers from the South poured into Chicago, they could at least get work even if it was low paid. There is a significant difference between being poor but in work, and being poor but with no real prospect of a job. This situation is dangerously corrosive of the ties that bind communities and even those individuals who have escaped the worst ghetto problems are deeply affected by the crisis. Young black males involved in violence, criminality, vandalism, gang warfare, or drug dependency may be media stereotypes, but tragically all too often there is truth behind the images. Even those who have fled to the black middle-class enclaves of the suburbs will almost certainly know friends or relatives who have been in trouble or landed in jail.

Chicago Blues Today

This prolonged and deepening inner-city crisis has had its own impact on the blues in Chicago. It remains the blues capital of the world and there are still more clubs and bars in the city where live music can be heard than anywhere else. There are also still plenty of record companies in Chicago championing the blues, particularly the market leader, Alligator Records, which for over a quarter century has done more than any other label to keep the blues out of some kind of antiquarian backwater.

But there are unmistakable signs of decline in the city's blues culture, and it's hard to avoid the conclusion that it's partly the result of Chicago's immense social problems.

An internal migration has seen the better-off black people moving to the suburbs so that some of the poorest districts have seen their population halved since 1970. Large stretches of weed-ridden wasteland now cover what used to be thriving, if poor, communities. Shops, stores, churches, and blues clubs from the great days have now gone, along with apartments inhabited by many of the singers whose lives were virtually inseparable from those of their working class audiences.

The music from the classic period of Chicago blues in the 1950s typified by Muddy Waters, Howlin' Wolf, Elmore James, and many others who have also now passed—had an electrifying declamatory energy born of the pent-up feelings of the immigrants who came looking for a better life away from the cotton-picking South.

Many of the artists who came in behind them, like Koko Taylor, Junior Wells, Otis Rush, Buddy Guy, and countless others, are still very much alive and keeping the blues going with the same dynamic urgency. They all pushed back stylistic boundaries, creating new, more urban sounds. These were the people who did more than anyone else to define the modern blues at precisely the time when the mainstream was discovering the music. For Eric Clapton, the Rolling Stones, or any of the "British blues invasion," these were the sounds to emulate. The blues, then, was taken to be either an old black man with a battered guitar on a Southern back porch singing "I woke up this morning . . . " or a blistering Chicago blues band with fierce lead guitar, wailing amplified harmonica, rolling boogie piano, electric bass, and thunderous back-beat drumming. This was one of the most intoxicating sounds in twentieth century American music and it would be misleading to say that it had gone. It is still possible to hear plenty of magnificent music, live or on record, in Chicago. But what is far less easy to find is the new-direction innovator.

There are plenty of fine artists in Chicago reinterpreting the classic bar-blues sound, and they certainly deserve an audience at least as wide as some of the Southern soul-blues artists who have been more successful in reaching the black commercial market. Two in particular stand out. Magic Slim (Morris Holt) and his band The Teardrops have developed a rocking, percussive sound with a heavy beat and mellow smoky vocals, showing an obvious debt to Muddy Waters and old pals like Magic Sam and Freddie King. The other, even less well-known singer is Byther Smith, cousin of the late J.B. Lenoir and, like Magic Slim, a native of Mississippi. He approaches his music with a degree of seriousness thoroughly in keeping with spirit of the 1990s. Like his cousin, he's tackled contemporary social and political questions, as with his 1989 album *Addressing the Nation with the Blues*. There is a sustained emotional commitment and craftsmanship about his work which commands respect.

Where artists like these have a role to play is in keeping alive a vital blues tradition by bringing to it their own distinctive voices. Slim or Byther may never become international superstars like Muddy Waters or B.B. King, but it's people like them who give weight and solidity to the music as an embodiment of a sharing, supportive community.

The Strong Persuaders

The other significant feature of the last two decades has been the emergence—from virtually nowhere—of a major new blues superstar, Robert Cray. His career began slowly with a little-noticed album in 1979, *Who's Been Talkin'* (an old Wolf song), followed by the more successful *Bad Influence* in 1983 and *False Accusations* the following year. It was the Alligator production *Showdown!* with Albert Collins and Johnny Copeland in 1985 that then gave him his real breakthrough: he won the first of three Grammy Awards, and the album sold over a quarter of a million copies. By now he was suddenly being feted as the future of the blues. He was young, handsome in a smooth-skinned, clean sort of way, and highly intelligent in demeanor. In 1986 he clocked up over a million sales with his next album *Strong Persuader* (another Grammy winner), and did the same in 1989 with *Don't Be Afraid of the Dark*.

This was astonishing. In less than a decade he had overtaken virtually everyone in the field and was reaching the young audience, black and white, and even older, traditional blues fans (at least those who didn't dismiss him as a "yuppie soul singer"). His voice was indeed soulful, self-possessed, and had a certain "middle-class" quality, like a college-educated professional. He only came late to the blues, but tutored by Albert Collins, master of Texas "cool," he swiftly developed his own disciplined but emotive guitar techniques to enhance skillfully crafted songs. His band included whites and he was the marketing promoters' dream.

The "yuppie" tag is only misplaced if it is taken pejoratively. Cray was a success because he is extremely talented, but that success did symbolize a phenomenon with much wider social implications, the emergence of an ever-expanding black middle class. Although those in poverty are worse off than they were twenty years ago, and the gap between rich and poor has widened, the actual proportion of black Americans in federally defined poverty actually fell slightly between 1970 to 1995, from 33.5% to 29.3%. In the same period, those earning over $50,000 at 1970 prices nearly doubled, to over 20%. At some point in the not-too-distant future it is quite conceivable that the black middle classes will outnumber the very poor. Given the explosive discontents festering in the poorest ghetto neighborhoods that generate considerable social tensions, many of those blacks now entering the middle classes do so with an angry ambivalence. There are often acute feelings of guilt: if the prevailing historical experience of being black in America has been to be poor and oppressed it can feel like a betrayal to aspire to the lifestyle of the white middle classes.

All the old anxieties about "authenticity" and "black identity" return, along with perhaps a yearning for the calming solidarities of racial separation. What adds to the complexity of the situation is that despite their own greater relative prosperity, it is actually often middle-class blacks who have, or suspect, most direct experience of discrimination. Back in the ghetto, blacks have fewer points of contact with whites, so it's often the young professionals and suburbanites who face the invisible barriers. They find problems with housing and getting mortgages, with surveillance in stores, service in restaurants, and getting taxis, and above all getting promotions. Everywhere they find themselves regarded in the same light as the most threatening crack dealer from the housing projects, while ironically the penetrating and calculated put-ons of gangsta rap endorse the reputation of the "young-black-as-mugger." Meanwhile, in the wake of assaults on the legitimacy of affirmation action, and on the confusing assumption that blacks had somehow *got* civil rights in the '60s, political sympathy for the black community's problems has diminished significantly. There has been a tendency for some people, black and white, to blame the poor for their own poverty. And yet those who might like to convince themselves that racism is a thing of the past will have had a shock. In 1996, following the sudden and embarrassed settlement by Texaco of the largest-ever racial discrimination lawsuit, the oil giant had to pay out $176 million. This followed the release of secret recordings in which senior executives had discussed destroying evidence and ridiculed black employees as "black jelly beans."

The blues has always functioned as a form of cultural expression which not only provided real pleasure and uplifting entertainment, but also helped enable significant numbers of black people to negotiate their own sense of identity. At each stage in the history of the music this has been true— the personal creativity of individuals working within one of the many different blues forms has somehow captured a wider mood, or encapsulated a set of attitudes. In the 1980s it was Robert Cray: he managed to signify an unhesitating modernity while embodying real respect and love for older traditions. He never looked old-fashioned yet brought back to life a notion of the old blues community which could seem convincingly young again and draw in people of all ages and colors.

Cray's success was an encouragement to his black contemporaries. The college-educated Californian Joe Louis Walker, whose career began to take off in the mid-1980s, released a series of albums which showed a similar understanding of blues tradition. Like Cray he's a skilled musician, chooses excellent songs, and performs with real conviction. By the early '90s he was becoming a major attraction at home and abroad. The openings created by Cray showed that many others could venture forward, and not all in the same idiom. While Joe Louis Walker generated an almost Chicago-style electric blues-band urgency, there were other, more surprising approaches waiting in the wings.

In 1994 Okeh Records released the first album by another California-based singer, the previously unknown acoustic guitar player Keb' Mo' (Kevin Moore), whose instrument featured the big metal resonator favored by some of the old country blues artists of the '30s.

The young Keb'—he was in his thirties—showed a remarkable adeptness with this archetypal bluesman's guitar. On this and his equally striking second album two years later, *Just Like You*, he demonstrated that he was a thoughtful songwriter and an accomplished interpreter of other peoples' material. He even risked covering Robert Johnson numbers, including "Come On In My Kitchen," nearly sixty years after the originals. His version of "Last Fair Deal Gone Down" was performed in a lilting waltz tempo, accompanied by a small traditional jazz band including exquisitely mournful clarinet. Some songs are backed by amplified instruments while others, like the pointedly topical "Momma, Where's My Daddy?" he sings alone to his own guitar.

The first album won the 1995 W.C. Handy Award for "Country/Acoustic Blues Album of the Year." Nothing about his work feels contrived, derivative or mechanically copied. Nor does it feel like a self-conscious pastiche of a once powerful artform. It sounds like an intelligent and engaged piece of work by a young man who understands the conventions of blues well enough to be able to depart from them for purposeful effect, without ever losing that real bluesy feel. He could be that mythical figure, "the future of the blues."

There are some blues artists who have survived long enough in the business to have recorded over four or five decades, and have been performing for even longer. It is fascinating to contemplate what will happen to some of today's talented young black blues singers, like Keb' Mo'. Will he still be singing the blues in half a century's time? (And will he still call himself Keb'?)

One of the veterans of the blues who has been recording almost continuously over nearly five decades is John Lee Hooker, who now stands alone alongside B.B. King as an elder statesman of the blues. In a curious way he has benefited from *all* the different developments which have preserved, revived and re-created the blues in the 1990s. Taken up by folkies and British R&B groups in the '60s, supported by the white American rock-blues band Canned Heat in the '70s, he then benefited in the late '80s from the Robert Cray connection. Cray contributed to what became the surprise hit album of 1989, *The Healer*. This has been the best-selling album Hooker has ever had, winning him a Grammy and then induction into the Rock'n'Roll Hall of Fame. Next, together with other rock luminaries, Cray again helped out on *Mr. Lucky*, another big-selling album, which proved that Hooker's hushed vocals and mesmeric deep-blues guitar still generated an emotional resonance with audiences. That's why recordings by him (and other blues artists) have frequently been used on TV advertisements in the last decade, capitalizing on the old man's reputation as the funky embodiment of hip wisdom and relaxed truth-telling.

So, as we approach the end of the millennium, when we can expect all manner of apocalyptic prognostications, the blues is still in remarkably good shape. The music has renourished its rooted connections in the working class black community, not as the dominant musical genre, but one with its own secure validity. It has also become a possible vehicle for the new generation of younger, more prosperous, college-educated African Americans to sustain a certain black authenticity at a time of contradictory emotional demands.

And for the wider American society the blues has become a heartbeat music which reminds the nation of its own humanity, shared by citizens of every class and color of skin. For the rest of the world, the blues has become part of everyone's heritage, one of the great reminders that everybody, even poor, ill-educated people, has a capacity for great creativity. As Gus Cannon remarked with a twinkle in his eye, "I learnt by ear. Taught it by ear, and picked it up by the nose."

Sources and Acknowledgements

The following list of references is given to help those wishing to find out more about the blues and their social background. At the same time I would like to extend my thanks to the many authors and musicians whose work I have made use of and enjoyed.

I would also like to thank my university tutor Dr Bob Reinders who first inspired me to write about American history.

Apart from published sources and records, this book also draws on material gathered in a research and filming trip to America in January 1976, and I would like to express my gratitude to all those who advised in various ways: in Sweden, Bengt Olsson; in Britain Mike Rowe and Bill Greensmith of *Blues Unlimited*, Tony Russell of *Old Time Music*, Derrick Stewart-Baxter of *Jazz Journal*, David Meeker of the British Film Institute and John Cowley; in Chicago Jim and Amy O'Neal of *Living Blues*, Bruce Iglauer of Alligator Records, Bob Koester of Delmark Records (who spent long hours through the night showing me his blues films), Joe Carter, Good Rockin' Charles, Fenton Robinson, Edith Wilson and Pervis Spann. I am particularly grateful to Thomas Dorsey (Georgia Tom), Little Brother Montgomery, The Aces and Eddie Shaw, who allowed us to film in his 1815 Club, and to Billy Boy Arnold who acted as a guide through a tour of blues sites past and present.

In St Louis our filming was helped by Sgt Charlie O'Brien, a blues- and soccer-loving policeman who introduced us to Vernell and Henry Townsend and to Henry Brown. We are most grateful to Charlie and the Townsends for their hospitality and kindness. One of the highspots of our visit to St Louis was filming James DeShay in his Santa Fe Lounge. Delighted to meet people from England who knew of his boyhood hero Charley Patton, he and his club patrons turned the occasion into something like a party.

In Memphis and in long hours of driving through Mississippi

and Arkansas we were helped by George Larrimore and Ken DeCell and particularly Harry Godwin. A true gentleman, Harry does much to promote the blues in Memphis and he introduced us to Sonny Blake, Mose Vinson, L. T. Lewis, Piano Red, Furry Lewis, Rev. Robert Wilkins, Booker White, Laura Dukes, Joe Willie and Carrie Wilkins, Houston Stackhouse and Gus Cannon. Harry also has an endless fund of Southern stories – like the one about the very undemonstrative husband who for once waxed sentimental about his wife on the occasion of their 50th wedding anniversary. 'I'm proud of you, honey,' he told her. Being deaf, she cupper her hand to her ear and shouted: 'What's that, dear?' 'I'm proud of you, honey,' he shouted back. 'I'm tired of you too,' she replied. To all the people like Harry, Laura, Booker and Gus in Memphis, Big Joe Williams and Sam Chatmon in Mississippi, who invited us into their homes, our grateful thanks, not forgetting Judy Peiser of the Center for Southern Folklore in Memphis who showed us an invaluable collection of films made by her, William Ferris Jr. and others. We also very much appreciated the welcome given us by Bishop Rogers and the Lambert Church of God in Christ when we filmed some very fine Gospel singing.

In New York our thanks go to Victoria Spivey – Queen Victoria – and to Lennie Kunstadt of *Record Research*. They also go to Barbara Benedek of the BBC New York office for her brilliant work in tracking down photos and films for both the book and television series. For their help via Barbara I would also like to thank Nick Perls of Yazoo Records, Chris Albertson and John Baker and many others.

Our filming trip was a harmonious and successful operation, in no small part thanks to the skill and good nature of our team – cameraman John Turner, his assistant Richard Adam, sound recordist Stan Nightingale and lights Vincent Price.

I also want to thank the many others who helped the preparation of this book: my flatmates Mary and Richard Fountain and Sarah Hodges for their tolerance; our cats for their company (one sat on my shoulder and one on my lap as I wrote); my mother for her encouragement; Barry Bright who typed the final manuscript; Paula Gilder who worked with endless good humour on such dreary tasks as proof checking, typing sources and compiling the index; Pamela Wood for typing new material for the second edition.

Above all I would like to thank the series producer Maddalena Fagandini for her faith, enthusiasm and kindly support. As Booker White said to her, 'You're a *real* blues lady!'

Finally this book is dedicated to the many blues singers whose work I have admired. A large proportion of song lyrics quoted are traditional or folk blues items, but every effort has been made to trace possible copyright owners to give credit where due. If by chance we have failed to quote the appropriate copyright we ask the indulgence of the music publisher concerned.

Introduction

1 HANDY, W. C. *Father of the blues: an autobiography* ed. A. Bontemps New York: Macmillan, 1941; London: Collier Books, 1970. p. 78.

2 OLIVER, P. *Conversation with the blues* London: Cassell, 1965. p. 26. *Kill that nigger dead* by Butch Cage and Willie Thomas. Issued on *Conversation with the blues* Decca LK 4664.

3 BBC interview: Booker White, Memphis, Tenn., 1976.

4 JONES, L. *Blues people* New York: William Morrow, 1963, p. 60.

Part One

Slavery

1 HUGHES, L. and MELTZER, M. *A pictorial history of the negro in America* New York: Crown Publishers, 3rd rev. edn. 1972. p. 171. Hymn sometimes known as *Miriam's song* by Thomas Moore, published in *Sacred songs* 1816.

2 FISHER, M. M. *Negro slave songs in the United States* New York: Citadel Press, 1953. p. 30. Quote PINCKARD, G. *Notes on the West Indies* 1816.

3 *Ibid*, p. 30.

4 *Ibid*. p. 11. Quote CRESSWELL, N. *Journal 1774–1777* New York, 1924.

5 SOUTHERN, E. ed. *Readings in black American music* New York: Norton, 1971. pp. 34, 35.

6 SYDNOR, C. S. *Slavery in Mississippi* American Historical Association, 1933; Louisiana State University Press, 1966, p. 86.

7 CONE, J. H. *The spirituals and the blues: an interpretation* New York: Seabury Press, 1972. p. 22. Quote BOTKIN, B. A. ed. *Lay my burden down* University of Chicago Press, 1945, pp. 89, 90.

8 BBC interview: Sam Chatmon, Hollandale, Miss., 1976.

9 *Ibid*. Booker White, Memphis, Tenn., 1976.

10 McPHERSON, J. M. *The negro's civil war* New York: Vintage Books, 1965. p. 55. Quote RUSSELL, Sir William H. *My diary north and south* London, vol. 1, 1863, p. 373.

11 LESTER, J. *To be a slave* New York: Dial Press, 1968; London: Puffin Books, 1973. p. 99.

12 BBC interview: Booker White, Memphis, Tenn., 1976.

13 CONE, J. H. *op. cit.* p. 23. Quote MEIER, A. and RUDWICK, E. eds. *The making of black America* New York: Atheneum, vol. 1 1961. p. 181.

14 *Ibid*. p. 23. Quote MATTHEWS, D. *Slavery and Methodism* Princeton University Press, 1965. p. 87.

15 *Ibid.* p. 41. Quote BOTKIN, B.
A. *op. cit.* p. 26.
16 McPHERSON, J. M. *op. cit.* p.
57. Quote TAYLOR, S. King
Reminiscences of my life in camp
Boston, 1902. pp. 7, 8.
17 SOUTHERN, E. ed. *op. cit.* p.
63. Quote WATSON, J. F.
*Methodist error or Friendly Christian
advice to those Methodists who
indulge in extravagant religious
emotions and bodily exercises* 1819.
18 OLIVER, P. *The story of the blues*
London: Barrie and Rockliff the
Cresset Press, 1969; Penguin
Books, 1972. p. 11. Quote Congressman Daniel C. De Jarnette, 1860.
19 *Let my people go* as quoted in
COURLANDER, H. *Negro folk
music U.S.A.* Columbia University
Press, 1963, p. 42.
20 SOUTHERN, E. ed. *op. cit.* p.
83. Quote DOUGLAS, F. *My
bondage and my freedom* 1855.
21 *Ibid.* pp. 71–72, 73, 77–78, 80.
Quote HUNGERFORD, J. *The
old plantation and what I gathered
there in an autumn month* 1859.

**Nigger Minstrels and coon
songs**
1 ROACH, M. *Black American
music past and present* Boston:
Crescendo Publishing Co., 1973. p.
33. Quote McILHENNY, E. A.
Befo' de War spirituals, 1933.
2 BLESH, R. and JANIS, H. *They
all played ragtime* Jazz Book Club
by arrangement with Sidgwick and
Jackson, 1960. p. 85. Quote
CHAFF, G. *Ethiopian glee book*
1849.
3 *Jump Jim Crow* as quoted in
OLIVER, P. *The story of the blues*
op. cit. p. 13.
4 BLESH, R. and JANIS, H. *op.
cit.* pp. 84, 85.

5 LOGAN, R. W. *Betrayal of the
American negro* New York: Collier-
Macmillan, 1965. pp. 242–5.
6 RUSSELL, T. *Blacks, whites and
blues* ed. P. Oliver (Blues paperback) London: Studio Vista, 1970.
pp. 19, 20.
7 LOGAN, R. W. *op. cit.* p. 244.
Quote *Studies in the south* by an
anonymous traveller, *Atlantic
Monthly* XLIX, Feb. 1882.

**From emancipation to
segregation**
1 BBC interview: Sam Chatmon,
Hollandale, Miss., 1976.
2 *Ibid.*

From minstrels to ragtime
1 HANDY, W. C. *Father of the blues*
op. cit. p. 36.
2 HANDY, W. C. ed. *Blues: an
anthology* rev. by J. Silverman New
York: Collier-Macmillan, 1972. p. 24.
3 *Old Zip Coon* as quoted in
LOMAX, A. *The folk songs of North
America* London: Cassell, 1960. p.
96.
4 *Illustrated London News* Feb. 27th
1897. Article by anonymous
English woman traveller.
5 BLESH, R. and JANIS, H. *op.
cit.* pp. 103, 104. Quote Rupert
Hughes, 1899.
6 *Ibid.* p. 23. Quote Tom Ireland re
Sedalia in 1898.
7 TRAILL, S. and LASCELLES,
the Hon. Gerald eds. *Just jazz*
London: Peter Davies, 1957. p. 17.
Quote Roy Carew in
BORNEMAN, E. *Boogie woogie.*
8 BLESH, R. and JANIS, H. *op.
cit.* p. 192. Quote Eubie Blake.

**Early New Orleans jazz and
blues**
1 LOMAX, A. *Mister Jelly Roll: the*

fortunes of Jelly Roll Morton, New Orleans creole and 'Inventor of jazz' London: Cassell, 1952; Pan Books, p. 29. Quote Jelly Roll Morton.
2 WILLIAMS, M. *Jazz masters of New Orleans* London, Collier-MacMillan 1967; pp. 11, 12.
3 SHAPIRO, N. and HENTOFF, N. *Hear me talkin' to ya: the story of jazz by the men who made it* New York: Rinehart, 1955; London: Peter Davies, 1955. p. 45. Quote Bunk Johnson re Buddy Bolden.
4 LOMAX, A. *Mister Jelly Roll op. cit.* p. 62. Quote Bunk Johnson.
5 *Ibid.* pp. 62, 63. Quote Jelly Roll Morton.
6 *Buddy Bolden's blues* by Jelly Roll Morton (1939). Orig. issue Circle 77–78. © Tempo Music.
7 BLESH, R. and JANIS, H. *op. cit.* p. 78. Work song as quoted in WHITE, N. I. *American negro folk-songs* Harvard University Press, 1928.
8 LOMAX, A. *Mister Jelly Roll op. cit.* p. 33. Quote Jelly Roll Morton.
9 SHAPIRO, N. and HENTOFF, N. *op. cit.* pp. 56, 57. Quotes Danny Barker re Chris Kelly.

Work and song
1 CHARTERS, S. B. *The country blues* New York: Rinehart, 1959; London: Michael Joseph, 1960. p. 22. Quote work song as in WHITE, N. I. *op. cit.*
2 HANDY, W. C. ed. *Blues: an anthology op. cit.* p. 12.
3 COURLANDER, H. *op. cit.* p. 82. Quote Frederick Olmsted, 1853.
4 *Ibid.* p. 83.
5 *Ibid.* p. 87 Quote *Bring me a lil'l water Silvie* by Huddie Ledbetter (Lead Belly). Issued on Disc 3001-A.

6 ODUM, H. W. and JOHNSON, G. B. *The negro and his songs* University of North Carolina Press, 1925. p. 258.
7 *Ibid.* p. 258.
8 *Ibid.* p. 252.
9 *Ibid.* pp. 254, 255.
10 OLIVER, P. *The story of the blues op. cit.* p. 21. Quote stanza collected by Lafcadio Hearn in 1870's, publ. in *The Cincinnati Commercial.*
11 *Down Beat* Dec. 14, 1967. Down Beat, Chicago. Quote Chester Burnett ('Howling Wolf') from 'I sing for the people: an interview with bluesman Howling Wolf' by Pete Welding.
12 BBC interview: Booker White, Memphis, Tenn., 1976.
13 CHARTERS, S. B. *The country blues op. cit.* p. 22. Quote early blues as in WHITE, N. I. *op. cit.*
14 METFESSEL, M. *Phonophotography in folk music* University of North Carolina Press, 1928. p. 88. Work song version of *John Henry.*
15 COURLANDER, H. *op. cit.* p. 280. Later version *John Henry.*
16 OLIVER, P. *The story of the blues op. cit.* p. 23. Further version *John Henry.*
17 *Spike Driver blues* by Mississippi John Hurt (1928). Orig. issue OKeh 8692. Re-issued on *Mississippi John Hurt 1928*, Biograph BLP C4. Words and music by John Hurt.
18 *Stack O'Lee blues* by Mississippi John Hurt (1928). Orig. issue OKeh 8654. Re-issued on *The story of the blues* CBS (M) 66218 and on *Mississippi John Hurt 1928* (see item 17 above).

W. C. Handy
1 HANDY, W. C. *Father of the blues op. cit.* pp. 80, 81.

2 EVANS, D. *Tommy Johnson* ed. P. Oliver, Blues paperbacks. London: Studio Vista, 1971. p. 19. Quote Rev. Ledell Johnson.

3 BBC interview: Sam Chatmon, Hollandale, Miss., 1976.

4 *Ibid.* Henry Townsend, St. Louis, Mo., 1976.

5 *St Louis blues* by W. C. Handy. © W. C. Handy. As quoted in HENDY, W. C. *Father of the blues op. cit.* p. 149.

6 BBC interview: Little Brother Montgomery, Chicago, Ill. 1976.

7 SHAPIRO, N. and HENTOFF, N. *op. cit.* p. 226. Quote T-Bone Walker.

8 CHARTERS, S. B. *The bluesmen* New York: Oak Publications, 1967. p. 22.

9 BBC interview: Gus Cannon, Memphis Tenn., 1976.

10 GINZBURG, R. *One hundred years of lynching* Lancer Books Inc., 1962. p. 63. Quote report in *The Vicksburg Evening Post* 1904.

11 JACKSON, J. *U.S. Negroes in battle: from Little Rock to Watts* Moscow: Progress Publishers, 1967, p. 75. Quote Civil Rights worker, 1963.

12 LOMAX, L. E. *The negro revolt* London: Hamish Hamilton, 1962. p. 47.

13 BBC interview: Booker White, Memphis, Tenn., 1976.

14 *Ibid.* Henry Townsend, St Louis, Mo., 1976.

15 *Ibid.* Houston Stackhouse, Memphis, Tenn., 1976.

16 *Ibid.* Henry Townsend, St Louis, Mo., 1976.

17 *Ibid.* Vernell Townsend, St Louis, Mo., 1976.

Part Two

Charley Patton

1 BBC interview: Sam Chatmon, Hollandale, Miss., 1976.

2 *Down Beat, op. cit.* Dec. 14, 1967. Quote Howling Wolf re Charley Patton.

3 FAHEY, J. *Charley Patton* ed. P. Oliver, Blues paperbacks, London: Studio Vista, 1970. p. 66. Quote Son House re Charley Patton.

4 *A spoonful blues* by Charley Patton (1929) Orig. issue Paramount 12869. Re-issued on *Charley Patton – Founder of the delta blues* Yazoo L1020.

5 *78 Quarterly* Vol. 1 no. 1, 1967. 78 Publishing Co., New York. Quotes Son House re Charley Patton, interviewed by Nick Perls.

6 *Prayer of death* by Charley Patton (1929). Orig. issue Paramount 12799. Re-issued on *Ten years of black country religion 1926–1936* Yazoo L1022. Also quoted in *Charlie Patton: Blues World* Booklet no. 2 ed. Bob Groom, Blues World, 1969 (defunct).

7 BBC interview: Sam Chatmon, Hollandale, Miss., 1976.

8 EVANS, D. *op. cit.* p. 39. Quote Rev. Rubin Lacey.

9 BBC interview: Sam Chatmon, Hollandale, Miss., 1976. *Pony Blues* by Charley Patton (1929), Paramount 12792. Re-issued on *Founder of the delta blues* (see item 4 above).

10 *Mississippi bo weavil blues* by Charley Patton (1929). Orig. issue Paramount 12805. Re-issued on *Founder of the delta blues* (see item 4 above).

11 *High water everywhere* by Charley Patton (1929). Orig. issue

Paramount 12909. Re-issued on
Founder of the delta blues (see item 4
above).
12 BBC interview: Booker White,
Memphis, Tenn., 1976.
13 CHARTERS, S. B. *The
bluesmen op. cit.* p. 37. Quote J. D.
'Jelly Jaw' Short.
14 *When your way gets dark* by
Charley Patton (1929) Orig. issue
Paramount 12998. Re-issued on
Founder of the delta blues (see item 4
above).
15 *Running wild blues* by Charley
Patton (1929. Orig. issue
Paramount 12924. Re-issued on
Founder of the delta blues (see item 4
above). Elements of this relate to
Runnin' Wild, 'an ebony jazz tune'.
Words and music by J. Grey, L.
Wood and A. H. Gibbs. © Leo
Feist Inc. (1922).

Henry Thomas
1 TWAIN, M. *Life on the
Mississippi* New York: Harper and
Row, 1957; New American Library
(Signet Books) 1961, p. 186.
2 GROSSMAN, S., GROSS-
MAN, H. and CALT, S. *Country
blues song book* New York: Oak
Publications, 1973. Introduction:
The country blues as meaning, by
Stephen Calt. Quote Mississippi
planter, lecturing in 1901.
3 ODUM, H. W. and JOHN-
SON, G. B. *The negro and his
songs op. cit.* p. 162.
4 *Henry Thomas 'Ragtime Texas' –
Complete recorded works 1927–1929
in chronological order* Herwin 209.
Quote G. T. Hardy interviewed by
Mack McCormick in album notes
'Biography Henry Thomas: Our
deepest look at the roots' by Mack
McCormick.
5 *Ibid.* Quote Mack McCormick.

6 *When the train comes along* by
Henry Thomas (Ragtime Texas)
(1927). Orig. issue Vocalion 1140.
Re-issued on *Complete recorded
works* (see item 4 above).
7 *Old country stomp* by Henry
Thomas (Ragtime Texas) (1928).
Orig. issue Vocalion 1230. Re-
issued on *Complete recorded works*
(see item 4 above). Words and
music by J. M. Williams.
8 *Honey, won't you allow me one more
chance* by Henry Thomas (Ragtime
Texas) (1927). Orig. issue Vocalion
1141. Re-issued on *Complete
recorded works* (see item 4
above).
9 *I'm Alabama bound* by Ferdinand
(Jelly Roll) Morton (1938). Orig.
issue Circle 67–68. Re-issued on
*Jelly Roll Morton: Library of Con-
gress recordings* vol. 1, Classic Jazz
Masters CJM 2. Words and music
by Ferdinand J. Morton. By
permission of Chappell/Morris
Ltd.
10 *Jazz Journal* vol. 10, no. 12, Dec.
1957. Jazz Journal, London. Quote
Roy Carew 'Of this and that and
Jelly Roll'.
11 *Don't ease me in* by Henry
Thomas (Ragtime Texas) (1928).
Orig. issue Vocalion 1197. Re-
issued on *Complete recorded works*
(see item 4 above). Words and
music by Henry Thomas and J. M.
Williams.
12 *Don't leave me here* by Henry
Thomas (Ragtime Texas) (1929).
Orig. issue Vocalion 1443. Re-
issued on *Complete recorded works*
(see item 4 above).
13 *Shanty blues* by Henry Thomas
(Ragtime Texas) (1927). Orig.
issue Vocalion 1139. Re-issued on
Complete recorded works (see item 4
above).

Lead Belly

1 ASCH, M. and LOMAX, A. eds. *The Leadbelly songbook* New York: Oak Publications, 1962; London: Music Sales, pp. 32 and 29, Quote Lead Belly.

2 *Down Beat op. cit.* Aug. 6, 1970. Quote Lead Belly from 'Illuminating the Leadbelly legend' by Ross Russell.

3 *Ox-driver's song* by Lead Belly (1935). Orig. issue Folkways FP-24. Re-issued on *The Leadbelly set* Xtra 1017. © Folkways Music.

4 *Corn bread rough* (Sukey jump). As quoted in ASCH, M. and LOMAX, A. eds. *op. cit.* p. 29. © Folkways Music.

5 *Poor Howard* by Lead Belly. As quoted *ibid.* p. 21. © Folkways Music.

6 *Down Beat op. cit.* Aug. 6, 1970. Quote Lead Belly.

7 ASCH, M. and LOMAX, A. eds. *op. cit.* pp. 14 and 32. Quotes Lead Belly.

8 *Down Beat op. cit.* Aug. 6, 1970. Quote Lead Belly.

9 *Fannin Street* by Lead Belly. As quoted in ASCH, M. and LOMAX, A. eds. *op. cit.* p. 33. © Folkways Music.

10 ASCH, M. and LOMAX, A. eds. *op. cit.* p. 13. Quote Lead Belly.

11 *Ibid.* pp. 32 and 14. Quotes Lead Belly.

12 *Down Beat op. cit.* Aug. 6, 1970. Quote Lead Belly.

13 *The Leadbelly set* (see item 3 above). Quote Lead Belly re Blind Lemon Jefferson on album notes.

14 *See see rider* by Lead Belly (1935). Orig. issue Folkways FP-24. Re-issued on *The Leadbelly set* (see item 3 above). © Folkways Music.

15 *Black girl* by Lead Belly (c. 1946). Orig. issue Folkways FA-2014.

Re-issued on *The Leadbelly set* (see item 3 above). © Folkways Music.

The barrelhouse circuit and the 'Piney Woods'

1 LOMAX, A. *Mister Jelly Roll op. cit.* pp. 53, 54. Quotes Jelly Roll Morton.

2 SHAPIRO, N. and HENTOFF, N. *op. cit.* pp. 60–61. Quote Bunk Johnson re Jelly Roll Morton.

3 LOMAX, A. *Mister Jelly Roll op. cit.* p. 55. Quote Jelly Roll Morton.

4 *I'm a levee man* as on *Jelly Roll Morton*, Library of Congress Recordings.

5 LOMAX, A. *Mister Jelly Roll op. cit.* p. 110.

6 Zur HEIDE, K. G. *Deep south piano: the story of Little Brother Montgomery* ed. P. Oliver, Blues paperbacks. London: Studio Vista, 1970. pp. 17, 18. Quotes Little Brother Montgomery.

7 BBC interview: Little Brother Montgomery, Chicago, Ill., 1976.

8 *The first time I met you* by Little Brother Montgomery (1936). Orig. issue Bluebird B6766. Re-issued on *Little Brother Montgomery* Collectors Classics CC35.

9 BBC interview: Little Brother Montgomery, Chicago, Ill., 1976.

10 *Ibid.* Big Joe Williams, Crawford, Miss., 1976.

11 *Down Beat op. cit.* Feb. 13, 1964. Quote Big Joe Williams, interviewed by Pete Welding.

12 *Arkansas Mill blues* by Elzadie Robinson (1928). Orig. issue Paramount 12701. Words and music by Will Ezell. Also quoted in *Jazz Journal op. cit.* April 1964, 'Blues on record' by Derrick Stewart-Baxter.

Migration

1 *Rhythm and Blues Monthly* (now

defunct) no. 2, Mar. 1964. Quote
Curtis Jones to Neil Slaven.
2 SPEAR, A. H. *Black Chicago: the
making of a negro ghetto 1890–1920*
University of Chicago Press, 1967.
p. 133. Quote 'Letters of negro
migrants of 1916–1918' collected
under direction of SCOTT, E. J.
Journal of Negro history no. 4,
Washington, October 1919.
3 *Rhythm and Blues Monthly op. cit.*
Further quote Curtis Jones.
4 SPEAR, A. H. *op. cit.* p. 137.
Quote Mississippi preacher interviewed by U.S. Dept of Labor as in
'Negro migration in 1916–17'.
5 *Ibid.* p. 134. Quote article in
Chicago Defender Oct. 7, 1916.
6 OLIVER, P. *The story of the blues
op. cit.* p. 75. Quote poem in *Chicago
Defender* May 28, 1917.
7 GINZBURG, R. *op. cit.* p. 129.
Quote *The Atlanta Constitution*
Oct. 1919.
8 BBC interview: Thomas Dorsey
(Georgia Tom), Chicago, Ill.,
1976.

Part Three

Crazy blues

1 BRADFORD, P. *Born with the
blues* New York: Oak Publications,
1965. pp. 117, 118, 119. *That thing
called love* by Mamie Smith (1920).
Orig. issue OKeh 4113. Words and
music by Perry Bradford.
2 *Crazy blues* by Mamie Smith and
her Jazz Hounds (1920). Orig issue
OKeh 4169. Re-issued on *Ma
Rainey and the classic blues singers*
CBS 52798. Words and music by
Perry Bradford. By permission of
Leeds Music Ltd.
3 BBC interview: Victoria Spivey,
Brooklyn, N.Y., 1976.
4 *Ibid.*

5 DIXON, R. M. W. and
GODRICH, J. *Recording the blues*
ed. P. Oliver, Blues paperbacks.
London: Studio Vista, 1970. p. 10.
Quote Mamie Smith advertise-
ment.
6 *Arkansas blues* by Lucille
Hegamin (1921). Orig. issue Arto
9053. Re-issued on *Blue flame:
Lucille Hegamin early recordings*
VJM Vintage Series VLP 50.
Words and music by Anton Lada
and Spencer Williams. By per-
mission of Leeds Music Ltd.
7 STEWART-BAXTER, D. *Ma
Rainey and the classic blues singers*
ed. P. Oliver, Blues paperbacks.
London: Studio Vista, 1970, p. 24.
Quote from early catalogue re
Lucille Hegamin.
8 *Ibid.* p. 19. Quote Lucille
Hegamin, interviewed by author.
9 SHAPIRO, N. and HENTOFF,
N. *op. cit.* p. 224. Quote Alberta
Hunter re Lil Hardin.
10 *Ibid.* pp. 88–89. Quote Lil
Hardin.
11 *Ibid.* p. 84. Quote Alberta
Hunter re Dago Frank's nightclub.
12 BBC interview: Little Brother
Montgomery, Chicago, Ill., 1976.
13 ANDERSON, N. *The hobo: the
sociology of the homeless man; a study
prepared for the Chicago Council of
Social Agencies.* (Phoenix Books)
University of Chicago Press, 1961.
Used as source for data.
14 *Don't mess with me* by Sister
Harris (1923). Orig. issue Pathe-
Actuelle 020911. Possibly: words
and music by Sam Gold. As
quoted in *Jazz Report* (The Record
Collector's Magazine) vol. 1,
no. 9, May 1961. Ventura, Calif.
'Nobody knows', article by Brian
G. Davis.

Showbiz blues 1: The tent shows

1 BBC interview: Sam Chatmon, Hollandale, Miss., 1976.
2 WATERS, E. and SAMUELS, C. *His eye is on the sparrow* New York: Doubleday, 1951, pp. 82, 83.
3 *Ibid.* p. 19.
4 *Ibid.* p. 17.
5 *Ibid.* p. 46.
6 *Ibid.* p. 84.

Ma Rainey

1 ALBERTSON, C. *Bessie* London: Barrie & Jenkins, 1972. p. 101. Quotes Billy Gunn and Ma Rainey.
2 BBC interview: Little Brother Montgomery, Chicago, Ill., 1976.
3 *Ibid.* Thomas Dorsey, Chicago, Ill., 1976.
4 *Chain gang blues* by Ma Rainey (1926). Orig. issue Paramount 12338. Re-issued on *Blame it on the blues: Ma Rainey* Milestone MLP 2008. Words by Charles Parker, music by Spencer Williams. By permission of Leeds Music Ltd.
5 *Storyville* no. 47. Quote Lucien Brown re Pa Rainey as in 'Lucien Brown' by John Randolph.
6 BBC interview: Little Brother Montgomery, Chicago, Ill., 1976.
7 *Ibid.* Laura Dukes, Memphis, Tenn., 1976.
8 *Ibid.* Thomas Dorsey, Chicago, Ill., 1976.
9 *Black cat hoot owl blues* by Ma Rainey (1928). Orig. issue Paramount 12687. Re-issued on *Ma Rainey* Riverside RLP 12-108. Words and music by Thomas Dorsey. By permission of Leeds Music Ltd.
10 BBC interview: Little Brother Montgomery, Chicago, Ill., 1976.
Bo Weavil Blues by Ma Rainey (1923). Orig. issue Paramount 12080. Re-issued on *'Gertrude "Ma" Rainey – Queen of the Blues'*, Biograph BLP 12032. Words and music by Gertrude Ma Rainey.
11 *Ibid.* Victoria Spivey, Brooklyn, N.Y., 1976. Quote *Bo Weavil Blues* (see item 11).
12 *Moonshine blues* by Ma Rainey (1927). Orig. issue Paramount 12603. Re-issued on *Blame it on the blues* (see item 4 above). Words and music by Gertrude Ma Rainey.

Showbiz blues 2: The theatres

1 BBC interview: Laura Dukes, Memphis, Tenn., 1976.
2 *Ibid.* Thomas Dorsey, Chicago, Ill., 1976.

Bessie Smith

1 ALBERTSON, C. *op. cit.* p. 52. Quote re Bessie Smith from un-named fellow performer.
2 *Ibid.* p. 133. Quote Bessie Smith to Ku Klux Klansmen.
3 BBC interview: Victoria Spivey, Brooklyn, N.Y., 1976.
4 *Poor man's blues* by Bessie Smith (1928). Orig. issue Columbia 14399-D. Re-issued on *Bessie Smith: empty bed blues* (double album) CBS M 64287/8. Words and music by Bessie Smith. © Chappell & Co. Ltd.
5 *Back water blues* by Bessie Smith (1927). Orig. issue Columbia 14195-D. Re-issued on *Bessie Smith: nobody's blues but mine* (double album) CBS 64719/21. Words and music by Bessie Smith. © Chappell & Co. Ltd.
6 ALBERTSON, C. *op. cit.* p. 66. Quote Ruby Walker.
7 SHAPIRO, N. and HENTOFF, N. *op. cit.* p. 221. Quote Zutty Singleton re Bessie Smith.

8 *Ibid.* pp. 223, 223. Quote Mezz Mezzrow re Bessie Smith.
9 *Ibid.* p. 219. Quote May Wright Johnson.
10 *Jazz Journal op. cit.* vol. 11, no. 12 Dec. 1958. Quote Harry Dial in 'The story of Harry Dial as told to Franklin S. Driggs.'
11 *Please help me get him off my mind* by Bessie Smith (1928). Orig. issue Columbia 14375-D. Re-issued on *Bessie Smith: empty bed blues* (see item 3 above). Words and music by Bessie Smith. © Chappell & Co. Ltd.
12 *Blue spirit blues* by Bessie Smith (1929). Orig. issue Columbia 14527-D. Re-issued on *Bessie Smith: any woman's blues* (double album) (CBS) M64177/8. Words and music by Spencer Williams. By permission of B. Feldman & Co. Ltd.
13 *Young woman's blues* by Bessie Smith (1926). Orig. issue Columbia 14179-D. Re-issued on *Bessie Smith: nobody's blues but mine* (see item 4 above). Melody by Bessie Smith. © Chappell & Co. Ltd.
14 BBC interview: Little Brother Montgomery, Chicago, Ill., 1976.

Women's blues
1 DIXON, R. M. W. and GODRICH, J. *op. cit.* p. 28. Quote advertisement in *Chicago Defender* July 1924.
2 ODUM, H. W. and JOHNSON, B. G. *Negro workaday songs* University of North Carolina Press, 1926; New York: Negro University Press, 1969, p. 33.
3 SHAPIRO, N. and HENTOFF, N. *op. cit.* p. 19. Quote Jelly Roll Morton.
4 *Ibid.* p. 21. Quote Bunk Johnson.

5 WILLIAMS, M. ed. *Jazz panorama* New York: Crowell-Collier Press, 1962. pp. 22, 23. Copyright *Jazz Review*. Quote SOUCHON, Edmond, M.D. 'King Oliver: a very personal memoir'.
6 SHAPIRO, N. and HENTOFF, N. *op. cit.* p. 226. Quote T-Bone Walker.
7 *Ibid.* pp. 223, 224. Quote Alberta Hunter.
8 *Ibid.* p. 227. Quote T-Bone Walker.
9 BBC interview: Thomas Dorsey, Chicago, Ill., 1976.
10 SHAPIRO, N. and HENTOFF, N. *op. cit.* p. 221. Quote Danny Barker.
11 *'Fore day creep* by Ida Cox (1927). Orig. issue Paramount 12488. Words and melody by Ida Cox. Also quoted in LANG, I. *Jazz in perspective: the background of the blues* London: Hutchinson, 1947. p. 118.
12 ALBERTSON, C. *op. cit.* p. 107. Quote Carl Van Vechten re Bessie Smith.
13 BBC interview: Victoria Spivey, Brooklyn, N.Y., 1976.
14 *Dirty no-gooder's blues* by Bessie Smith (1929). Orig. issue Columbia 14476-D. Re-issued on *Any woman's blues* (see under: Bessie Smith, item 11). Words and melody by Bessie Smith. © Chappell & Co. Ltd.
15 *Section hand blues* by Sippie Wallace (1925). Orig. issue OKeh 8232. Also quoted in BLESH, R. *Shining trumpets: a history of jazz* London: Cassell, 1949. p. 140.
16 *Mean tight mama* by Sara Martin (1928). Orig. issue QRS R7043. Re-issued on *Louis Armstrong plays the blues.* London AL 3501. Words

and music by Andy Razaf. By permission of B. Feldman & Co. Ltd.

17 WATERS, E. and SAMUELS, C. *op. cit.* p. 97.

18 OLIVER, P. *Conversation with the blues op. cit.* p. 114. Quote Victoria Spivey.

19 *Dirty T.B. blues* by Victoria Spivey (1929). Orig. issue Victor V38570. Re-issued on HMV 7EG-8190. Words and music by Victoria Spivey. © Victoria Spivey.

20 *How do you do it that way?* by Victoria Spivey (1929). Orig. issue OKeh 8713. Re-issued on *The Victoria Spivey recorded legacy of the blues* Spivey Records LP 2001.

21 *You can't sleep in my bed* by Mary Dixon (1929). Orig. issue Columbia 14415-D. Re-issued on *Gladys Bentley and Mary Dixon* Collector's Classics CC 52. Words and music by John Rose.

22 *Worn down daddy blues* by Ida Cox (1928). Orig. issue Paramount 12704. Re-issued on *Ida Cox sings the blues* Riverside 1019. Words by Selma Davis, music by Ida Cox.

23 *Strange lovin' blues* by Sara Martin (1925). Orig. issue OKeh 8214. Also quoted in OLIVER, P. *The meaning of the blues* 1st publ. as *Blues fell this morning* London: Cassell, 1960; Collier Books, 1963 edn. p. 118. Lyric related to a hymn by J. A. Carney, 1845. Published in *Songs of Praise*, O.U.P., 1925.

24 *Whip it to a jelly* by Clara Smith (1926). Orig. issue Columbia 14150-D. Re-issued on *The story of the blues* vol. 2. CBS 66232. Words and melody by Clara Smith. ©

Part Four

The men start recording

1 *Living blues* no. 22, July/August 1975. Living Blues Publications, Chicago. Quote Johnny Shines interviewed by Pete Welding in 'Ramblin' Johnny Shines'.

2 *Barrelhouse blues* by Ed Andrews (1924). Orig. issue OKeh 8137. Also quoted in *Jazz and Blues* vol. 2, no. 3, June 1972 (now incorporated in *Jazz Journal*). 'Talking blues' by Tony Russell.

3 *Paramount book of blues* New York Recording Laboratories Inc., 1927. Quote advertisement Papa Charlie Jackson.

4 *Georgia bound* by Blind Blake (1929). Orig. issue Paramount 12824. Re-issued on *Blind Blake: blues in Chicago* Riverside RM-8804.

5 *Jazz and Blues op. cit.* Dec. 1971. Quote Bill Williams re Blind Blake in 'Too tight: Bill Williams in person' by Paul Oliver.

6 *Early morning blues* by Blind Blake (1926). Orig. issue Paramount 12387. Re-issued on *Blues in Chicago* (see item 4 above). Words and melody by Arthur (Blind) Blake.

7 *Son House – Blind Lemon Jefferson* Biograph Records BLP 12040. Quote Son House from sleeve notes by Arnold S. Caplin.

8 CHARTERS, S. B. *The country blues op. cit.* p. 60. Quote Alec Jefferson re Blind Lemon Jefferson.

9 CHARTERS, S. B. *The bluesmen op. cit.* p. 182. Quote Henry Townsend re Blind Lemon Jefferson.

10 *'Lectric chair blues* by Blind Lemon Jefferson (1928). Orig.

issue Paramount 12608. Re-issued on *Blind Lemon Jefferson* vol. 2 Roots RL-306. Words and melody by Lemon Jefferson. Also quoted in *Blues World* Booklet no. 3 ed. Bob Groom, 1970.

11 *Record Research* no. 76, New York, May 1966. Quote 'Blind Lemon and I had a Ball' by Victoria Spivey.

12 BBC interview: Sam Chatmon, Hollandale, Miss., 1976.

13 RUSSELL, T. *op. cit.* p. 48. Quote Roscoe Holcomb re Blind Lemon Jefferson.

14 *Down Beat op. cit.* Dec. 14, 1967. Quote Howling Wolf re Blind Lemon Jefferson, interviewed by Pete Welding.

15 *Living Blues op. cit.* no. 11, Winter 1972–3. Quote T-Bone Walker re Blind Lemon Jefferson.

16 BBC interview: Victoria Spivey, Brooklyn, N.Y., 1976.

17 *Lonesome house blues* by Blind Lemon Jefferson (1927). Orig. issue Paramount 12593. Re-issued on *Blind Lemon Jefferson* vol. 2. Milestone MLP 2007. Words and melody by George Perkins.

18 CHARTERS, S. B. *The bluesmen op. cit.* p. 180. Quote Paramount advertisement.

19 *Low down mojo blues* by Blind Lemon Jefferson (1928). Orig. issue Paramount 12650. Re-issued on *The immortal Blind Lemon Jefferson* Milestone MLP 2004.

20 *Dynamite blues* by Blind Lemon Jefferson (1929). Orig. issue *Son House – Blind Lemon Jefferson* (see item 7 above). Words by Selma Davis, music by Lemon Jefferson.

21 *Bakershop blues* by Blind Lemon Jefferson (1929). Orig. issue Para-

mount 12852. Re-issued on *Blind Lemon Jefferson* vol. 3 Roots RL-331.

22 *Son House – Blind Lemon Jefferson* (see item 7 above). Quote Son House re Blind Lemon Jefferson from sleeve notes.

23 *Mosquito moan* by Blind Lemon Jefferson (1929). Orig. issue Paramount 12899. Re-issued on *Black snake moan* Milestone MLP 2013.

24 *That black snake moan* by Blind Lemon Jefferson (1926). Orig. issue Paramount 12407. Re-issued on *Black snake moan* (see item 23 above).

25 *Oil well blues* by Blind Lemon Jefferson (1929). Orig. issue Paramount 12771. Re-issued on *Penitentiary blues* London AL-3564. Words and music by Lemon Jefferson.

26 *Prison cell blues* by Blind Lemon Jefferson (1928). Orig. issue Paramount 12622. Re-issued on *The immortal Blind Lemon Jefferson* (see item 19 above). Words and melody by Lemon Jefferson.

27 *Lock step blues* by Blind Lemon Jefferson (1928). Orig. issue Paramount 12679. Re-issued on *The immortal Blind Lemon Jefferson* (see item 19 above). Words by Hyman Rosen, music by Lemon Jefferson.

28 *That crawlin' baby blues* by Blind Lemon Jefferson (1929). Orig. issue Paramount 12880. Re-issued on *Black snake moan* (see item 23 above) (track mistitled *That growling baby blues*).

Field recordings

1 BBC interview: Henry Townsend, St Louis, Mo., 1976.

2 *Mississippi John Hurt: the original 1928 recordings* Spokane Records SLP 1001. Quote Mississippi John Hurt from sleeve notes.

3 CHARTERS, S. B. *The country blues op. cit.* p. 61. Quote recording director.

4 BBC interview: Gus Cannon, Memphis, Tenn., 1976.

Atlanta

1 *Blues World* (now defunct) no. 26, Jan. 1970. Quote Jesse Fuller.

2 *Ibid.* Further quote Jesse Fuller.

3 *Living Blues op. cit.* no. 20 March–April 1975. Quote Georgia Tom Dorsey interviewed by Jim O'Neal.

4 BBC interview: Thomas Dorsey, Chicago, Ill., 1976.

5 *Ibid.* Further quote Thomas Dorsey.

6 BRADFORD, P. *op. cit.* p. 18.

7 BBC interview: Thomas Dorsey, Chicago, Ill., 1976.

8 *Statesboro blues* by Blind Willie McTell (1928). Orig. issue Victor V38001. Re-issued on *Blind Willie McTell: the early years* Yazoo L1005. Words and music by Willie McTell. ©Southern Music.

9 LEADBITTER, M. ed. *Nothing but the blues* London: Hanover Books, 1971. pp. 258, 259. Quote Peg Leg Howell.

10 *Low down rounder blues* by Peg Leg Howell (1928). Orig. issue Columbia 14320-D. Re-issued on *The country blues* RBF RF-1.

11 LEADBITTER, M. ed. *op. cit.* p. 259. Further quote Peg Leg Howell.

12 *Barbecue blues* by Barbecue Bob (1927). Orig. issue Columbia 14205-D. Re-issued on *Kings of the twelve-string* Piedmont 13159.

13 *We sure got hard times now* by Barbecue Bob (1930). Orig. issue Columbia 14558-D. Re-issued on SBS EP 1.

Memphis

1 *Going back to Memphis* by Charlie Nickerson and the Memphis Jug Band (1930). Orig. issue Victor 23310. Re-issued on *Memphis Jug Band* Collector's Classics CC-2. Words and melody by Will Shade. By permission of Southern Music Publishing Co. Ltd.

2 *Blues Unlimited* no. 52, April 1968. Quote Rev. Robert Wilkins interviewed by Pete Welding.

3 RAVEN-HART, Major R. *Canoe errant on the Mississippi* London: Methuen, 1938. p. 123.

4 OLIVER, P. *Conversation with the blues op. cit.* pp. 85, 86. Quote Will Shade.

5 RAVEN-HART, Major R. *op. cit.* pp. 110, 111.

6 OLIVER, P. *Conversation with the blues op. cit.* p. 89. Further quote Will Shade.

7 HANDY, W. C. *Father of the blues op. cit.* p. 97. 'Unofficial' lyrics *Mr. Crump* by W. C. Handy. © W. C. Handy.

8 *Blues Unlimited op. cit.* no. 100, April 1973. Further 'unofficial' version *Mr. Crump* by Frank Stokes, collected by Bengt Olsson in 'Frank Stokes – the Beale Street Sheik'.

9 GUNTHER, J. *Procession* London: Hamish Hamilton, 1965. pp. 283–287.

10 OLIVER, P. *Conversation with the blues op. cit.* p. 92. Further quote Will Shade.

11 HANDY, W. C. *Father of the Blues op. cit.* p. 17. Words of ditty sung as children.

12 *Beale Street mess around* Revival RVS 1004. Quote jug-band player from sleeve notes by Bengt Olsson.

13 HANDY, W. C. *Father of the blues op. cit.* p. 17.

14 HEMPHILL, P. *The Nashville sound* New York: Simon & Schuster, 1970. p. 167. Quote De Ford Bailey.

15 BBC interview: Big Joe Williams, Crawford, Miss., 1976.

16 *Gator wobble* by The Memphis Jug Band (1934). Orig. issue OKeh 8958. Re-issued on *Memphis Jug Band* (see item 1 above). Melody by Will Shade. © Southern Music. Quote member Memphis Jug Band.

17 *Move that thing* by the Caroline Peanut Boys (The Memphis Jug Band) (1930). Orig. issue Victor R23274. Re-issued on *Memphis Blues* vol. 1 Roots RL-323. Words and music by the Carolina Peanut Boys. © Southern Music. Various interjections by musicians.

18 *Stealin' stealin'* by The Memphis Jug Band (1928). Orig. issue Victor V38504. Re-issued on *The country blues* (see under Atlanta, item 10). © Southern Music.

19 *Complete works of Cannon's Jug Stompers* Herwin LP 208. Quote Gus Cannon re Noah Lewis from sleeve notes by Bengt Olsson.

20 *Viola Lee blues* by Cannon's Jug Stompers (1928). Orig. issue Victor V38523. Re-issued on *Complete works* (see item 18 above). Words and music by Noah Lewis. © Peer International.

21 *Complete works* (see item 18 above). Further quote Gus Cannon from sleeve notes.

22 *Ibid.* Further quote Gus Cannon.

23 *Feather bed* by Cannon's Jug Stompers (1928). Orig. issue Victor V38515. Re-issued on *Complete works* (see item 18 above). Words and music by Gus Cannon. © Peer International.

24 BBC interview: Gus Cannon, Memphis, Tenn., 1976.

25 *Jazz Journal op. cit.* June 1960. Quote Speckled Red in 'Speckled Red' by David Mangurian.

26 *Blues Unlimited op. cit.* no. 100, April 1973. Quote Lincoln Jackson interviewed by Bengt Olsson.

27 *Ibid.* no. 54, June 1968. Quote Robert Wilkins interviewed by Pete Welding.

28 *Ibid.* no. 53, May 1968. Quotes Robert Wilkins interviewed by Pete Welding.

29 *Falling down blues* by Robert Wilkins (1929). Orig. issue Brunswick 7125. Re-issued on *Ten years in Memphis* Yazoo L1002.

30 EVANS, D. *op. cit.* p. 22. Quote Rev. Ledell Johnson re Tommy Johnson.

31 *Ibid.* p. 43. Quote Rev. Rubin Lacey.

32 *Cool drink of water blues* by Tommy Johnson (1928). Orig. issue Victor 21279. Re-issued on *The great Tommy Johnson – Ishman Bracey 1928 session* Roots RL-330 (and elsewhere). Words and music by Tommy Johnson. © Peer International.

33 *Hard time killin' floor blues* by Skip James (1931). Orig. issue Paramount 13065. Re-issued on *Skip James: early blues recordings 1931* Biograph BLP 12029. Words and music by Nehemiah 'Skip' James.

34 GROSSMAN, S. *Delta blues guitar* New York: Oak Publications, 1969. p. 111. Quote Skip James.

35 *Cypress Grove blues* by Skip James (1931). Orig. issue Paramount 13088. Re-issued on *Early blues recordings 1931* (see item 31 above). Words and music by Nehemiah 'Skip' James.

Part Five

The Depression

1 HUGHES, L. and MELTZER, M. *op. cit.* p. 280. Quote *Chicago Defender*, early 1929.

2 *No dough blues* by Blind Blake (1928). Orig.issue Paramount 12723. Words and music by Arthur (Blind) Blake. Also quoted in LOMAX, A. with GUTHRIE, W. and SEEGER, P. *Hard-hitting songs for hard-hit people* New York: Oak Publications, 1967. p. 52.

3 *Starvation blues* by Big Bill Broonzy (1928). Orig. issue Paramount 12707. Re-issued on *The young Bill Broonzy 1928–1936* Yazoo L1011.

4 BBC interview: Thomas Dorsey, Chicago, Ill., 1976.

5 *Ibid.* Little Brother Montgomery, Chicago, Ill., 1976.

6 *Ibid.* Thomas Dorsey, Chicago, Ill., 1976.

7 *Depression blues* by Tampa Red (1931). Orig. issue Vocalion 1656. Also quoted in LOMAX, A., GUTHRIE, W. and SEEGER, P. *op. cit.* p. 45.

8 *It's hard time* by Joe Stone (1933). Orig. issue Bluebird B5169. Re-issued on *St Louis town (1929–1933)* Yazoo L1003. Words and music by Joe Stone. © Southern Music.

9 *President blues* by Jack Kelly and his South Memphis Jug Band (1933). Orig. issue Banner 32857. Re-issued on *Jack Kelly: South Memphis Jug Band* Flyright KP114.

10 *CWA blues* by Walter Roland (1934). Orig. issue Banner 33136. Also quoted in LOMAX, A., GUTHRIE, W. and SEEGER, P. *op. cit.* p. 194.

11 *Let's have a New Deal* by Carl Martin (1935). Orig. issue Decca 7114. Re-issued on *Country blues classics* vol. 4 Blues Classics BC 14.

12 *Don't take away my PWA* by Jimmy Gordon (1936). Orig. issue Decca 7230. Also quoted in LOMAX, A. GUTHRIE, W. and SEEGER, P. *op. cit.* p. 191.

13 BBC interview: Sam Chatmon, Hollandale, Miss., 1976.

14 Student lecture notes, 1967. (Dr. Robert Reinders, University of Nottingham.)

15 *New working on the Project* by Peetie Wheatstraw (1937). Orig. issue Decca 7379. Also quoted in GARON, P. *The devil's son-in-law* ed. P. Oliver, Blues paperbacks. London: Studio Vista, 1971, p. 75.

16 *Don't take away my PWA* by Jimmy Gordon (see item 12 above).

17 *Welfare blues* by Speckled Red (1938). Orig. issue Bluebird B8069. Also quoted in LOMAX, A., GUTHRIE, W., and SEEGER, P. *op. cit.* p. 198.

18 BBC interview: Big Joe Williams, Crawford, Miss., 1976.

19 *F.D.R. blues* by Champion Jack Dupree (c. 1946). Orig. issue Joe Davis 5102. Also quoted in OLIVER, P. *The meaning of the blues op. cit.* p. 311.

City blues

1 *Jazz Journal op cit.* June 1960. Further quote Speckled Red in 'Speckled Red' by David Mangurian.

2 *Rugged piano classics* Origin OJL. 15. Quote Romeo Nelson interviewed by Pete Welding and Erwin Helfer, reproduced on sleeve notes by Tracy Nelson.

3 BBC interview: Little Brother Montgomery, Chicago, Ill., 1976.

4 *Jazz Journal op. cit.* May 1959. Quote Cow Cow Davenport in

'Cow Cow Davenport' by Art Hodes.

5 *Pinetop's boogie-woogie* by Clarence Pinetop Smith (1928). Orig. issue Vocalion 1245. Re-issued on *Piano Jazz* Brunswick BL 58018. Words and music by Clarence Pinetop Smith. Quote spoken interjections on recording by Pinetop Smith.

6 *Jazz Journal op. cit.* May 1959. Further quote Cow Cow Davenport.

7 RAMSEY, F. Jr. and SMITH, C. E. eds. *Jazzmen* London: Sidgwick & Jackson, 1957. Quote Pinetop Smith to Albert Ammons in 'Boogie-woogie' by William Russell.

8 BBC interview: Little Brother Montgomery, Chicago, Ill., 1976.

9 *How long – how long blues* by Leroy Carr (1928). Orig. issue Vocalion 1191. Words and music by Leroy Carr and J. M. Williams. © Leeds Music.

10 *Hustlers blues* by Leroy Carr (1934). Orig. issue Vocalion 03034. Re-issued on *Blues before sunrise* CBS BPG 62206. Words and music by W. R. Caloway and C. Williams. © Leeds Music.

11 *Blues before sunrise* by Leroy Carr (1934). Orig. issue Vocalion 02657. Re-issued on *Blues before sunrise* (see item 10 above). Words and music by Leroy Carr. © Leeds Music.

12 *It's tight like that* by Georgia Tom and Tampa Red (1928). Orig. issue Vocalion 1216. Re-issued on *Rare blues of the twenties* vol. 1, Historical Records ASC 5829-1. Words and music by Thomas Dorsey and Hudson Whittaker. © T. Dorsey and H. Whittaker.

13 BBC interview: Thomas Dorsey, Chicago, Ill., 1976.

14 *It feels so good* by Lonnie Johnson and Spencer Williams (1929). Orig. issue OKeh 8664. Words and music by Spencer Williams. Also quoted in CHARTERS, S. B. *The country blues op. cit.* p. 57.

15 *Jazz Monthly* (now defunct) Dec. 1963. Quote Lonnie Johnson interviewed by Valerie Wilmer.

16 OLIVER, P. *Conversation with the blues op. cit.* p. 166. Quote Emma Williams (Mary Johnson's mother).

17 *Ibid.* p. 114. Quotes Mary Johnson.

18 *Barrelhouse flat blues* by Mary Johnson (1930). Orig. issue Paramount 12996. Re-issued on *Fabulous trombone of Ike Rodgers* London AL 3512.

19 *When I was lovin' changed my mind blues* by Lonnie Johnson (1926). Orig. issue OKeh 8309. Also quoted in *Blues World op. cit.* no. 35, Oct. 1970. 'It's too late to cry – a tribute to Lonnie Johnson' by Bob Groom.

20 *When you fall for someone that's not your own* by Lonnie Johnson (1928). Orig. issue OKeh 8635. Words and music by Lonnie Johnson. Also quoted in CHARTERS, S. B. *The country blues op. cit.* p. 56.

21 *Hard times ain't gone nowhere* by Lonnie Johnson (1937). Orig. issue Decca 7388. Re-issued on *The blues of Lonnie Johnson* Swaggie 5-1225.

22 *Rattlesnake blues* by Mary Johnson (1932). Orig. issue Champion 16570, re-issued on *Mr. Sykes blues 1929–32* Riverside RLP 8819.

23 *Mary Johnson blues* by Mary Johnson (1932). Orig. issue and re-issue: see item 22 above.

24 *Why women go wrong* by Lonnie Johnson (1939). Orig. issue Bluebird B8363. Also quoted in *Blues World op. cit.* no. 35, Oct. 1970.

25 *She's only a woman* by Lonnie Johnson (1939). Orig. issue Bluebird B8363. Also quoted *ibid.*

26 *She's my Mary* by Lonnie Johnson (1939). Orig. issue Bluebird B8322. Also quoted in LANG, I. *op. cit.* pp. 123, 124.

Blues in St Louis

1 *Jazz Journal op. cit.* vol. II, no. 12. Dec. 1958. Quote Harry Dial from '*The story of Harry Dial as told to Franklin S. Driggs*'.

2 JOHNS, O. *Times of our lives* New York: Stackpole, 1937; New York: Farrar, Straus & Giroux, 1973. p. 98.

3 *Nut factory blues* by Hi Henry Brown (1932). Orig. issue Vocalion 1692. Re-issued on *St Louis town (1929–1933)* (see under Depression, item 8).

4 OLIVER, P. *Conversation with the blues op. cit.* p. 105. Quote Henry Townsend.

5 *Keep it clean* by Charley Jordan (1930). Orig. issue Vocalion 1511. Re-issued on Origin OJL-8. Words and music by Charley Jordan. Also quoted in *78 Quarterly op. cit.* 'The conspiracy against Charley Jordan?' by Bernard Klatzko.

6 BBC interview: Henry Townsend, St Louis, Mo., 1976.

7 JOHNS, O. *op. cit.* pp. 336, 338.

8 BBC interview: Big Joe Williams, Crawford, Miss., 1976.

9 *Ibid.* Henry Townsend, St Louis, Mo., 1976.

10 HUGHES, L. and MELTZER, M. eds. *op. cit.* p. 266. Quote newspaper report, July 3, 1917.

11 GARON, P. *op. cit.* p. 19. Quote librarian re Peetie Wheatstraw.

12 *Peetie Wheatstraw stomp no. 2* by Peetie Wheatstraw (1937). Orig. issue Decca 7391. Re-issued on *Peetie Wheatstraw and Kokomo Arnold* Blues Classics BC-4

13 *Doin' the best I can* by Peetie Wheatstraw (1934). Orig. issue Decca 7007. Re-issued on *Peetie Wheatstraw 1930–1936* Flyright III.

14 *Froggie blues* by Peetie Wheatstraw (1936). Orig. issue Vocalion 03249. Also quoted in GARON, P. *op. cit.* p. 59.

15 ELLISON, R. *Invisible man* New York: Random House, 1952; London: Gollancz, 1953; Penguin Books, 1965. p. 144.

16 GARON, P. *op. cit.* p. 74. Quote Henry Townsend and Yank Rachel.

17 ELLISON, R. *op. cit.* p. 144.

Blues in Chicago

1 STRACHWITZ, C. and WELDING, P. eds. *The American folk music occasional* New York: Oak Publications, 1970. pp. 60, 61. 'My life in recording' by Lester Melrose.

2 BRUYNOGHE, Y. *Big Bill blues* New York: Oak Publications, 1964. pp. 141, 142. Quote Big Bill Broonzy.

3 *Tampa Red – the Guitar Wizard* RCA Bluebird AXM2-5501. Quote Blind John Davis on sleeve notes by Jim O'Neal.

4 *I'm just a bum* by Big Bill Broonzy (1935). Orig. issue Bluebird B6111. Re-issued on *Big Bill and Sonny Boy* RCA Victor RD-7865. © Leeds Music.

5 *Jazz Journal op. cit.* May 1962. Quote Kokomo Arnold interviewed by Paul Oliver.

6 *Milk cow blues* by Kokomo Arnold (1934). Orig. issue Decca 7026. Re-issued on *Peetie Wheatstraw and Kokomo Arnold* (see under: Blues in St Louis, item 10). Words and melody by Kokomo Arnold. © Leeds Music. Also quoted *ibid.*

7 *Blues by Jazz Gillum* Xtra 1111. Quote sleeve notes based on interview with Jazz Gillum by Roy and Lola Freelace, 1961.

8 *Key to the highway* by Jazz Gillum (1940). Orig. issue Bluebird B8529. Re-issued on *Jazz Gillum* RCA 130.257. Words and melody by Willie Broonzy and Charles Segar. © Wabash Music.

9 *I'm not the lad* by Washboard Sam (1941). Orig issue Bluebird B8878. Re-issued on *Feeling lowdown: Washboard Sam* RCA Victor RD 8274 (LPV 577).

10 *I've been treated wrong* by Washboard Sam (1941). Orig. issue Bluebird B9007. Re-issued on *Feeling lowdown* (see item 9 above).

11 *Insurance man blues* by Sonny Boy Williamson (1938). Orig. issue Bluebird B8034. Re-issued on *Bluebird blues: Sonny Boy Williamson* RCA International Int. 1088. Words and music by Yank Rachel. © Leeds Music.

12 *Christmas morning blues* by Sonny Boy Williamson (1938). Orig. issue Bluebird B8094. Re-issued on *Bluebird blues* (see item 11 above).

13 *I been dealing with the devil* by Sonny Boy Williamson (1940). Orig. issue Bluebird B8580. Re-issued on *Big Bill and Sonny Boy* (see item 4 above). Words and music by Robert Brown. © Wabash Music.

14 *My black name blues* by Sonny Boy Williamson (1941). Orig. issue Bluebird B8992. Re-issued on *Sonny Boy Williamson* Blues Classics BC-3.

15 ROWE, M. *Chicago Breakdown* London: Edison Bluesbooks 1, 1973. p. 24. Quote Billy Boy Arnold.

16 *Million years blues* by Sonny Boy Williamson (1941). Orig. issue Bluebird B8866. Re-issued on *Big Bill and Sonny Boy* (see item 4 above). Words and music by Sonny Boy Williamson.

17 *Tuff luck blues* by Big Maceo (1941). Orig. issue Bluebird B8973. Re-issued on *Big Maceo: Chicago breakdown* RCA AXM2-5506.

18 *County jail blues* by Big Maceo (1941). Orig. issue Bluebird B8798. Re-issued on *Chicago breakdown* (see item 17 above).

19 *Worried life blues* by Big Maceo (1941). Orig. issue Bluebird B8827. Re-issued on *Chicago breakdown* (see item 17 above). Words and music by Maceo Merriweather. © Wabash Music.

20 *Living blues op. cit.* no. 19 Jan./Feb. 1975. Quote *Chicago Defender*, 'Here to yonder – music at year's end'. Langston Hughes.

The rural South

1 SHANNON, D. A. ed. *The Great Depression* (Spectrum Book) Engelwood Cliffs, N.J.: Prentice-Hall, 1960. p. 29. Quote Congressman George Huddleston of Alabama, speaking to U.S. Senate Committee for Federal Aid for Unemployment, 1932. Taken from U.S. Congressional Record.

2 *Sing Out* New York, no. XV, 1965. Quote Son House interviewed by Julius Lester.

3 SCHLESINGER, A. M. *The age of Roosevelt* vol. 2. *The coming of the*

New Deal London: Heinemann,
1959. Ch. 22, Section IV. Quote
Franklin D. Roosevelt.
4 *High fever blues* by Bukka White
(1940). Orig. issue Vocalion 05489.
Re-issued on *Bukka White* CBS
Realm Jazz Series 52629.
5 SCHLESINGER, A. M. *op. cit.*
Quote plantation owner's descrip-
tion of sharecropper's needs.
6 *Ibid.* Quote Georgia farmer.
7 BBC interview: Sam Chatmon,
Hollandale, Miss., 1976.
8 LEUCHTENBURG, W. E.
*Franklin D. Roosevelt and the New
Deal* (Harper Torchbook) New
York: Harper & Row, 1965. p. 138.
Quote letter from cropper's wife to
Norman Thomas.
9 MACK, R. W. ed. *The changing
South* (Transaction Books)
Chicago: Aldine Publishing Co.,
1970. pp. 27, 28. Quote KESTER,
H. *Revolt among the sharecroppers* in
'The changing realm of King
Cotton' by Joseph S. Vandiver.
10 SCHLESINGER, A. M. *op. cit.*
Section V. Quote words spoken to
Norman Thomas.
11 *We shall not be moved* orig. pre-
Civil War spiritual. As quoted in
LOMAX, A. GUTHRIE, W. and
SEEGER, P. *op. cit.* p. 348.
12 SCHLESINGER, A. M. *op. cit.*
Section IV. Quote description
cropper's cabin by Erskine
Caldwell.
13 AGEE, J. *Let us now praise
famous men* Boston: Houghton,
1941; London: Peter Owen, 1965;
Panther Books, 1969. Photographs
by Walker Evans.
14 *Working man blues* by Sleepy
John Estes (1940). Orig. issue
Bluebird B8950. Re-issued on
Kings of the blues RCA RCX-
204.

15 BBC interview: Sam Chatmon,
Hollandale, Miss., 1976.

Blues in the South
1 *The death of Blind Boy Fuller* by
Brownie McGhee (1941). Orig.
issue OKeh 06265. Also quoted in
CHARTERS, S. B. *The country
blues op. cit.* pp. 150, 151.
2 *Living Blues op. cit.* no. 13 Summer
1973. Quote Sonny Terry interviewed with Brownie McGhee by
Barry Elmes.
3 *Jazz Monthly op. cit.* Aug. 1958.
Quote Brownie McGhee in 'Key
to the highway' by Paul Oliver.
4 *Worn out engine blues* by Blind Boy
Fuller (1940). Orig. issue Vocalion
05575. Re-issued on *Blind Boy
Fuller on down* vol. 1 Saydisc SDR
143. Also quoted in BASTIN, B.
Crying for the Carolines ed. P.
Oliver, Blues paperbacks. London:
Studio Vista, 1971. pp. 29, 30.
5 *Pistol Snapper blues* by Blind Boy
Fuller (1938). Orig. issue Vocalion
04106. Re-issued on *Blind Boy
Fuller* Blues Classics BC-11.
6 TRAUM, H. ed. *Guitar styles of
Brownie McGhee* New York: Oak
Publications. 1971. pp. 13 and 15.
Quote Brownie McGhee.
7 *Blues Unlimited op. cit.* no. 95, Oct.
1972. Quote Hound Dog Taylor
interviewed by Wesley Race.
8 BBC interview: Houston Stackhouse, Memphis, Tenn., 1976.
9 *Living Blues op. cit.* no. 22,
July/Aug. 1975. Quote Johnny
Shines interviewed by Pete Welding
in 'Ramblin' Johnny Shines'.
10 *Fixin' to die blues* by Bukka White
(1940). Orig. issue Vocalion 05588.
Re-issued on *Bukka White* (see
under: The Rural South, item 4).
Words and melody by Booker
White. © Leeds Music.

11 LEADBITTER, M. ed. *op. cit.* p. 251. Quote Bukka White interviewed by David Evans.

12 *Sleepy man blues* by Bukka White (1940). Orig. issue OKeh 05743, re-issued on *Bukka White* (see item 10 above).

13 *Down Beat op. cit.* Aug. 7, 1969. Quote Muddy Waters in 'Father and son: an interview with Muddy Waters and Paul Butterfield' by Don De Michael.

14 *Jazz Journal op. cit.* Feb. 1959. Quote Muddy Waters in 'Muddy Waters in London' part 2 by Tony Standish.

15 JOHNSON, C. S. *Growing up in the black belt* Washington D.C.: American Council on Education, 1941; New York: Schocken Books, 1967. p. 76.

16 *Down Beat op. cit.* Oct. 8, 1964. Quote Muddy Waters in 'Last King of the South-Side?' by Pete Welding.

17 BBC interview: Houston Stackhouse, Memphis, Tenn., 1976.

18 *Preachin' the blues* part 1 by Son House (1930). Orig. issue Paramount 13013. Re-issued on *Son House – Blind Lemon Jefferson* (see under: The men start recording, item 7). © Son Dick Music.

19 *Preachin' blues* by Robert Johnson (1936). Orig. issue Vocalion 04630. Re-issued on *Robert Johnson, King of the Delta Blues singers* CBS Archive Series 62456. ©.

20 *Hellhound on my trail* by Robert Johnson (1937). Orig. issue ARC 7-09-56. Re-issued on *Robert Johnson* (see item 18 above). ©.

21 STRACHWITZ, C. and WELDING, P. eds. *op. cit.* p. 32. Quote Johnny Shines in 'The Robert Johnson I knew'.

22 *Come on in my kitchen* by Robert Johnson (1936). Orig. issue ARC 7-07-57. Re-issued on *Robert Johnson* (see item 18 above). ©.

23 STRACHWITZ, C. and WELDING, P. eds. *op. cit.* p. 32. Further quote Johnny Shines.

24 *Living Blues op. cit.* no. 17, Summer 1974. Quote Houston Stackhouse interviewed by Jim O'Neal.

25 *Genesis: the beginnings of rock* vol. 2: *Memphis to Chicago* Chess Records 6644 1125. Opening announcement for *King Biscuit Time* Radio Station KFFA, Helena, Arkansas. As quoted in sleeve notes by Mike Leadbitter.

26 *Living Blues op. cit.* (see item 23). Further quote Houston Stackhouse.

27 FERRIS, W. Jr. *Blues from the delta* ed. P. Oliver, Blues paperbacks. London: Studio Vista, 1970. p. 90. Quote Southern black interviewed by author.

Part Six

Post-war blues

1 SIMMONS, H. *Corner boy* Boston: Houston Mifflin, 1957; London: Methuen. The song quoted is similar to many records of the time, e.g. *No Rollin' Blues* by Jimmy Witherspoon (1949). Orig. issue Modern 20-721. Re-issued on *Jimmy Witherspoon: spoonful of blues* Crown CLP 5156 and Ember EMB 3369.

2 *Down Beat op. cit.* Nov. 18, 1965. Quote Joe Turner in 'Boss of the blues' by Valerie Wilmer.

3 *Ibid.* Further quote for Joe Turner.

4 *Blues Unlimited op. cit.* no. 106, Feb./Mar. 1974. 'The Otis Tapes: 1, Louis Jordan' by Johnny Otis.

5 *Hard luck blues* by Roy Brown
(1950). Orig. issue De Luxe 3304.
Re-issued on *25 years of rhythm-
and-blues hits* Ember EMB 3359.
Words and music by Roy Brown.
© Blue Ridge Music.
6 BROVEN, J. *Walking to New
Orleans: the story of New Orleans
rhythm-and-blues* Blues Unlimited, 1974. pp. 22, 23.
7 *Good rockin' tonight* by Roy Brown
(1948). Words and music by Roy
Brown. © Blue Ridge Music.
8 *Living Blues op. cit.* no. 12, Spring
1973, Quote T-Bone Walker interviewed by Jim and Amy O'Neal.
9 *Sounding Out* BBC TV, Jan. 31,
1972, prod. by Tony Cash. Quote
B.B. King interviewed by Charlie
Gillett.
10 HARALAMBOS, M. *Right on:
from blues to soul in Black America*
(Eddison bluesbooks, 2) Eddison
Press, 1974. New York: Drake
Pubs., 1975. p. 24. Quote Little
Milton re T-Bone Walker.
11 *Sunday Times Colour Supplement*
June 3, 1973. Quote B.B. King in
'Soul on fire' by Phillip Norman.
12 *Blues Unlimited op. cit.* no. 76.
Oct. 1970. 'Midnight in the barrel-
house' by Johnny Otis.
13 MILLAR, B. *The Coasters*
London: W. H. Allen, 1974. p. 16.
Quote Johnny Otis interviewed by
Rob Finnis.
14 *Blues Unlimited op. cit.* (see item
12 above). Further quote Johnny
Otis.
15 *Living Blues op. cit.* no. 6,
Autumn 1971. Quote Lowell
Fulson.
16 *Drifting blues* by Charles Brown
(1945). Re-issued on *A world of
blues* London HA-P 8099. Words
and music by Charles Brown. ©
Pamco Music.

The end of an era
1 GILLETT, C. *The sound of the
city: the rise of rock-and-roll*
London; Souvenir Press, 1970;
Sphere Books, 1971. p. 168.
2 LEADBITTER, M. ed. *op. cit.* p.
206. Quotes J. R. Fullbright.
3 *Goin' back and talk to mama* by
Sam Lightnin' Hopkins (c.
1947–1951). Orig. issue *Lightnin'
Hopkins early recordings* Arhoolie
LP 2007. Re-issued in U.K. on
Bluebird blues – Lightnin' Hopkins
Fontana 688803. Words and music
by Bill Quinn.
4 LEADBITTER, M. ed. *op. cit.* p.
121. Quote John Lee Hooker interviewed by Pete Welding.
5 *Jazz Journal op. cit.* vol. 13, no. 5,
May 1960. Quote 'Land of the
blues' by Jacques Demetre and
Marcel Chauvard.
6 LEADBITTER, M. ed. *op. cit.* p.
123. Further quote John Lee
Hooker.
7 *I can't be satisfied* by Muddy
Waters (1948). Orig issue Aristocrat 1305. Re-issued on *Genesis: the
beginnings of rock* Chess Records
6641 047. Words and music by
Muddy Waters. © ARC Music.
8 GURALNICK, P. *Feel like going
home* (Fusion Books) New York:
Outerbridge and Dienstfrey, 1971.
p. 46. Quote Muddy Waters.
9 ROONEY, J. *Bossmen: Bill
Monroe and Muddy Waters* New
York: Dial Press, 1971. p. 108.
Quote Muddy Waters.
10 GURALNICK, P. *op. cit.* p. 108.
Quote Marshall Chess.
11 BBC interview: Pervis Spann,
Chicago, Ill., 1976.
12 *The legend of Elmore James*
United Artists UAS 29109. Quote
Georges Adins from sleeve notes
by Frank Scott.

13 *They call me lazy* by Lazy Lester (1958). Orig. issue Excello 2107. Re-issued on *Lazy Lester: made up my mind* Blue Horizon Postwar Masters 2431 0. Words and music by J. Miller. © Excellorec Music.

Say it loud

1 *Down Beat op. cit.* Aug. 7, 1969. Quote 'The B.B. King Experience' by James Powell.
2 *Sunday Times Colour Supplement op. cit.* Further quote 'Soul on fire' by Phillip Norman.
3 KING, B.B. *Personal instructor* Amasco Music Publishing Co., New York. Quotes B.B. King interviewed by Stanley Dance. 1st publ. *Jazz* (magazine).
4 OLSSON, B. *Memphis Blues* ed. Paul Oliver, Blues paperbacks. London: Studio Vista, 1970. p. 94.

Quote Willie Cobbs.
5 BBC interview: Pervis Spann, Chicago, Ill., 1976.
6 *Living Blues op. cit.* no. 20, Mar./April 1975. Quote Little Johnny Taylor in 'You can't beat the original Little Johnny Taylor' by Dick Shurman.
7 *Ibid.* vol. 1, no. 4. Winter 1970–71. Quote Bobby Bland in 'Bobby Bland backstage' by Jim O'Neal.
8 BBC interview: Pervis Spann, Radio Station WVON, Chicago, Ill., 1976.
9 *Down Beat op. cit.* Aug. 7, 1969. Quote 'Time for Bobby Bland' by J. B. Figi.
10 BBC interview: Pervis Spann, Chicago, Ill., 1976.
11 HARALAMBOS, M. *op. cit.* p. 124. Quote WVON disc-jockey Butterball.

Selected Bibliography

Blues
ALBERTSON, Chris *Bessie* London: Barrie and Jenkins, 1973; Sphere, n.e. 1975, o.p. *Thoroughly researched biography of Bessie Smith.*
BROVEN, John *Walking to New Orleans: the story of New Orleans rhythm and blues* Blues Unlimited, 1974; n.e. Flying Records, 1978, *Blues, R-&-B, rock 'n' roll. Excellent coverage of artists, clubs, recordings etc.*
CHARTERS, Samuel Barclay *The country blues* (Roots of Jazz) N.Y.: Rinehart, 1959; London: Michael Joseph, 1960; Da Capo, n.e. 1976. *Highly readable history; now somewhat superceded by recent research.*
CHARTERS, Samuel Barclay *The Poetry of the blues* N.Y.: Oak Publications, 1963; Avon, paperback, 1970, o.p.
CHARTERS, Samuel Barclay *The bluesmen* N.Y.: Oak Publications, 1967, o.p. *Pre-war country blues in Mississippi, Texas and Alabama. Excellent.*
FERRIS, William Jnr *Blues from the Delta* (Blues paperbacks) Studio Vista, 1970; Doubleday, paperback, 1979. *Study of black folklore from the Mississippi Delta; examines creative processes of the blues through inter-*

views and recording sessions with singers.
GROOM, Bob *The blues revival* (Blues paperback) Studio Vista 1971; Legacy, paperback n.d. *The growth of blues appreciation and scholarship described by the former editor of the now defunct journal Blues World.*
JONES, Le Roi *Blues people: negro music in white America* N.Y.: William Morrow, 1963: London: MacGibbon and Kee, 1965, o.p. *By poet and playwright LeRoi Jones, this is one of the most important books on the subject. A work which combines insight with wit and readability.*
KEIL, Charles *Urban blues* University of Chicago Press, 1966; paperback 1968. *A sociological study of the modern blues and the role of the blues singer. Vivid chapters on B.B. King and Bobby Bland, skilfully intertwined with analysis.*
LEADBITTER, Mike *Delta country blues* Blues Unlimited, 1968, o.p. *Very readable booklet concentrating on the 1940's and early 50's.*
LEADBITTER, Mike ed. *Nothing but the blues* Hanover Books, 1971, o.p. *An anthology of articles and interviews from Blues Unlimited (8 Brandram Road, Lewisham, London SE13 5EA). The late Mike Lead-*

*itter was a founder editor of B.U.
and helped make it the leading
journal of blues research. He died
suddenly in 1974 at the age of 32.*
MIDDLETON, Richard *Pop
music and the blues: a study of the
relationship and its significance*
London: Victor Gollancz, 1972;
Atlantic Highlands, N.J.
Humanities, 1974, o.p. *Original and
valuable cultural analysis based on
the study of the blues and blues-
influenced pop as musical form. A
book which has not yet received the
critical attention and discussion it
warrants.*
OLIVER, Paul *Blues fell this
morning* Cassell, 1960. Repub-
lished as *The meaning of the blues*
N.Y.: Collier Books, 1963;
Horizon, paperback, 1982. *An
important and pioneering study of the
blues related to the quoted lyrics of
350 songs. As with all his books, it
shows an unrivalled depth of
scholarship.*
OLIVER, Paul ed. *Conversation
with the blues* London: Cassell,
1965, o.p. *A superb book based on
Oliver's field-recording trips of 1960.
It contains an introductory essay and
the words of musicians and others he
interviewed talking about their lives,
attitudes and music. Brief biographical details are given of the
speakers and there are many evocative photographs by Oliver himself.
This book conveys more of the essence
of the blues than any other.*
OLIVER, Paul *Screening the
blues: aspects of the blues tradition*
London: Cassell, 1968, o.p. *A
series of illuminating essays on a
number of themes, including a major
study of the 'blue' blues, blues and
religion, etc. Extensive lyric
quotations.*

OLIVER, Paul *The story of the
blues* London: Barrie and Rockliff
the Cresset Press, 1969; Penguin
Books, n.e. 1972. *The definitive
history. Accurate in detail and
balanced in scope, it is an invaluable
reference work, enhanced by more
than 500 illustrations.*
OLIVER, Paul *Savannah synco-
pators: African retentions in the blues*
(Blues paperbacks) Studio Vista,
1970; Stein and Day, (Blues) 1970.
*An examination of the relationship
between African music and the blues.
Oliver was himself editor of the
Studio Vista Blues paperbacks, a
series of short, scholarly monographs.
Many have been quoted and referred
to in this book, including those by
Bruce Bastin, R. M. W. Dixon
and J. Godrich, David Evans,
John Fahey, Paul Garon, Bengt
Olsson, Tony Russell, Karl Gert
Zur Heide and Derrick Stewart-
Baxter. See Sources and Acknow-
ledgements.*
ROWE, Mike *Chicago Break-
down* (Roots of Jazz) Eddison
Press, 1973, N.Y.: Drake Pubs,
1975; Da Capo, 1979. *Well-
researched and detailed study of
post-war Chicago blues, by one of the
Blues Unlimited team.*

Related music
CONE, James H. *The spirituals
and the Blues: an interpretation*
N.Y.: Seabury Press. 1972;
Greenwood Press, 1980. *Mainly
on spirituals. A good introduction.*
COURLANDER, Harold *Negro
folk music USA* Columbia
University Press, 1963; paperback
1975. *Excellent survey; section on
blues slight.*
FOX, Charles *Jazz in perspective*
British Broadcasting Corporation,

1969, o.p. *A good short introduction.*
GAMMOND, Peter *Scott Joplin
and the rag-time era* London:
Angus Robertson, 1975; Abacus
Sphere Books, 1975, o.p.
GARLAND, Phyl *The sound of
soul* N.Y. Henry Regnery, 1969.
GILLET, Charlie *The sound of the
city: the rise of rock and roll*
London: Souvenir Press, 1971;
Sphere Books, 1971. *R-&-B, rock
'n' roll, soul and rock, etc.; the best
history.*
HEILBUT, Tony *The gospel
sound: good news and bad times*
N.Y.: Simon and Schuster, 1971.
LOMAX, Alan *The Folk songs of
North America* London: Cassell
1960; N.Y.: Doubleday 1960;
Doubleday, 1975. *Words, music and
annotations. Good section on blues.*
MALONE, Bill C. *Country Music,
USA: a fifty years history* American
Folklore Society and University of
Texas Press, 1968; n.e. paperback,
1974. *The best history of white
country music – sometimes known as
'white man's blues'.*
STEARNS, Marshall W. *The
story of jazz* London O.U.P., 1956;
Sidgwick and Jackson 1957; N.Y.:
O.U.P., Galaxy Books, n.e. 1971.
Highly readable and expert survey.

Historical and social background

ABRAHAMS, Roger D. *Deep
down in the jungle: negro narrative
folklore from the streets of Philadelphia* Chicago: Aldine, 1970.
Vivid and often funny.
ABRAHAMS, Roger D. *Positively
black* Engelwood Cliff, N.J.:
Prentice-Hall, 1970. *An examination of black culture and urban
folklore, including reference to
the blues. Surveys the soul movement and especially looks at the
performer as culture hero. Entertaining and full of insight.*
ALLSOP, Kenneth *Hard
travellin': the hobo and his history*
London: Hodder and Stoughton,
1967; N.A.L. 1970; Penguin
Books, 1972, o.p. *Very readable.
Includes material on the blues.*
BRADY, Terence and JONES,
Evan *The fight against slavery*
British Broadcasting Corporation
1975; Norton, 1977. *Deals specifically
with the British involvement in the
slave trade. Also points to the consequences of the trade on African
civilization and to the origins of
racial prejudice.*
CARMICHAEL, Stokely and
HAMILTON, Charles V. *Black
power: the politics of liberation in
America* N.Y.: Random House,
1967; London: Jonathan Cape,
1968; Penguin Books, 1969.
DAVIS, John P. ed. *The American
negro reference book* Engelwood
Cliff, N.J.: London: Prentice-
Hall, 1966, o.p. *Essays and extracts
from books on black history, politics,
culture, sociology, economics, etc.
LeRoi Jones on blues. Valuable.*
FRAZIER, E. Franklin *The negro
in the United States* N.Y.: London:
Macmillan, 1946; rev. edn. 1957,
o.p. *A standard work.*
GENOVESE, Eugene D. *Roll,
Jordan, roll: the world the slaves
made* N.Y.: Pantheon, 1974;
London: Andre Deutsch, 1975;
Random paperback, 1976 *The best
recent study of slave society.*
HERNTON, Calvin C. *Sex and
Racism* N.Y.: Doubleday, 1965;
London: André Deutsch, n.e.
1969; Paladin, 1970, o.p.
HUGHES, Langston and
MELTZER, Milton *A pictorial*

history of the negro in America 3rd
rev. edn. by C. Eric Lincoln and
Milton Meltzer. N.Y.: Crown,
1968, o.p.
LERNER, Gerda ed. *Black women
in white America: a documentary
history* N.Y.: Pantheon Books,
1972; Vintage Books, 1973 *A collection of source materials.*
LESTER, Julius *To be a slave*
N.Y.: Dial Press, 1968; London:
Kestrel, 1970; Puffin Books, 1973.
*Simple and effective collection of slave
memories.*
RAINWATER, Lee *Behind ghetto
walls: black families in a federal slum*
Chicago: Aldine, 1970; London:
Allen Lane, 1971; Penguin Books,
1973. *Study of a St Louis Federal
housing project in the 1960's. Based
on case studies; gives a good insight
into ghetto life.*
WOODWARD, C. Vann *The
strange career of Jim Crow* N.Y.:
Oxford University Press, 1966; 3rd
edn. cased and paperback 1974.
*Good introductory history of segre-
gation.*
WRIGHT, Richard *Native Son*
N.Y.: Harper, 1940, reprinted
1969; London: Cape, 1970;

Penguin Books, 1972. *A classic
novel.*
WRIGHT, Richard *Black boy: a
record of youth and childhood* N.Y.:
Harper, 1945, reprinted 1969:
London: Cape, 1970; Longman,
paperback, 1970. *Autobiography.*
WRIGHT, Richard *Twelve
million black voices: a folk history of
the negro in the United States* With
photographs by Edwin Rosskam.
N.Y.: Viking, 1941, reprinted by
Arno, 1969: London: Lindsay
Drummond, 1947.

Musical instructors
GLOVER, Tony 'Little Sun'
*Blues harp: an instruction method for
playing the blues harmonica* N.Y.:
Oak Publications, 1966; Music
Sales 1973. *One of Oak's excellent
series.*
GROSSMAN, Stefan *The country
blues guitar* N.Y.: Oak Publi-
cations, 1968. o.p. *Guitar instruc-
tion with examples and lyrics from
early records.*
KING, B.B. *The personal instructor*
N.Y.: Amasco Music Publishing
Co., 1970. *Interviews, songs and
guitar solos.*

Booknote to the new edition

Since *The Devil's Music* was written several valuable new books about the
blues have been published. Among them the following are recommended.

GARON, Paul *Blues and the Poetic
Spirit* Eddison Bluesbooks,
Eddison Press, 1975. *Thought
provoking polemical work which
doesn't always convince.*
GURALNICK, Peter *Lost
Highway* Boston: David R.
Godine, 1979. *Further portraits of*

*blues, rock 'n' roll and country artists,
by the author of* Feel
Like Going Home.
HARRIS, Sheldon. *Blues Who's
Who* New York: Arlington House,
1979. *A huge biographical dictionary
which is an astonishing feat and a
major work of reference.*

McKEE, Margaret and
CHISENHALL, Fred. *Beale
Black and Blue* Baton Rouge:
Louisiana State University Press.
1981. *Useful study of life and music
on Beale Street.*
MURRAY, Albert *Stomping the
Blues* New York: McGraw Hill,
1976. London: Quartet, 1978.
*Mainly about instrumental jazz,
arguing that blues is good-time music
rather than the expression of personal
anguish.*

PALMER, Robert *Deep Blues*
New York: Viking Press, 1981 *Well
written account, mainly covering
Delta blues of the '40's and '50's.*
SHAW, Arnold *Honkers and
Shouters* New York: Macmillan,
1978. *A vibrant, sprawling history of
rhythm and blues.*
TITON, Jeff Todd *Early Down-
home Blues* Chicago: University of
Illinois Press, 1977. *Scholarly work
including musical analysis and tran-
scriptions.*

Selected discography

There have been a bewildering number of records issued and re-issued not only in America, Britain and on the continent but also in Australia and Japan. Some issues remain in catalogues for only a short time before deletion, only to reappear under a new release number or under a new label. The best way to keep track of new releases is through the regular reviews in *Blues Unlimited*, *Living Blues* and *Picking the Blues*.

Indispensable to the serious collector are the two standard discographies, which list all releases by artists, giving recording details and the names of accompanying musicians:

DIXON, R. M. W. and GODRICH, J. *Blues and good gospel records 1902–1943* London: Storyville Publications, 3rd edn. 1982.
LEADBITTER, Mike and SLAVEN, Neil *Blues records, 1943–1966* London: Hanover Books, 1968; Music sales, paperback 1974.

The most helpful and authoritative guide through the maze of blues records can be found in:
McCARTHY, Albert, MORGAN, Alun, OLIVER, Paul and HARRISON, Max *Jazz on record: a critical guide to the first 50 years, 1917–1967* London: Hanover Books, 1968.

Paul Oliver covers all the major individual blues artists, and reviews the countless miscellanies and anthologies under different categories such as blues festivals, classic blues, gospel songs and spirituals, jug and washboard bands, Northern blues, piano blues, Southern blues, work songs and field hollers.
GURALNIK, Peter *The Listener's Guide to the Blues* Blandford, 1982.

This is a potted history of the blues as a framework for listings of recommended blues albums under various categories. Subjective but useful.

Records

The following selection is intended to give a range of artists of different styles and periods and of course leaves out many important singers. Foreign issues are easily available through the larger record shops and specialist jazz and folk outlets, many of which also have large secondhand sections.

Collections

The Devil's Music (Double album) Red Lightnin' RL 003
Sound tracks leased from the BBC featuring Mississippi, Memphis and Chicago blues. Artists include Big Joe Williams, Sam Chatmon, Booker White, Houston Stackhouse, Sonny Blake, Joe Willie Wilkins, Mose Vinson, Little Brother Montgomery, Edith Wilson, The Aces, Joe Carter, Billy Boy Arnold, Fenton Robinson and Good Rockin' Charles.
More Devil's Music Red Lightnin' RL 0038
Companion to the above, featuring blues from St Louis. Artists include Victoria Spivey, Henry Townsend, Big Joe Williams, James DeShay and his band.
The Story of the Blues Vol. 1 CBS 66218
The Story of the Blues Vol. 2 CBS 66232
(These two double-album sets, compiled by Paul Oliver, are the best starting point, covering blues from the 20's, 30's, World War II and after in Vol. 1, and guitarists, women, pianists and groups in Vol. 2).
Barrelhouse Blues Yazoo L-1028
Rugged piano classics Origin OJL-15
Really! The Country Blues Origin OJL-2
The Mississippi Blues 1927–1940 Origin OJL-5

Lake Michigan Blues 1934–1941 Nighthawk 105
Buddy Boy Hawkins and his Buddies Yazoo L-1010
The Country Girls 1927–35 Origin OJL-6
The Great Jug Bands Origin OJL-4
Blues Roots – The Atlanta Blues RBF RF15
Ten Years in Memphis 1927–1937 Yazoo L1002
St.Louis Town Yazoo L1003
The Blues come down from Memphis Charly CR 30125
Memphis and the Delta – 1950's Blues Classics 15
Chicago Blues –The Early 1950's Blues Classics 8
Chess Masters Chess (UK) CXMD-4010
The Roots of Rock 'n' Roll Savoy SJL-2221
The Johnny Otis Show Live at Monterey Epic 66295

Individual artists and groups

BIG MACEO *Chicago Breakdown* RCA Bluebird AXM 2-5506
BLIND BLAKE *Search Warrant Blues* Biograph BLP 12023
BOBBY BLAND *Greatest Hits* Fairway BBB-1400
BIG BILL BROONZY *The Young Big Bill* Yazoo L1011
GUS CANNON'S JUG STOMPERS *Complete Works* Herwin LP 208
LEROY CARR AND SCRAPPER BLACKWELL *Naptown Blues 1929–1934* Yazoo L1036
BO CARTER *Greatest Hits 1930–1940* Yazoo L1014
IDA COX *Vol. 1* Fountain FB 301

BLIND BOY FULLER *Blues
Classics* BC-11
LOWELL FULSON *Hung Down
Head* Chess LP 408
WYNONIE HARRIS *Oh
Babe!* Route 66 KIX-20
TED HAWKINS *Watch Your
Step* Rounder 2024
JOHN LEE HOOKER *No Friend
Around* Red Lightnin' RL 003
LIGHTNIN' HOPKINS *Early
Recordings* Arhoolie R2007
PEG LEG HOWELL AND HIS
GANG Origin OJL-22
HOWLING WOLF *Chester
Burnett AKA Howling Wolf*
Chess 2CH 6016
IVORY JOE HUNTER *Jump-
ing at the Dew Drop* Route 66
KIX-15
MISSISSIPPI JOHN HURT
1928 – His First Recordings
Biograph BLP-C4
ELMORE JAMES *The Legend of
Elmore James* Kent KST 9001
BLIND LEMON JEFFER-
son Milestone M47022
LONNIE JOHNSON *1927–
1932* Origin OJL-22
ROBERT JOHNSON *King of the
Delta Blues Singers* CBS BPG
62456
ALBERT KING *Live Wire/Blues
Power* Stax STX 4128
B.B. KING *Live at the Regal*
ABC ABCS-724
LEAD BELLY *Library of Congress
Recordings (3 records)* Elektra
EKL 301/2/3
J. B. LENOIR *Natural Man*
Chess 410
JOE LIGGINS AND HIS
HONEY DRIPPERS *Juke Box
Lil* 1067
LITTLE WALTER *Boss Blues
Harmonica* Chess 2CH 60014
BLIND WILLIE McTELL *The

early years 1927–1933* Yazoo
L1005
MEMPHIS JUG BAND Yazoo
1067
MEMPHIS MINNIE *Vol. 2*
Blues Classics BC-13
MISSISSIPPI SHEIKS *Stop and
listen* Herwin 53804
LITTLE BROTHER
MONTGOMERY Collectors
Classics CC 35
MUDDY WATERS *McKinley
Morganfield AKA Muddy
Waters* Chess 2CH 6006
CHARLEY PATTON *Founder of
the Delta Blues* Yazoo L1020
JUNIOR PARKER *I wanna
ramble* Ace Ch 42
PROFESSOR LONGHAIR
Crawfish Fiesta Alligator 4718
MA RAINEY Milestone M47021
JIMMY REED *Big Boss Man*
DJM DJD 28033
JIMMY ROGERS *Chicago
Bound* Chess 407
OTIS RUSH *Right Place Wrong
Time* Bulldog 301
BESSIE SMITH *Nobody's blues
but mine* CBS 67232
VICTORIA SPIVEY *Recorded
legacy of the blues* Spivey LP 2001
HOUSE DOG TAYLOR *And
the Houserockers* Alligator 4701
LITTLE JOHNNY TAYLOR
Part Time Love Charly CRB 1012
MONTANA TAYLOR *Mon-
tana's Blues* Oldie Blues OL 2815
IKE TURNER'S KINGS OF
RHYTHM *I'm Tore Up*
Red Lightnin' RL 0016
JOE TURNER *His Greatest
Recordings* Atlantic 40525
PHILLIP WALKER *The bottom
of the top* Playboy PB 118
T-BONE WALKER *T-Bone
Jumps Again* Charly CRB 1019
JUNIOR WELLS *Blues hit Big

Town   Delmark DL-640
PEETIE WHEATSTRAW AND
KOKOMO ARNOLD Blues
Classics BC-4
BUKKA WHITE CBS Realm
Jazz 52629
BIG JOE WILLIAMS *Early
Recordings 1935–41*   Mamlish
S-3810

SONNY BOY WILLIAMSON
(NO. 1) *Blues Classics Vol. 2* Blues
Classics 20
SONNY BOY WILLIAMSON
(NO. 2) *This is my story*   Chess
2CH 50027
JIMMY YANCEY AND
CRIPPLE CLARENCE
LOTTON *Gannet*   GEN 5137

General index

Index of song titles and first quoted lines

Acknowledgment is due to the following for permission to reproduce photographs:
CHRIS ALBERTSON plates 13, 14; BLUES UNLIMITED plate 30; MADDALENA FAGANDINI plates 11, 12, 16, 23, 24, 27, 31, 35; JAZZ MONTHLY plate 15; MAX JONES (MELODY MAKER) plate 8; KEYSTONE PRESS AGENCY plate 5; LIBRARY OF CONGRESS, WASHINGTON D.C. plates 1, 3, 4, 22, 25; PAUL OLIVER plate 2; JAN PERSSON plate 26; GIUSEPPE PINO plate 28; SYLVIA PITCHER plates 32, 36; POPPERFOTO plate 6; VALERIE WILMER plates 29, 33, 34; YAZOO RECORDS plate 7, 20.

Acknowledgment is due to the following whose permission is needed for multiple reproduction:
Mean Tight Mama Blues (words and music by Andy Razaf) p. 108, © copyright 1928 by MCA Music, a division of MCA Inc, New York, NY. Used by permission. All rights reserved. Reproduced in British Commonwealth (excluding Canada & Australasia), Eire and Europe, by permission of B. Feldman & Co. Ltd; *Blue Spirit Blues* (words and music by Spencer Williams) p. 101, © copyright 1930 by MCA Music, a division of MCA Inc, New York, NY. Used by permission. All rights reserved. Reproduced in British Commonwealth (excluding Canada &

Australasia), Eire and Europe, by permission of B. Feldman & Co. Ltd; *Going Back To Memphis* (Will Shade) p. 128/129, © Southern Music Publishing Co. Ltd; *I'm Alabama Bound* (Jelly Roll Morton) p. 61, © Chappell Morris Limited; *Crazy Blues* (Perry Bradford) p. 84, *Arkansas Blues* (Anton Lada/Spencer Williams) p. 85, *Chain Gang Blues* (Thomas Dursey/Charles Parker) p. 92, and *Black Cat Hoot Owl Blues* (Thomas Dursey) p. 94, all reprinted by kind permission of MCA Music Ltd.

The front cover illustration is by JAMES WRIGHT and the map on p. 44 by CATHERINE CAUFIELD.

Other titles of interest

BIG BILL BLUES
William Broonzy's Story
as told to Yannick Bruynoghe
176 pp., 4 drawings, 15 photos
80490-5 $10.95

THE ARRIVAL OF B. B. KING
Charles Sawyer
274 pp., 99 photos
80169-8 $12.95

BLUES: AN ANTHOLOGY
Edited by W. C. Handy
228 pp., 14 illus.
80411-5 $15.95

BLUES FROM THE DELTA
William Ferris
New introduction by
Billy Taylor
226 pp., 30 photos
80327-5 $11.95

THE BLUES MAKERS
Samuel Charters
New preface and new
chapter on Robert Johnson
416 pp., 40 illus.
80438-7 $16.95

BLUES WHO'S WHO
Sheldon Harris
775 pp., 450 photos
80155-8 $35.00

CHICAGO BLUES
The City and the Music
Mike Rowe
226 pp., 147 photos
80145-0 $13.95

THE COUNTRY BLUES
Samuel B. Charters
288 pp., 45 illus.
80014-4 $12.95

I AM THE BLUES
The Willie Dixon Story
Willie Dixon with Don Snowden
288 pp., 44 photos
80415-8 $12.95

I'D RATHER BE THE DEVIL
Skip James and the Blues
Stephen Calt
400 pp., 13 pp. of illus.
80579-0 $14.95

I SAY ME FOR A PARABLE
**The Oral Autobiography of Mance
Lipscomb, Texas Bluesman**
as told to and compiled by
Glen Alyn
Foreword by Taj Mahal
508 pp., 45 illus.
80610-X $16.95

LOVE IN VAIN
A Vision of Robert Johnson
Alan Greenberg
New foreword by Martin Scorsese
272 pp., 9 photos
80557-X $13.95

MEETING THE BLUES
Alan Govenar
248 pp., over 250 illus.
80641-X $17.95

STORMY MONDAY
The T-Bone Walker Story
Helen Oakley Dance
302 pp., 56 illus.
80413-1 $13.95

Available at your bookstore

OR ORDER DIRECTLY FROM

DA CAPO PRESS, INC.

1-800-321-0050